D0945433

Sexuality in the Later Years
ROLES AND BEHAVIOR

Sexuality in the Later Years
ROLES AND BEHAVIOR

Edited by Ruth B. Weg

Andrus Gerontology Center
University of Southern California
Los Angeles, California

With a Foreword by Robert N. Butler, M.D.
National Institute on Aging
Washington, D.C.

1983

ACADEMIC PRESS
A Subsidiary of Harcourt Brace Jovanovich, Publishers
New York London
Paris San Diego San Francisco São Paulo Sydney Tokyo Toronto

ACADEMIC PRESS, INC.
111 Fifth Avenue, New York, New York 10003

United Kingdom Edition published by
ACADEMIC PRESS, INC. (LONDON) LTD.
24/28 Oval Road, London NW1 7DX

Library of Congress Cataloging in Publication Data

Main entry under title:

Sexuality in the later years.

Includes bibliographical references and index.
1. Aged--Sexual behavior--Addresses, essays, lectures.
2. Age discrimination--Addresses, essays, lectures.
I. Weg, Ruth B.
HQ30.S484 1982   306.7'0880565   82-11395
ISBN 0-12-741320-0

PRINTED IN THE UNITED STATES OF AMERICA

83 84 85 86   9 8 7 6 5 4 3 2 1

In Memoriam

To the memory of our colleague and friend,
Flo Livson, whose life was spent too soon . . .

Once more to share and question
New ideas, old dreams and hopes
With a loving, caring friend.

Once more to work together
In search of fact and feeling
Of how we change and grow.

Once more we meet on this small plateau
To rest, to look beyond
And savor what we know.

Ruth B. Weg

Contents

9 Range of Alternatives
Paula L. Dressel and W. Ray Avant

III   Issues in Research and Therapy

10 Research: Status, Gaps, and Design
Alex Finkle

11 Dysfunction: Origins and Therapeutic Approaches
Ivor Felstein

IV   A View from Other Countries

12 Continuity of Self-Actualization: Womanhood in the Climacterium and Old Age
Erika Landau and Benjamin Maoz

Contributors

Numbers in parentheses indicate the pages on which the authors' contributions begin.

W. RAY AVANT[1] (185), DeKalb Community Council on Aging, Decatur, Georgia 30030

NAN CORBY (131), Andrus Gerontology Center, University of Southern California, Los Angeles, California 90089-0191

NANCY DATAN (279), Department of Psychology, West Virginia University, Morgantown, West Virginia 26506

PAULA L. DRESSEL (185), Department of Sociology and Gerontology Center, Georgia State University, Atlanta, Georgia 30303

IVOR FELSTEIN (223), Department of Geriatric Medicine, Bolton Group Hospitals, Bolton, Lancashire, United Kingdom

ALEX FINKLE (211), Department of Urology, University of California School of Medicine, San Francisco, California 94115

BIRGITTA GUSTAVII (271), Clinic for Sexual Therapy, University Hospital, Lund, Sweden

MARY HOTVEDT (13), Department of Family and Community Medicine, University of Arizona, Health Sciences Center, Tucson, Arizona 85724

VICTOR KASSEL (167), 60 South 4th East, Suite 16, Salt Lake City, Utah 84111

ERIKA LANDAU (251), Department of Psychotherapy, Tel Aviv University, Tel Aviv, Israel

FLORINE B. LIVSON[2] (105), Institute of Human Development, University of California, Berkeley, California 94720

BENJAMIN MAOZ (251), Ben Gurion University of the Negev, Soroka Medical Center, Beer-sheva, Israel

---

[1] Present address: 112 Glenn Circle, Decatur, Georgia 30030.
[2] Deceased.

PAULINE K. ROBINSON (81), Employment and Retirement Division, Andrus Gerontology Center, University of Southern California, Los Angeles, California 90089-0191

DEAN RODEHEAVER (279), Department of Psychology, West Virginia University, Morgantown, West Virginia 26506

BENJAMIN SCHLESINGER (259), University of Toronto, Faculty of Social Work, Toronto M5S 1A1, Ontario

RUTH B. WEG (1, 39), Andrus Gerontology Center, University of Southern California, Los Angeles, California 90089-0191

LAWRENCE J. WEISS (147), Project OPEN, Geriatric Services, Mt. Zion Hospital and Medical Center, San Francisco, California 94115

JUDY MAES ZARIT[1] (131), Department of Psychology, University of Southern California, Los Angeles, California 90007

[1] Present address: Didi Hirsch Community Mental Health Center, Los Angeles, California 90230.

Foreword

As long as society takes a negative view of sexuality among the elderly, the overall lot of older people is worsened. The many jokes and stories that ridicule sexuality in the later years accurately reflect our society's hostile, insulting attitudes toward both sex and old age. The stereotyping of older men and women as sexless is the ultimate example of ageism. But, as with other forms of prejudice, this devastating myth about the nature of aging can be laid to rest, once we obtain and disseminate correct information.

Additional biomedical and behavioral studies on the sexuality of later life will confirm the continuing desire and capacity of the aged for physical intimacy. Once we transfer this knowledge to health care providers, it will be possible to eliminate some of the discriminatory attitudes that often prohibit the old from seeking and receiving real help for sexual problems. Research on the specific sexual difficulties faced by older people will provide information on the impact of various diseases and disabilities, of adverse side effects of drugs, and of fears associated with a potential heart attack or stroke. I would like to see medical school departments of medicine (especially divisions of endocrinology), gynecology, and urology develop special emphasis on sexual medicine in general, with stress on the middle and later years. Armed with a knowledge of the older person's interest in and need for intimate relationships and with better information on the medical, emotional, and social problems that may interfere with sexual satisfaction, the health care provider can offer genuine assistance to the aged individual.

Particular attitudes toward and needs of older women must also be examined carefully. Since women currently live an average of 8 years longer than men, many of the problems of old age are the specific problems of older women. The National Institute on Aging has identified this differential life expectancy as an area of high priority in its research programs. An increase in male life expectancy that would equalize the survivorship of the sexes would result in fewer women spending years as widows, with accompanying loneliness and lack of intimacy.

As the body of factual information about the sexuality of the later years grows, our researchers, scholars, and policymakers must involve writers, artists, and other cultural leaders in the effort to eradicate ageism. This comprehensive volume's contribution toward an increased awareness of sexuality in the later years makes it an important addition to the small but growing list of works in the field. It is especially pleasing that this volume represents a commitment to the importance—to the whole person—of sensuality and sexuality beyond intercourse.

Robert N. Butler
National Institute on Aging

Preface

A significant gap exists between the reality and meaning of sexuality–sensuality for the elderly and the persistent, widespread mythology and destructive stereotypes associated with this age group. There is a formidable history that indicates the importance and centrality of sexuality throughout the development of the human family from primitive to modern times. Research (although still rudimentary) has repeatedly provided data demonstrating that our interest in and our need and capacity for sexual expression continue into the ninth decade of life. Yet, the images of "dirty old man" and "dirty old woman" remain.

Most of the early sex research focused on the physical acts of intercourse and orgasm and ignored the whole person. It has become increasingly evident that the whole person—personality, physiology, and integrated life experiences—is involved in sensual–sexual behavior. There is little doubt that gender identity, role ascription, and the qualities of femaleness and maleness contribute to the sexual behavior of every human being; yet these attributes are largely submerged in the neuterdom assumed to be the state of the late middle-aged and the elderly.

The powerful and pervasive influence of sexuality continues to be seen in the world of commerce, as demonstrated by advertising, sales, television, film, the print media, and so-called beauty products. At the same time, scientific interest in the meaning of human sexuality for the individual has increased measurably. The examination of sensual–sexual behavior beyond procreation, orgasm, and technique appears most appropriate now, when the perception of human beings is becoming more holistic.

This exploration of human sexuality is a multidimensional presentation in keeping with the essentially multidisciplinary, complex nature of the topic. This volume pulls together evidence from the anthropological, psychological, social, and physiological disciplines and represents an effort to present a coherent picture of sexual roles and behavior in the later years. My colleagues and I see this approach as particularly appropriate in a contemporary society that is witnessing considerable female–male role change and confusion.

This work does not pretend to answer all questions that could be raised concerning sexuality and aging but attempts rather to concentrate on issues that have been relatively neglected, primarily options, potentials, and possibilities for the individualization and humanization of sex roles and sexual behavior of older persons. For these issues, there has been an identifiable gap in research and clinical application.

I wish to extend my appreciation to all the contributors for sharing their work and to Academic Press for its confidence in gerontology and especially in this volume.

My special thanks go to Mrs. Jean Carver, without whose consistent support and tireless efforts in rewriting, proofreading, and communicating with contributors this book could not have been completed.

Introduction: Beyond Intercourse and Orgasm

Ruth B. Weg

SIGNIFICANT NUMBERS, SIGNIFICANT CAPACITIES, AND NEEDS

Until fairly recently, a volume addressing itself to sex roles and sexual behavior in the later years could not and would not have been written. Even at the turn of this century, only 3 of 76 million Americans were over 65 (Brotman, 1981; Weg, 1981). In the early 1900s the consequences of denial to elders of sexuality as part of being would have been diluted, unnoticed in the backwash of Victorian morality.

Today's reality of more than 25 million people over 65 and almost 34.5 million over 60 alters the consequences and dimensions of society's "sexless" designation. Not only are more people reaching 65 than ever before, but today's average life span (74.3 years) has increased 30 years since 1900. Moreover, levels of education and health status have improved—old age is no longer an isolated phenomenon, but an expected

1

stage of life (Weg, 1982). The new knowledge derived from the various fields of inquiry that are part of gerontology and geriatrics requires dissemination to the public, students, educators, policy makers, and medical and allied clinicians.

Old age and aging can no longer be perceived as "problems," but rather as major landmarks in the evolutionary progress of the human family. Existing problems and difficulties faced and presented by elders and the aging are the unique concerns of a previously nonexistent, rapidly burgeoning group of the population engaged in previously nonexistent experiences: age-related psychosocial and physiological changes (among these changes asexuality is a myth), accompanying pathologies and risks to health, and the power of widespread, negative societal attitudes and ignorance.

Ignored or underemphasized in the scientific literature, sensationalized, misrepresented and/or shut out in the lay media are the remaining capacities, desires, needs, and strengths of the later years (Butler, 1975; Weg, 1982). These failures in sensitivity, recognition, and reliability are no accident. Rather, they are functions of the internalization of learned ageism among scientists and other professionals and the tacit assumption that research, theory, and clinical application concerning aging hold little interest and are of minor impact.

Ongoing demographic shifts, attributes of elders, and changing health emphases would appear to ensure the certainty of an ever-increasing older population as the world moves toward the twenty-first century (Weg, 1981). Various studies from different perspectives provide data that document statistics and trends: continuation of the decline in birth rates (Brotman, 1981; Weg, 1981); reduction in death rates from cardiovascular and cerebrovascular disease (Walker, 1977); a postponement of symptoms and dysfunctions of the major chronic diseases (Fries, 1980); increasing numbers of better-educated, healthier elders (Weg, 1981, 1982); greater numbers of old and young in advocacy organizations for the improved quality of life in aging (Hendricks and Hendricks, 1981; Hess and Markson, 1980); a growing realization of a national lack of regard and a waste of a necessary human resource—the aging and aged (Troll, 1982; Sheppard and Rix, 1977).

The older and old increase and will continue expanding. Society will learn to plan and incorporate this segment of the populace at many levels, but will the sexual continuum into the later years be nurtured? Will options in sexual behavior be encouraged? Will love, affection, and intimacy be considered, as they increasingly appear to be in the literature, human needs that begin in infancy and remain throughout life? Will the changing perceptions of gender identity, sex roles, and sexual expression in which all ages are now immersed confer benefit or further disadvantage on the old? What questions can be asked? From what directions will some answers come?

HISTORICAL PERSPECTIVE OF HUMAN SEXUALITY: YOUTH AND AGE

The human family has long associated life, and especially long life, with sexuality. This apparent interdependence has, however, been involved in a self-defeating contradiction. Though perceived among the ancients as the essence of life and a prescription for long life, even immortality, sexual activity soon became synonymous with youth and the maintenance of youthful vigor. Since a lifetime then was frequently short, the deprivation was minimal for those labeled "no longer young." As the life span grew longer, and people of greater years were more in evidence, the expectation of an active sexual life stayed behind with youth, creating an unnatural discontinuity that persists to varying degrees today (Bullough, 1976).

Prehistory, contemporary history, archeology, anthropology, and the diverse cultures around the world provide bases for a relatively clear statement (Beach, 1977; Davenport, 1977; Tannahill, 1980). There has been and is a wide-ranging variation among peoples (and within cultures as well) in sexual behavior and orientation and in the interconnections and translation of gender identity, sex roles, and physical sexual activities (Marshall and Suggs, 1971). The correlations among particular cultural norms, expectations, and mores related to gender, role, and sexuality and their reflection in behavior are legion (Gagnon and Henderson, 1975). Individual sexual behavior develops on a bedrock of biology, then is molded, constrained, encouraged, or disallowed by each culture's rules. These proscriptions are laid down in early socialization, and continue throughout life via societal institutions, interpersonal relationships, law, and the media. It is inescapable that gender identity, sex role, and sexual activity are largely learned, in keeping with a time, place, and culture. So persuasive is this early learning that many persons remain locked into lifelong beliefs and patterns that neither serve individual needs and/or satisfactions, nor are consistent with the changing reality of living. What are some of the salient far and near historical steps taken to create the current prevailing views of human sexuality in general, and sexuality and age more particularly?

HUMAN SEXUALITY: THE SEARCH FOR FACTS

The mid-twentieth century was notable as a period of the emergence and legitimatization of the scientific study of human sexuality. Even this early period of sexual liberation was built on a past of repression and acceptance, ignorance and discovery, and finally persuasive leadership. The path from Judaism, early Greek sexual philosophy and behavior, Christianity, Eastern thought (Islam, Hindu, and ancient Oriental), medieval and Renaissance life, the Protestant Reformation, and the eighteenth-century Puritan ethic is marked by change and continuity. Characterizations of sexuality were multiple. St. Augustine (354-540), moralist of the Christian Church for more than 1000 years, described sex as a necessary evil for the perpetuation of the human race with predetermined male and female roles. A more contemporary perception of sex as pleasure, which also had adherents among the ancient Jewish people, as a "good" of life in a permissive milieu, depicts gender identity and sex role as learned (Gagnon and Simon, 1973; Fisher, 1980). Both views had their origins in the early anthropological and moral beginnings of human beings; both exist today, as do more eclectic perceptions combining elements of each (Tannahill, 1980).

Two philosophical and theoretical pioneers born in the last half of the nineteenth century were successful in chipping away the hyprocrisy and vacuum of knowledge in human sexuality. They were the Viennese physician Sigmund Freud (1856-1939), founder of psychiatry and psychoanalysis, and Henry Havelock Ellis (1859-1939), an English physician turned sex researcher and essayist. This was a time when Victorianism reigned and sexual matters were discussed in hushed voices, if at all.

Freud's contention that libido and the instinct for self-preservation represented the "driving force behind all human activity" (Gagnon and Henderson, 1975, p. 20), his explanations of "normal" sexuality, of sexual repression as essential to normal development, and the declaration concerning the nature of female sexuality and development as incompletely male, dominated psychoanalytic theory and practice through the 1950s. His theories of female and male sexuality grew from clinical practice and his traditional moral upbringing and lifestyle.

Ellis, on the other hand, can more appropriately be remembered as the father of the scientific study of human sexuality. His major mission was to seek and disseminate knowledge and critically address many of the repressive, ignorant mores of that period. In a six-volume work "Studies in the Psychology of Sex" Ellis (1940) stressed the essentially multidisciplinary character of sexuality—historical, anthropological, biological, psychological, and sociological. He maintained that sex is not an unnatural drive that needs to be curbed, but rather a natural, instinctive human quality (Leiblum and Pervin, 1980). He departed from the Victorian ethos in his rejection of the notions that masturbation led to illness or insanity and that homosexuality was degenerate. Ellis was supportive of female sexuality and stood alone among his colleagues in his consideration of sexual activity as that which "could and should be enjoyable" (Leiblum and Pervin, 1980, p. 5). In contrast to Freud's clinical perspective of illness and dysfunction, Ellis's emphasis was on the sexuality of relatively average, normal persons. The works of both Freud and Ellis stood in sharp opposition to the Victorian psychiatrist Richard von Krafft-Ebing, whose major contribution to the understanding of human sexuality was the categorization and description of sexual perversion and degenerates (Brecher, 1969).

Documentation of Americans' sexual behavior, rather than theoretical projections, awaited the massive (18,000 individual histories) survey of Kinsey and colleagues (1948, 1953). These works confirmed the remarkable variation and range in sexual practices, put the lie to the supposedly natural lack of interest and anorgasmia of the female, and shocked professionals and lay readers alike with the information that 37% of all males reported at least one homosexual encounter to orgasm. Admittedly, methodological problems and biases are found in these data (e.g., only Caucasians are included), but there is agreement that Kinsey's investigations were significant in the development of normative standards of American adult sexual behavior. Kinsey's findings were contrary to the expected behavior of persons who were still living with widespread restrictions and taboos imposed by law, religion, and social expectations (Leiblum and Pervin, 1980; Brecher, 1969). While these investigations remain a primary source of generally relevant information, it is useful to recognize that, in an attempt to be dispassionate and scientific, Kinsey focused on a quantifiable entity—the number of encounters and/or orgasms from a range of sexual activities including self-stimulation, fellatio or cunnilingus, intercourse, and homosexual or heterosexual interactions. The quality and meaning of human relationships were not considered, and the importance of such information escaped major recognition.

Masters and Johnson (1966, 1970) extended the scientific approach directly into the physiology of sexual arousal and response among adult volunteers. Their research was the first extensive laboratory examination of sexual intercourse from arousal to resolution. They studied the physiology of response using a range of stimuli—"masturbation, coitus with a partner, artificial coition, and stimulation of the breasts alone" (Crooks and Baur, 1980, p. 25). There was, for the first time, careful visualization of the anatomy and physiology of male and female internal and external genitalia during arousal and intercourse. Interviews were conducted with each participant as well. The work of Kinsey and colleagues, which stimulated considerable professional interest and received some favorable public acceptance, should logically have better prepared the professional and lay communities for the Masters and Johnson reports, but the reception was tentative and critical. Persons who expected the sensational in "Human Sexual Response" (Masters and Johnson, 1966) were disappointed in the scientific presentation of the physiology of sexual arousal and stages of response. Scientific colleagues pointed to the "bias" in the originally studied group of prostitutes, and later the volunteers. Despite pervasive sexual references and sexual excitement in society—in adverstising, books, film, television, magazines, etc.—there appeared to be resistance to the open and public exposure of physiological specifics of sexual behavior. This resistance and indignation persists, and sex research continues to meet with difficulties whether the questions are physiological, psychological, or sociological. Although sexual behavior exerts a significant impact on society economically, emotionally, socially, and politically, recognition of and support for studies to understand human sexuality in a changing society and to develop sex education and therapeutic approaches, have been and remain minimal.

Nevertheless, the efforts of Masters and Johnson led not only to the development of new therapeutic techniques for sexual problems and dysfunction but also to the unequivocal demonstration of the identical physiological nature of clitoral and vaginal orgasms. This information served to liberate women who had concluded (according to Freudian dogma) they were inadequate or immature because they had not experienced the vaginal orgasm (Leiblum and Pervin, 1980). Masters and Johnson emphasized the generally psychogenic nature of sexual dysfunction, which could be resolved through short-term reeducation (2 weeks) of couple interaction rather than individual psychotherapy. One of the unique ways in which the Masters and Johnson therapy differs from other therapeutic modes is in its attention to the responsibility of each of the partners for the sexual pleasure or dysfunction of the couple. Masters and Johnson proceeded to develop the "dual therapy team" and sensate focus exercises, which have been used, in part or whole, by many sex therapists who followed them (Kaplan, 1974; Lazarus, 1976; Heiman, 1978). A number of these more recent therapies involve only one person who has come for help and the use of techniques beyond those directly related to sexual dysfunction. Among such therapists, there is the conviction that sexual problems are just symptoms of a more pervasive intrapsychic or interpersonal disorder.

In spite of the work of Kinsey and colleagues and Masters's and Johnson's data, which included the middle-aged and old (albeit in small numbers), the neuter image of old age has been slow to die. Perhaps these important studies, which have contributed so much to the liberalization of sexual attitudes and practices, still suffer from a narrow view of human sexuality. These inquiries were, as so much therapy and so many self-help groups still are, concentrated on the physical aspect of human sexuality. "How to" illustrated pamphlets and manuals by writers and therapists are countless, largely technique oriented, and addressed to the eradication of physical sexual dysfunction and the ensurance of orgasm. It would appear that the aforementioned research has played a major role in the gradual erosion of sexual taboos and the explosion of some myths about roles and behavior. Yet, this progress has been perceived as directed primarily toward increased physical–sexual satisfaction rather than toward the improved quality of interpersonal relationships with sexual expression as a part of the whole.

Specific, age-related longitudinal studies investigating many mental and physical parameters have more recently provided additional data on human sexuality. Other investigations, that are one-time explorations of sexual behavior of groups of older men and women, also have recorded useful information. Yet, even this kind of age-related research has continued to survey the "numbers": How many times per month or per year did the subjects engage in sexual intercourse? How often have the encounters resulted in orgasm (Pfeiffer *et al.*, 1969; Christenson and Gagnon, 1965; Christenson and Johnson, 1973; Martin, 1981)?

BEYOND ORGASM: CHANGING PERSON AND RELATIONSHIPS

A recent review of the available literature on the sexuality of elders (Ludeman, 1981) confirms what has been stated earlier by Weg (1977, 1978)—most of the studies report primarily on genital sex among biased samples. This accumulated information has had some positive consequences, perhaps the most important of which is the realization that the capacity for the physical aspects of sexual expression is lifelong, into the eighth and ninth decades. Though genital and other systematic anatomical and physiological changes with time are real and moderate the physical–sexual experience, they are gradual and minimal. Rather than age alone as the limiting factor, it has become clear that pathology and psychosocial ambiance (both individual and societal) are most often the critical, limiting variables. These appear as the barriers to the aging and the old in the opportunities for, and pleasure derived from sexual activities.

What has also become clear is that the presence or absence of orgasm, masturbation, and intercourse, as the most reportable facts among the old as among the young, has overshadowed the emotional, sensual, and relationship qualities that give meaning, beyond release, to sexual expression. What has been largely missed are studies of changing love patterns with time, the meaning of friendships over the years, and the importance of affection and intimacy in same-sex and different-sex relationships among older persons (Saflios-Rothschild, 1977; Reedy, 1978).

What has been overlooked are the continuing "sexual dreams, hopes and fantasies and satisfactions" of older men and women (Renshaw, 1982, p. 139). What has been ignored are the walking hand-in-hand or arm-in-arm; the caring for one another; the touching and holding, with or without intercourse.

What has been looked at marginally are the frustrations, needs, and emotional starvation of many older women who, in accordance with early socialization, must face the present and the future alone with little contact warmth and probable abstinence.

Both relationships among elders called companionable, friendly, supportive, and happy by them, and those among persons who have apparently put aside the physical expressions of human sexuality have barely been explored. The antecedents of the latter are likely to be diverse: Victorian background and sex education, illness in one or both partners, religious training, lack of knowledge, or a conviction that intercourse and orgasm are not central to their affectional or intimacy needs and expressions.

SUMMARY

Modest forward movement in the acceptance of the old as human and of old age as a reasonable, livable reality, and an equally modest, but steady growth of knowledge of human sexuality in all its multiple dimensions require research in aging and in sexuality. The speed and depth of these probes into heretofore taboo concerns are predicated on enlightened professional and lay communities. This enlightenment can only proceed in an atmosphere of open and continued exhange of information and ideas.

The present transformations in sex roles and the blurring of the hard lines separating so-called appropriate gender behavior patterns among adults augurs growth. During this transition in societal assignations of male–female, and feminine–masculine there are signs of apparent confusion and some fear and questioning. Differences in theoretical developments and sexual practices feed the ferment. Also there is evidence that a number of encounter groups and therapy situations increasingly emphasize total body effects of sexual activity beyond genitalia and encourage engaging the whole person, beyond the sex object (Gagnon and Henderson, 1975). Long-term benefits, not yet perceptible, would logically accrue to the young, the middle-aged, and the old alike.

By encouraging concern with more than the physical acts of intercourse and orgasm and uncovering androgyny in people, sexual activity can be perceived as a part of the whole person, of relationships, intimacy, love, caring, touching, and friendship, more appropriately an integral part of humanness—another behavior susceptible to personal option, learning, and change in a particular situation. Rather than behavior regulated by law, religion, tradition, or fixed and pervasive social, political, and economic norms, sexuality will be as it begins: a personal quality, part of a total personality in communication with other personalities. Rather than an evil to be monitored, sublimated, or eradicated, or a moral good only for the procreation of the human population into the future, sexuality can be one of the human expressions that protects against alienation, coldness, and terror of an instrumental, cost-accounting culture; a connection with the humanity in people for the celebration of being alive.

REFERENCES

Beach, F. A., (1977). "Human Sexuality in Four Perspectives." Johns Hopkins Press, Baltimore.

Brecher, E. M. (1969). "The Sex Researchers." Little, Brown, Boston.

Brotman, H. (1981). "Every Ninth American," prepared for "Developments in Aging." Special Committee on Aging, U.S. Senate, Washington, D.C.

Bullough, V. L. (1976). "Sexual Variance in Society and History." Wiley, New York.

Butler, R. N. (1975) "Why Survive? Being Old in America." Harper & Row, New York.

Christenson, C. V., and Gagnon, J. H. (1965). *J. Gerontol.* 20, 351.

Christenson, C. V., and Johnson, A. B. (1973). *J. Geriatr. Psychiatry* 6, 80.

Crooks, R., and Bauer, K. (1980). "Our Sexuality." Benjamin/Cummings, Menlo Park, California.

Davenport, W. H. (1977). In "Human Sexuality in Four Perspectives" (F. A. Beach, ed.), pp. 115-163. John Hopkins Press, Baltimore.

Ellis, H. (1940). "Studies in the Psychology of Sex." Random House, New York.

Fisher, L. E. (1980). In "Handbook of Human Sexuality" (B. B. Wolman and J. Money, eds.), pp. 164-189. Prentice-Hall, Englewood Cliffs, New Jersey.

Fries, J. F. (1980). N.Engl. J. Med. **303**, 130-135.

Gagnon, J., and Henderson, B. (1975). "Human Sexuality." Little, Brown, Boston.

Gagnon, J., and Simon, W. (1973). "Sexual Conduct: The Social Sources of Human Sexuality." Aldine, Chicago.

Heiman, J. R. (1978). In "Handbook of Sex Therapy" (J. LoPiccolo and L. LoPiccolo, eds.), pp. 123-135. Plenum, New York.

Hendricks, J. and Hendricks, C. D. (1981). "Aging in Mass Society: Myths and Realities." Winthrop, Englewood Cliffs, New Jersey.

Hess, B. B., and Markson, E. W. (1980). "Aging and Old Age." Macmillan Co., New York.

Kaplan, H. S. (1974). "The New Sex Therapy." Brunner/Mazel, New York.

Kinsey, A., Pomeroy, W. B., and Martin, C. I. (1948). "Sexual Behavior in the Human Male." Saunders, Philadelphia.

Kinsey, A., Pomeroy, W. B., Martin, C. I., and Gebhard, P. H. (1953). "Sexual Behavior in the Human Female." Saunders, Philadelphia.

Lazarus, A. (1976). "Multimodal Behavior Therapy." Springer Publ., New York.

Leiblum, S. R., and Pervin, L. A. (1980). "Principles and Practice of Sex Therapy." Guilford Press, New York.

Ludeman, K. (1981) Gerontologist **21**, 203-208.

Marshall, D. S., and Suggs, R. C., eds. (1971). "Human Sexual Behavior." Basic Books, New York.

Martin, C. E. (1981). Arch. Sex. Behav. **10**, 339-420.

Masters, W. H., and Johnson, V. (1966). "Human Sexual Response." Little, Brown, Boston.

Masters, W. H., and Johnson, V. (1970). "Human Sexual Inadequacy." Little, Brown, Boston.

Pfeiffer, E., Verwoerdt, A., and Wang, H. S. (1969). J. Gerontol. **24**, 193-198.

Reedy, M. N. (1978). In "Sexuality and Aging" (R. Solnick, ed.), rev. ed., pp. 184-195. Andrus Gerontology Center, Univ. of Southern California Press, Los Angeles.

Renshaw, D. C. (1982). Med. Aspects Hum. Sex. **16**, 132-139.

Saflios-Rothschild, C. (1977). "Love, Sex and Sex Roles." Prentice-Hall, Englewood Cliffs, New Jersey.

Sheppard, H. L., and Rix, S. E. (1977). "The Graying of Working America." Free Press, New York.

Tannahill, R. (1980). "Sex in History." Stein & Day, New York.

Troll, L. E. (1982). "Continuations: Adult Development and Aging." Brooks/Cole, Monterey, California.

Walker, W. (1977). N. Engl. J. Med. **297**, 163-165.

Weg, R. B. (1977). In "Looking Ahead" (L. Troll, J. Israel, and K. Israel, eds.), pp. 22-34. Prentice-Hall, Englewood Cliffs, New Jersey.

Weg, R. B. (1978). In "Sexuality and Aging" (R. L. Solnick, ed.), rev. ed., pp. 48-65. Andrus Gerontology Center, Univ. of Southern California Press, Los Angeles.

Weg, R. B. (1981). "The Aged: Who, Where, How Well." Andrus Gerontology Center, Leonard Davis School of Gerontology, Los Angeles.

Weg, R. B. (1982). J. Am. Optom. Assoc. **53**, 21-29.

PART **I**

CONCEPTS OF SEXUALITY
IN LATER YEARS

2

The Cross-Cultural and Historical Context

Mary Hotvedt

Now Abraham and Sarah were old and well-stricken in age; and it ceased to be with Sarah after the manner of women. Therefore Sarah laughed within herself, saying, After I am waxed old shall I have pleasure, my lord being old also?
Genesis 18:11–12

INTRODUCTION

Throughout our youth we are given direct and indirect messages about our culture's code of appropriate sexual behavior. The most obvious ones are statements about the right circumstances for beginning sexual

SEXUALITY IN THE
LATER YEARS

13

experiences with another, the reproductive functions of both sexes, the characteristics of good partners, and the ways in which we can be attractive to potential mates. The opinions, coming from disparate sources such as parents and peer groups, often conflict, but today the sexual concerns of the young are at least discussed. The indirect message is that sexuality is the domain of young adults. It may be an area of interest, anxiety, and experimentation for children and adolescents. For mature adults, sexuality should be a settled matter that declines in importance with the years.

The heavier emphasis on sexuality in the first 25 years of the life cycle, the "formative" years, is poor preparation for the life crises that must be faced by many of us. The man going through a mid-life crisis, the woman leaving a loveless marriage after the children have grown, the older couple whose cherished sexual relationship is disrupted by serious illness, the woman who must decide on hormone treatments after menopause, the widowed and divorced, the mature couple wishing to add more variety to their sex life—all share two common problems. First, they are concerned about their sexuality. Second, they have been told indirectly since childhood that they should not be concerned about sex after youth is past.

In the absence of knowledge, we call upon our folklore about sexuality in the later years. Three repeated themes in these myths stand out:

1. In the later years, we are not sexually desirable.
2. In the later years, we are not sexually desirous.
3. In later life, we are not sexually capable.

The rest of this volume contains information contrary to these three themes. The purposes of this chapter are to delve into the sources of the mythology, to demystify the myths by understanding their cultural and historical roots, to compare several cultures' attitudes and behaviors in order to broaden the perspective of our own culture, and, finally, to suggest the reasons why a book such as this is so timely.

CROSS-CULTURAL DATA

Limits of the Data

It is possible that much of the anthropological literature, with some notable exceptions, reflects the cultural biases with which we were raised. Little, if anything, is said about the sexuality of older people, and, often, sexuality itself is not examined much. Furthermore, a researcher who has made a serious attempt to get such information is faced with other difficulties. Much of the most revealing expressions of sexuality take place in private, so that the fieldworker must rely on reported, more than seen, behavior. Thus, informants may state ideal rather than actual behaviors or attitudes (Gebhard, 1971a). Last, the segregation of the sexes is far greater in many other cultures than it is in our own; as a result, a researcher can discuss intimate topics with same-sex informants only, making for useful but uneven ethnographies.

This chapter is not an exhaustive discussion of all the literature available. Examples cited either illustrate commonly seen patterns, supported by other ethnographics done for the same culture, or are unique for their emphasis on sexuality. Research for this chapter involved a search of the Human Relations Areas Files (HRAF), periodicals on gerontology and comparative family studies, and current readings in the social sciences.

A Model for Studying Sexuality

Sexual identity can be seen as having three major components: core morphological identity, sex-role behavior, and sexual orientation (Green, 1974). Core morphological identity, the sense that one is male or female, is the first to form in the individual and the part of sexual identity least likely to change over the life span.

Related to core identity is sex-role (or gender-role) behavior, the individual's conduct that is culturally ascribed to either females or males. While much of the dichotomy of sex roles relates to the reproductive functions and the division of labor in the culture, the exact traits considered desirable for each sex vary among cultures and within the life span for many cultures.

The third component, perhaps the last to develop, is sexual orientation. It embodies not only the sexual experience of the individual but also his/her fantasies, desires, and self-description as a sexual being. Cultures help to channel much of the sexual impulse toward reproductive ends, yet there are great variations between cultures in preferred sexual acts, levels of intimacy between partners, and allowances for homosexual and nonmarital heterosexual experiences.

Much of the data presented here are concerned with continuities and shifts in sex roles as well as sexual activity in the later years. The roles, changing throughout life, are pervasive for almost every aspect of the culture and channel the ways an individual acts or reacts toward others as well as his/her own needs and emotions.

What Are "Later Years?"

There is no cultural universality about the point at which someone passes into the status of "old man" or "old woman." There are trends, however. In many cultures the climacteric in a woman marks a change in her status and roles, as will be discussed in this chapter. No such change is marked in a man, although a man monogamously married to a woman who has experienced menopause may be seen as sharing her status change. In other cases, the marriage of children or the appearance of grandchildren are demarcations of age. Another major change, particularly in extended family situations, is the point at which an adult child and spouse—usually an oldest son and a daughter-in-law—become the practical heads of the household, although the parents may maintain positions of respect. Still another more commonly recognized transition is reached when individuals, usually by this point widowed, are no longer capable of caring for themselves physically and must become dependent on relatives.

The mortality and life expectancy rates for each sex in each culture must be considered. In rural Ireland and France, for example, 18 to 25% of a village's population lives to age 60 or older (Arensberg and Kimball, 1961; Wylie, 1965). Much attention has been given by the press to Eastern European mountain communities whose members live in the range from their 80s to over 100 (Gutmann, 1977). In America, although 11.3% of the total population is 65 or older (Brotman, 1981), only 3.7% of the Mexican American population is over 65 (U.S. Bureau of Census, 1972). The figure for Mexican Americans approximates those reported for several tribal societies (e.g., Murphy and Murphy, 1974) and agricultural societies (e.g., Lewis, 1951; Martin and Voorhies, 1975), reflecting the ravages of disease, the dangers of childbirth, and the perils of warfare and certain occupations.

Thus, the concept of "older" is a relative one, measured against the usual life expectancy of one's sex in the culture and against the perceptible bodily changes that occur sooner in a difficult environment.

Sex Roles and Sexual Behavior

Several researchers have reported shifts in both private and public sex roles for both sexes in later adulthood in many cultures. Factors that affect these shifts for women are the cultural attributions of power to menstruation and the role content of wife, mother, and mother-in-law. For men, sex role changes are related to the father–son and husband–wife reciprocal roles and the seniority system for public power. For both sexes, individual and family economic status, health, religion, and respect are important in determining the exact position of the person.

Whether or not there is a concomitant change in sexual behaviors and attitudes for older people depends on the sex-role content as well as such factors as cultural concepts of beauty, potency, the female orgasm, sexuality in youth, and religious ideals about the nature of sexuality. For men and, to a lesser extent; for women, wealth and power may greatly affect the availability of partners in later years. Thus, partner availability, for both heterosexual and homosexual experiences, should be examined. The economic base of the culture, with which the family is completely intertwined, must be examined for patterning of cultural attitudes toward virtually all aspects of sexual expression.

TRIBAL, AGRARIAN, AND INDUSTRIALIZED SOCIETIES

A lengthy list of variables has been presented, and they must be organized logically for the discussion. A progression from tribal through agrarian to industrialized societies will be used, as it approximates the prehistory and history of the cultures that have contributed to our own.

Tribal Structures

Examples here are drawn from cultures in which all members consider themselves related, at least by mythical ancestry, and in which lineage and family form the basis for the power structure of each community. The economic base may be hunting and gathering, horticulture (simple gardening), herding, or a combination of these elements. Tribal societies dependent on irrigation agriculture and a developed class structure, such as certain Middle Eastern groups, are discussed with other agrarian societies.

Recent research using the HRAF files indicates that overall status of the aged in a society is correlated with the type of subsistence base. Balkwell and Balswick (1981) proposed that the status of older people is low in hunting and gathering societies in which there are great fluctuations in food supply and that their status is high in those economies that have a stable herding and/or agricultural production.

In tribal life, men and women occupy different spheres by division of labor. The tasks that each sex is trained for vary from culture to culture; some are the exclusive responsibility of one gender, whereas others are simply more commonly performed by one group than by another. The division of labor can be visualized as two bell curves overlapping to varying degrees for each tribe (see Figure 2.1). At the median point in each curve are the activities that all or almost all men or women must perform in order to be considered an adequate member of their sex. The non-intersecting tails are the specialized, segregated roles for each sex. The overlapping tails represent the activities shared by adult members, regardless of sex.

The division of labor is bound up with reproduction, particularly on the women's part, and forms the bases of sex roles. In small children, the curves of activities would be far more overlapping, with distance increasing drastically as an Ibibio boy of Nigeria, for example, is drawn away from his mother and is taught traditionally male occupations such as hunting, warfare, and religious rituals in preparation for his initiation into manhood. His sister, at an even earlier age, is being trained in

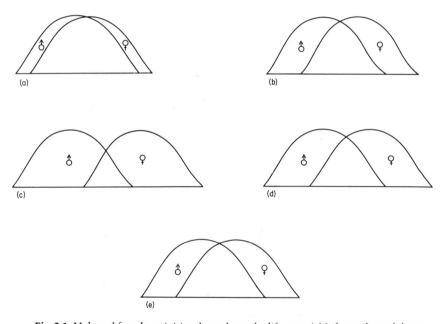

Fig. 2.1 Male and female activities throughout the life span. (a) Infancy through breast feeding: children suckled, kept close to mother. (b) Early childhood: boys engaged in rough-and-tough play; girls trained in household tasks and infant care. Mother still key figure for both sexes. (c) Puberty through young adulthood: males and females initiated into separate adult activities. Courtship and marriage are an area of overlap. (d) Mature adulthood: shared householding and parental responsibilities. (e) Late adulthood: androgynization of sex roles.

gardening and household tasks that remove her from male playmates and eventually bring her to her own initiation (Andreski, 1970). Marriage, a necessity in most tribes for the true achievement of adulthood, serves the interests of both sexes eventually as they contribute the skills and abilities of each of their spheres to parenthood and householding. The curves begin to move closer together for the more mature adults. In later years, the overlap is significantly greater than it is for young adults, though it is still smaller than the overlap for small children.

The psychological context of sex roles undergoes this melting effect as well, so that women and men could be said to be androgynized with age (Gutmann, 1977). In some cultures, this process is a fairly benign one, based on the recognized respect each sex accords the other. Among the Lepcha of Nepal, studied by Gorer (1967), the sexual division of labor is slight, the major features being that women, the childbearers, are barred from hunting. Sexual antagonism is minimal; both yin and yang are seen as necessary for life.

Despite the complementarity of labor always necessary for a tribe's survival and growth, in many cultures such a deep antagonism exists between the sexes that the sex-role changes of later life signify major power shifts for a man and a woman rather than a solely congenial recognition of common goals and abilities. Andreski (1970) has described this state as a "cold sex-war" in which the power and higher status men consider rightfully theirs is challenged by the women who can make equivalent claims to it. In such cultures, the mythology alludes to a time in which women knew the rituals of power until the men, usually through trickery, stole the knowledge needed for control. The men feel, however, that they must always be vigilant in order to keep women from recapturing their leadership over them. Women view the functioning of the culture quite differently from men, despite their observances of the taboos on them (Murphy and Murphy, 1974), and older women pay only token tribute to men's dominance (Mead, 1950).

The status of an Ibibio man as he ages is dependent on his economic situation and the size of his household, as it is for a woman. Working adult children and a prosperous farm or business allow the man to hold public office, all of which requires resources for financing necessary ceremonies and the arts of hospitality. Until his death he is the pater-familias, the head of the compound, which includes his wife or wives, his unmarried daughters and sons, his married sons and their wives and children, and often his relatives who are less fortunate. Even a widower or a man with many daughters but no sons can enlarge his family by appointing his youngest child as "home-daughter." Instead of marrying into another family, she remains with her parent and is allowed to have lovers so that her children are of her own rather than their fathers' lineages (Andreski, 1970). Thus, a man of any wealth can fulfill all male sex roles in the later years, freed to do so in part by the death or infirmity of his father, the prior head of the family.

The conflict between an aging father and a maturing son is difficult to resolve when it occurs. In some senses a father is an obstacle to a younger man's own success; in other ways, he is a valuable ally and teacher. Personalities and child-rearing practices of the tribe affect each household, so that warm, nurturing fathers fare better than men who were little more than persons to be feared and respected by their children. Domestic tension may be increased by the technological and educational changes in a society. It is useful and prestigious for a man to send his children to school, his sons to universities, perhaps, in America or Europe. Educated sons have returned with skills their fathers will never have. The aging father's roles as decision maker for the compound and as the oral historian and teacher to children and grandchildren are eroded. Achebe's trilogy of Ibo life in Nigeria (1959, 1960, 1967) is a moving fictional depiction of this process.

A variety of cultural mechanisms handle male intergenerational conflict in the sphere of public power. In many East African tribes, for example, a formal age-grade system assures that at certain points all authority is turned over to a somewhat younger group of men, so that older men assume a passivity in public affairs that Gutmann (1977) sees as paralleling feminine roles. Another mechanism involves moving older men into special public positions that call on them to exercise personality characteristics that are traditionally feminine—nurturing, ameliorating, peaceful traits. For example, among the Comanche, war chiefs become peace chiefs in later years, trying to constrain the desires of younger men (Gutmann, 1977). Thus, even societies that are gerontocracies have rules by which the oldest members make way, prior to their deaths, for others.

As men age and as their health and householding situation require it—that is, widowhood, dependency on a son or daughter, life along with an aging wife—they may gradually do more "women's work" as part of their daily routine. Older men also may become more nurturing and indulgent with their grandchildren than they are with their own off-spring. Gutmann (1977) refers to this as a further androgynization of the male with age.

An older woman is in an enviable position. She has lived through the hazards of childbearing—no small feat. If she has adult children who love and respect her, she has assurance of support for some time and aid with her work. If she is a senior wife, as among the Ibibio of Nigeria, she has the right to respect from her junior cowives and their children and a legal status close to her husband's. She may have a profitable trading business, which her oldest daughter will inherit. Among the Ibibio and several other West African tribes, if she has no living children but does own a flourishing trading business, she may make a "woman-marriage" in which she is the legal "husband" to another women whose children, usually sired by the "husband's" husband or another male relative, will inherit their "father's business (Bohannon and Middleton, 1968; Andreski, 1970). She also can be involved, due to the wisdom gained from her experiences and her elaborate social network, in a number of special societies with religious, social, and economic prestige. Her daughter-in-law, particularly the senior wife of her oldest son, is her closest ally, having been raised in her home from late childhood as a kind of adopted daughter. Her son treats her with respect and love. These affectional ties with the younger generation benefit her economically as well as emotionally. If she is fortunate, her husband is still living and they are comrades in their various enterprises. The androngynization process as described earlier possibly contributes to greater husband–wife cooperation at this point.

In sex-antagonistic cultures an older woman assumes an interestingly contradictory position regarding the public and religious rule of men. On the one hand, she is the teacher of women's rituals, the initiator of young girls, and the trainer of younger wives; in these roles she is supportive of the male power structure. Also, as a wife she is deeply involved in the concerns of her husband; she is a guardian of his interests as well as her own. On the other hand, an older women has the knowledge and power within her own spheres, as well as within male spheres, to no longer fear male authority. For an old woman there are many more freedoms. She may sit in on councils of men from which she was once excluded. She may openly criticize or ridicule certain aspects of male roles. In some cases, she may become a ruler over men, as with the Ibibio uncrowned queen known as "Ma" (Andreski, 1970).

Menopause significantly alters women's status and roles in the male sphere. The sexual division of labor and authority is often supported by beliefs in the power of menstrual blood to severely affect the activities of men. No single word can describe that power, because the sense of it differs from culture to culture. Research for this review suggests that in sex-cooperative societies, such as the Lepcha, women's blood can be viewed as detrimental to hunting and that it has an awesome power of a separate sphere, but is not a source of disgust, for men. Sex-antagonistic societies, however, seem fraught with ideas of fear or disgust over pollution by a menstruating woman. In such societies a woman is shunned or placed in seclusion during each cycle until she ritually cleanses herself. In both types of societies a linkage between life and death exists in menstrual blood.

When a woman ceases to menstruate, therefore, she is no longer bound by men's fear of her pollution. She becomes "like a man" (Gutmann, 1977), though not quite, for she has knowledge of the women's sphere, which men cannot have. A woman, therefore, may be able to combine all these factors and become a witch (Gutmann, 1977), the penalty for which is often death if a charge is brought and proved true to the satisfaction of the community.

In a number of societies, men too, in later years, are thought to engage in magic (DeBeauvoir, 1973). Landes (1971) reports several Ojibwa life histories in which older married couples are in league in their sorcery, forcing unwilling families to marry their children to their own for fear of illness or death. The sources of these magical attributes are multiple. First, the older men and women are androgynized; they have knowledge and abilities of both sexes. Second, they have the knowledge of a community through their long experience with it, and that knowledge can be used for their own ends or for their clients' interests. Third, they envy the young who are replacing them, or their success in life, which they lacked (Mead, 1950). Finally, they are closer to death symbolically, if not actually, than are the young, and their energies are attuned to the supernatural world, which they will soon join (DeBeauvoir, 1973; Gutmann, 1977).

The time comes for some people when they become physically unable to care for themselves. This is yet another phase of older life. By their own standards, those who are unable to care for themselves are the least respected. In cultures in which everyone marries and works to ensure life, the infirm person is considered less than a child. Children at least are a resource, but a sick old relative loses much respect and becomes another mouth to feed for no eventual reward. In some cultures, people choose to die before this time in order to avoid rejection or to feel they are contributing something through their death. In other cultures, the children abandoned the parent, as they knew in turn their children would abandon them. Another "solution" is to treat the sick, old persons so poorly that disease or deprivation will quickly take them (DeBeauvoir, 1973). Yet death brings an upward swing in one's status again; the deceased is remembered as an ancestor.

The paucity of data on the sexual lives of older tribal peoples most likely reflects a bias on the part of the researcher. Certain inferences can be drawn from life histories that include descriptions of enduring marital relationships. The more direct data come from cultures that encourage sexual expression throughout the life span, where only partner availability severely alters sexuality in the later years. First, we will examine data from marriages and approved extramarital relationships.

The research found no tribe in which menopause marked the end of sexual relations for couples who are married at the time of the woman's menopause. In Andreski's (1970) accounts of Ibibio women, informants in their 60s who have husbands imply that a sexual relationship exists. These are first to fourth marriages for the subjects,, made in some cases after divorced and widowhood. An estimated 40 to 60% of tribes permit a form of extramarital activity for women so that members have the opportunity of leaving arranged unions to find more compatible partners (Gebhard, 1971b). The Canadian Ojibwa, according to Landes (1971), place a high premium on individualism, romantic expression, and compatability. Among the Ojibwa, remarriage and divorce continue until compatible partners are found, and these unions last until death. Among the Eskimo, likewise, such remarriages occur. Additionally, mate sharing (the exchange of sexual partners between visitors and hosts or a husband's loan of his wife to an unmarried male visitor) brings about reciprocal relationships between the households for the rest of life, so that even children may ask favors and hospitality of old mate-sharing partners of their parents (Spencer, 1968). In Lepcha culture, remarriage and sexual expression are continued into a person's 80s, the expected life span, although younger people find such involvement humorous when new lovers are in their 70s (Gorer, 1967).

Menopause in patriarchal, sex-antagonistic societies seems to reduce the marriageability of widows who have no children. In many societies, sterility lowers the status of a woman. In some cases, a widow is remarried to her deceased husband's brother, although, if she is past child bearing and has adult children, she may remain with them.

A man of any wealth and vigor may continue to form marriage alliances as long as other families accept his offer of bride price. Ibibio men of substance who are not Christian may have two or more wives of varying ages. Only one of Andreski's informants had a non-Christian husband who felt he was too old to add another wife to his compound who felt he was too old to add another wife to his compound, despite his wife's urging (Andreski, 1970). Polygamy in certain African nations is practiced to varying degrees. Census figures show that 31% of all married men in Benin (1961) and 28% of married Senegalese men (1971) are polygamous (Welch and Glick, 1981).

Few statistics exist to indicate the frequency of marital intercourse. Among the Mangaians, a Polynesian people who have a history of divorce and remarriage similar to the Ojibwa, Marshall (1971) found that men over 48 expect to have at least one orgasm per night, whereas women may have more. Mangaian lovers show virtually no affectional or foreplay gestures in public. Sexual activity, however, is highly enjoyed from an early age, and Marshall (1971) reports that women are always orgasmic.

Among the Lepchas and some Oceanic societies, older women are the sexual teachers of the boys who have been initiated. Malinowski (1929) reported that the Trobiand Islanders, a Melanesian society, place a high value on youth and beauty and, therefore, do not seek out older sexual partners. In one case, however, several young men in the community contracted a venereal disease. No young women were infected. The common partner was a very old woman.

The literature search for data on the other sexual experiences was not a fruitful one. Data on homosexual encounters, extramarital sexuality, and masturbation among the elder generation were not found. What can be surmised is that within tribal cultures, even the sex-antagonistic ones, the continuation or cessation of sexual contact is a matter of individual circumstances for older members. In cultures that encourage female sexuality from youth, women may have more opportunities, despite widowhood, to continue being active. Older men in tribal life, being reproductively capable for a longer time then women, may continue to seek partners until they feel that they are no longer able or interested. Health and wealth, along with status, may be the significant factors here.

Sex Roles and Sexuality in Peasant Societies

Harris (1975 p. 300) defines peasants as "pre-industrial food-producers who pay rent or taxes." They are structurally inferior in the society, whether they are controlled by a nobility (who may in fact be their kin), a state, a conquering army, or a bank. Although the family may be as central to a peasant society as it is to a tribal one, the external pressure on the class as a whole seriously affects the way in which the sex roles and the sexuality of family members are expressed.

It is more common among peasant cultures to find an emphasis on female virginity at marriage, a low regard for female sexuality, and an emphasis on childbearing as the only legitimate reason for marital sex.

Among Catholics and Moslems, these attitudes are reinforced by religion. The economic reasons must not be overlooked, however.

A portion of peasants' production and time must go to at least one source that has some punitive control over the family. If payment of whatever kind is not met, aid from other relatives and members cannot be counted on for too long because resources are limited throughout the entire group. Failure to meet payments and to produce can mean loss of land. Marriage and children are essential to the family's continued control of its land. Through marriage, new wealth can be brought into the house as dowry; affines, kin by marriage, can be important allies; the new wife is an additional worker, and children will be both workers and heirs.

Martin and Voorhies (1975) note that in peasant, or agricultural, societies the sexual division of labor seen in tribal economies is extended.

> Agricultural societies, then, generally prefer to keep a woman as isolated from public interaction as possible. Indeed, her value as a potential spouse may depend upon the degree of innocence and mystery she is able to maintain. The social segregation of the sexes accompanying intensive cultivation thus surrounds the woman with a highly charged set of taboos. Perhaps more than any other economic adaptation, the behavioral sets of men and women in agricultural societies are diametrically opposed by culture. Sexuality is certainly one of the most dynamic examples of role complementarity. As the sexual life of women falls under the control of society, no sexual activity for women becomes a social obligation symbolically detached from individual gratification. For females, nonparticipation in extra domestic production, protective spatial isolation, premarital chastity, and institutionalized frigidity go hand in hand [p. 294].

As in sex-antagonistic tribes, peasant men consider themselves to be the rulers of the society. Unlike the tribal men, the peasant men see themselves as having "natural" superior abilities (Martin and Voorhies, 1975) as opposed to being the winners of a past battle between the sexes that could be rekindled if men are not wary.

Whereas the magic of menstrual blood keeps tribal women within their own sphere, the concept of female chastity is used by peasants to keep women under strict familial control until menopause. Women's power to disrupt men's positions lies in their possible sexuality. In a system in which land is at a premium and is desired by others and a few years of misfortune can deplete the resources and work of generations, any challenge to the rightful ownership of the land jeopardizes the family. Any decline in the allegiances between families is a threat. If a man were to die and his son's paternity were in dispute, his family could lose the land to the challenger or to the landlord. If families cannot assure that their daughters are virginal at marriage, no other families will want marriage alliances with them, because of this potential threat. In twelfth century western England, for example, any widow accused of postmarital sex lost her husband's land to the lord. Her only recourse was to ride into court on a black ram, singing:

> Here I am,
> Riding upon a black ram
> Like a whore, as I am . . . .
> Therefore, I pray of you, Mr Steward,
> Let me have my land again.
> [Bennett, 1969, p. 255]

The most common marriage pattern reported in rural Europe, the Middle East, China, Japan, and Latin America is one in which the bride lives with her husband, particularly if he is the oldest son, in the home of his parents. Eventually, she becomes mistress and her husband becomes master of the house, and, in turn, their son and his wife replace them. The system provides for a waxing and waning of authority for both sexes throughout the life span, with many reports of conflict between husband and wife, father and son, and mother-in-law and daughter-in-law, which have great effects on the later years.

The first major source of stress to look at is antagonism between husband and wife. The initial problem is often sexual in nature. In rural Taiwan, young women enter marriage with no preparation for love-making, and they hardly know their husbands. Mothers, remembering their own sad first experiences, say they do not have the heart to tell their daughters what it will really be like (Wolf, 1972). In Tepoztlan, Mexico, Oscar Lewis (1951) reported that a woman avoids sexual relations before marriage and restricts contact after marriage in order to limit pregnancies, and that men discourage their wives' sexual response so that the women will not be unfaithful.

Men are not under the same strictures, although, when they enter into their first marriage, they may not be experienced either. In Tepoztlan, men are expected to have extramarital sex, although wives are angered by the accompanying loss of income and attention to the family (Lewis, 1951). In rural Taiwan, as elsewhere, prostitutes provide safe sexual outlets for men (Wolf, 1972). Rural Ireland and the Aran Islands are among the few reported cultures in which men, as well as women, are expected to be chaste before and during marriage (Arensberg and Kimball, 1961; Messenger, 1971); also, the ages of first marriage are the highest reported. Here too, sex is mainly for procreation, and male orgasm is considered debilitating (Messenger, 1971).

The second major source of stress in the husband–wife relationship is combined male authority and absenteeism. Because young peasant men live more public lives than their wives, and because they may need to accept labor in another area to help the family, they do not have the same degree of contact with their children that women have. Furthermore, the male sex role often, though not always, requires the father to be more authoritarian than affectionate toward both his wife and his children, particularly toward his sons (Kiray, 1976; Lewis, 1951). Also, the home is the woman's sphere, and, in a sense, a husband is there to provide care but not to interfer in her activities (Campbell, 1974).

A daughter-in-law often has a respectful but minimal relationship with her husband's father (Wolf, 1972; Peristiany, 1976). Next to her husband, and the child who will supplant him, her mother-in-law is the most important person in her new household. In Taiwan there is a "honeymoon" period between the new wife and her mother-in-law (Wolf, 1972), but often the "outsider"—as she is called—very quickly becomes the apprentice of the older woman. The birth of a child, particularly a son, improves the new wife's status significantly (Campbell, 1974). The young woman is then on her way to becoming the head of the household and, eventually, a mother-in-law herself.

The third major source of stress comes with the father–son relationship changing drastically with time. In a Greek community, Campbell (1974) reports, fathers, unlike many in peasant societies, are indulgent and affectionate with their sons until the son becomes apprenticed to the father's work. The tension then begins. The son must maintain respect for his father, but he is anxious to be independent. The father knows that soon his son will marry and have a son, which will signify his own time for retirement—not a welcome event. They maintain a delicate balance for the sake of the family.

In rural Ireland the oldest surviving son is kept waiting for his parents' land a long time. He is referred to as "the boy" until he marries, the father and mother being reluctant to be assigned become secondary status in their home. Thus, many "boys" of 45 can be found working their farms with their still dominant fathers (Arensberg and Kimball, 1961). The combined effects of these three sources of stress on sex roles and sexual behavior can now be seen.

As in tribal societies, late adulthood can be divided into two periods. The first is the time in which an individual is still active and in charge of a multigenerational household. The second period is retirement, although in peasant society this may occur before illness or neglect force the issue.

In the active phase, men continue much as they have from young adulthood, assuming more authority with age until they are confronted with their sons' maturity and the true nature of their wives' power over the household through the sons as well as through the domestic sphere.

In a study of a Turkish community it was found, for example, that mothers were the intermediaries between sons and fathers, helping sons to achieve financial independence from their fathers (Kiray, 1976). Lewis' comments on Tepoztlan men illustrate this point:

> We have seen that frequently husbands are only nominally the heads of household.... As men grow older, and as their sexual powers and ability to work decline, their position of dominance is more difficult to maintain .... The life cycle of men and women takes an opposite course: Men in early life are in a comparatively favored position, but as they grow older they are weighed down by life situations, women begin with less freedom, lower aspiration levels, and earlier responsibilities, but as they mature after marriage, they slowly gain more freedom and often take a dominating position in the household [Lewis, 1951, pp. 419–420].

Gutmann (1977), in his cross-cultural analysis, notes these patterns in older men; a "feminization" or androgynization occurring that is similar in both tribal and peasant societies accompanied by a "masculinization" of older women as they come to dominate the household and, it should be noted, the social network outside the family.

In peasant societies, then, a woman's heyday occurs fairly late in life, while she is the head of a team of daughters-in-law and faithful sons and is freed of certain restrictions on her mobility and social life. Older women may engage in sexual joking and mimicry, showing less modesty than was required of them in their childbearing years (Arensberg and Kimball, 1971; Lewis, 1951; Wolf, 1972). Arensberg saw this joking by both sexes as in fact a means of reinforcing the strict sexual norms of the community. In rural France, the sexual urge is seen as compelling and natural in both sexes. Everyone jokes and chats about it, finding great hilarity in a younger man's joking pass at a good-natured 99-year-old widow. Nonetheless, actual sexual behavior is very private, and the humorists are careful to choose their subjects discreetly (Wylie, 1964).

Actual sexual behavior between older married partners is difficult to assess. In rural Ireland, menopause may end sexual activity.

> Among the old, if it (sexual interest) exists at all, it is only as a survival of embers that should far better off be long dead. For adults, in adult family life, sex is divested of any awesome, evil character. "God help us," said one woman in this regard," what is natural can't be wonderful" [Arensberg and Kimball, 1961, p. 208].

In an analysis of Indian Hindu fertility, Nag ascertained that Hindu wives over 44 had an average of about 1 coital experience every 21 days, whereas American white women of the same age group had an average of 1.3 experiences every week (1972). In Tepoztlan, men never encourage their wives to be too sexually interested, for fear they will be unable to satisfy them in later years (Lewis, 1951). Older widows in Tepoztlan often do not remarry, because the children disapprove of a new male being installed in the home (Lewis, 1951). Yet, men's premarital and extra-marital relations are often with widows (Lewis, 1951).

Religion encourages older people to turn away from sexual matters as well as from issues of power in the household. In Hinduism, for example, the older householders are encouraged to turn matters over to the next generation in order to spend the remainder of life in religious pursuit (Basham, 1954). In Catholicism, it is thought that the proximity of death should be felt by the old and that they should live a sanctified old age (Arensberg and Kimball, 1961).

A note on the respect accorded older parents in peasant societies: it is traditionally the sons' and daughters'-in-law responsibility to care for older parents, thereby reversing the dependencies of the generations. Parents, however, often do not trust that their children will do so properly (Lewis, 1951). When conflict between mother and daughter-in-law is severe, the older woman is forced out of the home (Arensberg and Kimball, 1961). If fathers' authority has been too keenly felt by sons, the care of aging parents may pass from the uninterested sons' hands to those of daughters, who have had more affectionate ties with the parents. In Moslem communities this is a new pattern, because only recently have some younger married couples lived separately from the husband's family (Kiray, 1976; Peristiany, 1976). In some cases, older parents are abandoned to poorhouses (Tentori, 1976).

As long as one can work and contribute useful advice, one retains some adult status, but respect diminishes with ill health, and the infirm old parent is treated as being worse than a child (Wylie, 1964). In some areas, such as Sicily, an old mother fares much better due to her close relationship with her children (Cronin, 1970), so that some of the achieved higher status of older women stays with them until death.

In summation of sexuality in peasant societies, the rule appears to be that the repression of interest and experience in female children and young women, regardless of its encouragement or discouragement in males, results in less sexual activity in later years. If men are permitted more sexual experience outside marriage, they nonetheless must shoulder the responsibility for sexual initiative and activity within the marriage, in some cases taking care *not* to create desire in women. Under that responsibility, male sexuality appears to become as repressed with age as does its female counterpart.

A Historical Perspective on Our Culture

Trends in both male and female sex roles and sexuality have been delineated for both tribal and peasant groups for two reasons: to impart an idea of patterning and variability in human cultures, and to provide background for understanding the sources of the earlier-mentioned mythology of sexuality and aging that has been a part of our culture.

We are the heirs of these tribal and peasant traditions. The United States has been formed by the incorporation of Dahomeans, Ibibio, Ibo, Ojibwa, Comanche, and Oceanic tribal peoples, to name but a few, and by influxes of European, Asian, and Latin American families from rural backgrounds. Our legal and religious systems share roots with these peasantries. Until recently, we were a rural, agricultural society with a minimal technology, under some of the influences described earlier. Our families of origin often fight to preserve a sense of our original cultural values regarding sexuality and female behavior. With that history in mind, let us now turn to some factors that have created new viewpoints as well as factors that reinforce older viewpoints.

The Development of Competing Norms

Stone (1977) notes three unusual features in the formation of Western society's sexual behavior and attitudes. Referring particularly to the seventeenth and eighteenth centuries, he points out the long gap—10 years or more—between an individual's age of sexual maturity and marriage, with a large percentage of the population never marrying. This is the pattern reported in the twentieth century by Arensberg and Kimball (1961) for rural Ireland. The usual reason for his was the inability of a family to finance all marriageable children (with dowries, land, or a trade) or to find suitable partners, due to limited assets.

Another feature was a religion that looked upon sexuality with hostility, except when the purpose of sex was procreation. Although Protestantism marked a break with the idealization of virginity, it emphasized virginity for women before marriage (Stone, 1977).

Finally, the ideology of romantic love became popularly adopted, Stone theorizes, as the major reason for marriage. In the twelfth century, the cult of romatic love was an upper class preoccupation divorced from the realities of arranged marriage. The fact that the idea was at least appealing to the masses might be indicated by the number of old folk ballads about love affairs that have survived. Love was a popular theme on the stage, in song, and in literature for centuries. In the seventeenth and eighteenth centuries, however, novels became far more accessible to a population that was more literate than ever before, and romantic love became a part of real life—in varying degrees for each class—in the middle 1700s.

In the American colonies, as well as in England, the concept of romantic love as a reason for marriage was gaining strength, although more pragmatic reasons were still important (Queen and Habenstein, 1967). In Massachusetts, for example, marriage was virtually a necessity for survival in the smaller frontier communities of the seventeenth and early eighteenth centuries. Although the single-parent family existed— Boston was once described as a city of "widows and orphans"—the norm was for as many people as possible to marry and to remarry after widowhood. Severe financial penalties were imposed on bachelors, and the early colonial practice of the government giving land to unmarried women as well as men was stopped in some communities. Both practices were meant to ensure the growth of the colony, where land was so plentiful that the European restrictions on inheritance and therefore marriage eligibility, did not hold.

In the same period in English history, and slightly later in America, the extended-family pattern, as described in the discussion of peasants, was breaking down (Queen and Habenstein, 1967; Stone, 1977). With the growing patterns of urban laiving, wage labor, and a mobile labor force, the rise of the nuclear family was seen. This pattern is replicated today in peasant societies that are being transformed into urban forces (Hotvedt, 1976; Kiray, 1976; Peristiany, 1976). Ireland, although far more agrarian than the U.S. and England, devotes 23.8% of its land to agriculture (Gordon et al., 1981), and a recent study showed that less than 50% of farming parents expected their sons to stay on the farm (Hannon, 1979).

The combined effects of these factors on the sexuality and sex roles of people in their later years are multiple. The structural changes of households and their economics provide the backdrop to the ideational dilemmas. We have noted that, in rural systems, beneath the ideal of male dominance, there exists a pattern of matrifocality; the household is considered mainly the domain of the senior woman, who has the most affectional relationships as well as a good number of authoritative roles. Thus a decline in the extended family that reduces the power of older men also reduces, though perhaps to a lesser degree, that of older women as well. In the early nineteenth century, more older people were forced to retire to almshouses than ever before, reflecting an unwillingness—or an inability—on the part of children in nuclear families to live by the older pattern of caring for infirm parents (Stone, 1977). A hale mother could be welcomed into a daughter's home as an additional helper and friend. She would have the knowledge of childrearing, "women's work," and health care to make a significant contribution (Kiray, 1976; Queen and Habenstein, 1967). Older men who must retire from their own enterprises because of failing strength may find a welcome place in a child's home, but they are at a disadvantage in continuing the fabric of their lives. The admission of their dependency and the loss of their strength and dominance are marks against their masculinity.

Older men today, according to Gutmann (1977), show a coping mechanism marked by a movement away from masculine activities and values in the face of conflict with a younger generation of men; a drift toward a more passive, congenial stance defined as feminine earlier in the life cycle. In another context, in the absorption of the members of some Native American tribes into modern American life, it has been found that women suffered less personality conflict with adaptation, because they could continue the preoccupations of traditional tribal women's roles, whereas men could no longer fulfil their own definitions of masculinity through their work (Georing, 1970).

In England, Stone (1977) argues, the value of the later years changed with the decrease in the extended family. Once it was a period respected as part of the life cycle where one's wisdom compensated for the loss of physical strength. However, it came to be seen as a period of physical and mental decay preceding death. As standards of health improved and people felt less at the mercy of fate, the process of aging was seen as proof of a failure of the individual.

Another erosion of later life was the loss of older people as teachers of the young family members. With the increase of science, literacy, and, finally, the mass media, the young can receive information as swiftly or more so than their elders, greatly reducing the value of the oral tradition and greatly increasing the independence of youth (Mead, 1970). The growth in the number and distribution of romantic novels (Stone, 1977) and their effects on the young can be seen as an early example of this trend.

DeBeauvoir (1973), in "The Coming of Age," sees two coexisting sexual images of older people. On the one hand there is the moralistic, religious ideal of the dignified older man or woman who no longer is interested in sex, the passions having died a natural death. On the other hand, there is the "dirty old man" or the "shameless old lady" (DeBeauvoir, 1973). Neither images stems from what we might now consider a healthy view of sexuality, but the images have long been with us. Indeed, both viewpoints appear in Greek drama and philosophy (DeBeauvoir, 1973).

Within our own history, religion and the older system of arranged marriage and residence with the extended family supported the decline of sexuality with age. For all classes, lust, even within marriage, was inveighed against as being dangerous to psychological and physical well-being (Stone, 1977). We know that the actual pattern of premarital sexuality, which in other cultures seems to be related to sexuality in the later years, varied from the ideal under new circumstances. In seventeenth and eighteenth century Massachusetts, cases of premarital sexual violations were extremely common (Queen and Habenstein, 1967). Extra-marital and postmarital sexual conduct was far more severely punished and, therefore, less likely to be confessed. And so, again, it is difficult to ascertain the conduct of older people outside or in marriage. Instead, we are left with the ideal of the couple (or widowed person) declining into graceful old age, living a natural celibacy after a family is created, and preparing to meet the Creator by shedding their "earthly desires."

Of the other image, we know a bit more, chiefly through the diaries of famous people who were interested in their sexual selves until death. The appearance of these first intimate diaries coincides with the rise in romantic love. The journals of Tolstoy and Madame Tolstoy, Victor Hugo and his mistress, Trotsky, and many others (DeBeauvoir, 1973) show people grappling with the three myths mentioned earlier: the sexual undesirability, lack of interest, and inability of the later years. Patterns emerge. First, romantic love, perhaps an artificial piece of culture designed to mask the sexual urge (Stone, 1977), figures into the passions of these middle-class and upper-class people in later life. Sometimes the preference is for one's spouse, while at other times it is a heterosexual or homosexual attachment to a new person. Second, the negative effect of aging on women as sex objects as compared to the prospects of older men are seen. If a man had fame as a creative person or wealth and standing, he was capable of attracting and keeping younger partners, although he might still have an involved marital relationship. Women, however, felt keenly the competition with younger women, and sometimes men, who came closer to the romantic ideals of youth and beauty. This jealousy showed, despite the fact that these women received attention from other men. Finally, the journals show that even when coitus became difficult or impossible because of health, sexuality required an outlet and that varieties of expression could be found by both sexes (DeBeauvoir, 1973). It should be noted that these are the accounts of active people to whom the spheres of creativity and work were vital to the self-concept.

Research on older Americans' (average age 68) sexuality and self-esteem was conducted by questionnaire, with 51 men and 99 women responding (Stimson *et al.*, 1981). Both men and women in the study felt that sex was acceptable for older people. Results showed that being sexually active was as critical a variable in self-esteem for older men as it was for younger male samples studied earlier by the same research team. A key difference was that for older men, the quality of sexual performance was related to good feelings of self, whereas the quantity of sexual activity was the important factor for the younger men.

Women in the sample viewed sexual activity as separate from issues of self-esteem, as did younger women in the authors' previous study. The crucial point was that women seem to accept youth as a prerequisite for "desirability" and use youthful standards to judge themselves. When a woman no longer feels attractive, she is no longer sure of her overall worth.

WHERE WE NOW STAND

A cross-cultural analysis on sexuality in the later years may be dismaying to the reader as well as to the researcher. Many of us were taught that the strict sexual mores of peasant life are "natural" and correct. The cases of abandonment when ill health occurs—whether in tribal, peasant, or early industrial society—strike uncomfortably close to many of our own fears for our own futures. The scarcity of detailed data on the subject echoes the long tradition we have known in which the personal concerns of older people are supposedly less interesting than those of the young.

It is hoped that this review will give some hope as well as some background through its tentative conclusions. We have seen that great personal and cultural variation exists throughout the life span regarding sexuality. Vital to the continuation of sexual expression in later years, on anything other than an idiosyncratic basis, is a cultural pattern that allows for sexual expression in youth as well. Real sexual and economic domination by men appears to be inimicable to the full expression of female sexuality, which in turn has limiting effects on later male heterosexual expression in traditional societies except, possibly, for the more wealthy, who have the influence necessary to experience new sexual partners. Finally, in tribal and early industrial societies, it is indicated that a sense of vitality and purpose in later years strengthens one's sexuality.

There may have been some gains from the often painful past. Although the demise of the extended family and the rise of romantic love vitiate many of the roles of later years, benefits arise as well. The changes in sex roles that are slowly developing are, in fact, a move to foreshorten the changes Gutmann (1977) and others see as occurring later in life; that is, an androgynization of both sexes so that the traditional values of masculinity and femininity might be more uniformly expressed by both sexes across the life span (Martin and Voorhies, 1975).

Although the cult of youth and beauty is still deep within our culture, older people are as literate and as verbal (or more so) as the young, and they have begun to influence the media to expand their standards of attractiveness to include a much older age group. In the later years, we may be more free to experience a continued or even new sense of sexuality without the presence of offspring to contradict and remind us of the dignity and asceticism proper to old age. We also feel more entitled to love and compatibility with a partner, regardless of age. Much is possible. To quote Goethe:

> So, lively brisk old man
> Do not let sadness come over you;
> For all your white hairs
> You can still be a lover.
>
> [DeBeauvoir, 1973, p. 488]

REFERENCES

Achebe, C. (1959). "Things Fall Apart." Fawcett, Greenwich, Connecticut.

Achebe, C. (1960). "No Longer at Ease." Fawcett, Greenwich, Connecticut.

Achebe, C. (1967). "Arrow of God." John Day, New York.

Andreski, I. (1970). "Old Wives' Tales: Life-Stories of African Women." Schocken Books, New York.

Arensberg, C., and Kimball, S., eds. (1961). "Family and Community in Ireland." Peter Smith, Gloucester, Massachusetts.

Balkwell, C., and Balswick, J. (1981). *J. Marriage and the Family* 43, 423–429.

Basham, A. L. (1954). "The Wonder That Was India." Grove Press, Inc., New York.

Bennett, H. S. (1969). "Life on the English Manor." Cambridge Univ. Press, London/New York.

Bohannon, P., and Middleton, J., eds. (1968). "Marriage, Family and Residence." Natural History Press, New York.

Brotman, H. (1981). Developments in Aging. "Every Ninth American," prepared for "Special Committee on Aging," U.S. Senate, Washington, D.C.

Campbell, J.K. (1974). "Honor, Family, and Patronage. "Oxford Univ. Press, London/New York.

Cronin, C. (1970). "The Sting of Change: Sicilians in Sicily and Australia." Univ. of Chicago Press, Chicago.

DeBeauvoir, S. (1973). "The Coming of Age." Warner Paperback Library, New York.

Gebhard, P. H. (1971a). In "Human Sexual Behavior" (D. S. Marshall and R. Suggs, eds.), p. xii. Basic Books, New York.

Gebhard, P. H. (1971b). In "Human Sexual Behavior" (D. S. Marshall and R. Suggs, eds.), pp. 207–217. Basic Books, New York.

Gearing, F. O. (1970). "The Face of the Fox." Aldine, Chicago.

Gordon, M., Whelan, B., and Vaughan, R. (1981). *J. Marriage and the Family 43*, 741–747.

Gorer, G., ed. (1967). "Himalayan Village." Basic Books, New York.

Green, R. (1974). "Sexual Identity Conflict in Children and Adults." Penguin, Baltimore.

Gutmann, D. (1977). In "Handbook of the Psychology of Aging" (J. E. Birren and K. W. Schaie, eds.), pp. 305–306. Van Nostrand-Reinhold, Princeton, New Jersey.

Hannon, D. F. (1979). "Displacement and Development: Class, Kinship, and Social Change in Irish Rural Communities." Economic and Social Research Inst., Dublin.

Harris, M. (1975). "Culture, People, Nature." T. Y. Crowell, New York.

Hotvedt, M. E. (1976). Dissertation, Department of Anthropology, Indiana University, Bloomington (unpublished).

Kiray, N. (1976). In "Mediterranean Family Structures" (J. G. Peristiany, ed.), pp. 266–267. Cambridge Univ. Press, London/New York.

Landes, R. (1971). "The Ojibwa Woman." Norton, New York.

Lewis, O. (1951). "Life in a Mexican Village: Tepoztlan Revisited." Univ. Of Illinois Press, Urbana.

Malinowsky, B. (1929). "The Sexual Life of Savages." Harcourt, Brace & World, New York.

Marshall, D. S. (1971). In "Human Sexual Behavior" (D. S. Marshall and R. Suggs, eds.), pp. 103–162. Basic Books, New York.

Martin, M. K., and Voorhies, B. (1975). "Female of the Species." Columbia Univ. Press, New York.

Mead, M., ed. (1950). "Sex and Temperament in Three Primitive Societies." Mentor Books, New York.

Mead, M. (1970). "Culture and Commitment." Doubleday, New York.

Messenger, J. C. (1971). In "Human Sexual Behavior" (D. S. Marshall and R. Suggs, eds.), pp. 3–37. Basic Books, New York.

Murphy, Y., and Murphy, R. F. (1974). "Women of the Forest." Columbia Univ. Press, New York.

Nag, M. (1972). *Curr. Anthropol.* **13**, 231–238.

Peristiany, J. G., ed. (1976). "Mediterranean Family Structures." Cambridge Univ. Press, London/New York.

Queen, S. A., and Habenstein, R. N. (1967). "The Family in Various Cultures." Lippincott, Philadelphia.

Spencer, R. F. (1968). In "Marriage, Family and Residence" (P. Bohannon and J. Middleton, eds.), p. 142. Natural History Press, New York.

Stimson, A., Wase, J., and Stimson, J. (1981). *Research on Aging* **3**, 228–239.

Stone, L. (1977). "The Family, Sex, and Marriage in England. 1500–1800." Harper & Row, New York.

Tentori, T. (1976). *In* "Mediterranean Family Structures" (J. G. Peristinay, ed.), pp. 273–286. Cambridge Univ. Press, London/New York.

U.S. Bureau of Census (1972). "Statistical Abstracts of the United States: 1972," Table 40. U.S. Govt. Printing Office, Washington, D.C.

Welch, C., and Glick, P. (1981). *J. Marriage and the Family 43*, 191–192.

Wolf. M. (1972). "Women and the Family in Rural Taiwan." Stanford Univ. Press, Stanford, California.

Wylie, L. (1964). "Village in the Vaucluse." Harper & Row, New York.

3

The Physiological Perspective

Ruth B. Weg

> *I will reveal to you a love potion,*
> *Without medicine, without herbs,*
> *without any witch's magic;*
> *If you want to be loved, then*
> *LOVE.*
>
> Hecaton of Rhodes[1]

INTRODUCTION

Love, and be loved. This familiar prescription suggests the typical advice to all men and women down through the centuries, except for the aging. Those who are wrinkling, graying, and over 65 have been assigned to a special category—sexually inert, uninterested, and dysfunctional. Young and old alike are uncomfortable with the reality that older persons (especially parents) are involved with the intimacy, pleasure, and tenderness of sexual expression that are associated primarily with the younger years. What in the human family's developmental history through the eons has brought the culture to the existing sexual mores and practices?

The long story of sexual relationships goes back to human beginnings. The available knowledge of prehistory based on surmise and archaeological detective work is necessarily varied, often ambiguous, and subject to various interpretations. But some fairly reliable facts have filtered through. Men and women were probably fairly equal in status prior to the neolithic revolution. But, by about 3000 BC, when recorded history begins, the sex roles of men and women had been more or less redefined, and man was master (Tannahill, 1980).

Intercourse in the usual nonhuman primate position (the female's dorsum to the male's venter) is "brief, crude and purposeful" (Tannahill, 1980, p. 16). When our early ancestors came down from the trees, added meat to their diet of fruit and vegetables, and began to use their hands for more than kneeling, the vertical, bipedal posture ushered in a new era of sexual expression. The new face-to-face position is thought to have led to human female orgasm, apparently absent in the nonhuman primate female (Ford and Beach, 1951). And so, in addition to the perpetuation of the species, the personal pleasure components were added to the human sexual experience.

Throughout much of prehistory, it was natural for men and women (as was true for other animals) to have sexual intercourse; it was a part of

[1] A philosopher of the second century BC, Stoic school who wrote on ethical subjects; often quoted by Cicero.

their physical fulfillment. It was also natural for the human female, "like the wild mare or the reindeer cow, to be either pregnant or nursing for much of her adult life" (Tannahill, 1980, p. 24). Humanity may have been promiscuous at first; "family" ties awaited the cave dwelling of about 250,000 years ago. Any connection between sexual activity and morality came much later in the development of civilization. Similarly, the ignorance of the connection between coitus and conception was widespread until about 9000 BC. Even in contemporary England, where the causal relationships between fatherhood and coitus are understood, a woman wrote to a column of a woman's magazine inquiring whether the "pill" would protect her from pregnancy by husband and/or lover (London, from a report in Sunday Times, 1977, in Tannahill, 1980).

The most common measures of youth and the potential for immortality were sexual capacity and performance (Trimmer, 1970). Sexual activity and potency were equated with vigor and long life. Human history is replete with magic, sorcery, and alchemy using plant and animal tissues; potions, elixirs, and topical concoctions to enhance sexual capacities. The search for the extension of sexual potency, youth, and finally immortality may be as old as humankind and extends to modern-day society. The biblical tale of King David of Israel describes the final treatment (typical of that time) to help revive the aging, ill king—the attention and body warmth of a young virgin. Aphrodisiac recipes were said to be written on a Babylonian cuneiform tablet from about 800 BC, the earliest record found so far (Gruman, 1966).

Taoism, the philosophy that developed during the third and second centuries BC (350–250 BC), dominated Chinese thought and behavior for more than 2000 years. Sexual activity was perceived as a sacred duty and a rejuvenator to be exercised often with great care in order to achieve the goal of harmony with the Supreme Path or the Way (Tao) (Tannahill, 1980). Elaborate, prescribed techniques (sexual disciplines) to augment and conserve semen, (the male, or young, "essence") related to the Chinese concern with a long, sexual life (Gruman, 1966). Such a regimen included breathing exercises, sun therapy, a balanced diet, full sexual activity, and finally, the elixir of immortality.

As recently as 1920, the concept of preservation of the male essence, or semen, was implemented and tested by Dr. E. Steinach (Guillerme, 1963, pp. 107, 108). He suggested that an internal accumulation of sex hormones, released into the blood, could be achieved by tying off the sperm ducts (vasa deferentia), thereby rejuvenating the individual. Sexual rejuvenators that promised success in love and sex were often plant or plant products such as sweet potatoes, orchids, mandrake, and ginseng;

the latter is currently in a period of renewed popularity (Trimmer, 1970).

The culmination of experimentation with animals and animal products (such as partridge brains, Chinese bird's nest soup, and sex glands and extracts) received the scorn of scientists. In 1889, Dr. Brown-Séquard, a French physician, injected himself with three volumes of guinea pig testes extract. He stated, at a meeting of the Société de Biologie, that he was "young again," and that he had turned the clock back 30 years. His Parisian colleagues dismissed his studies as "senile aberrations" (Trimmer, 1970).

"Monkey gland" grafting was the vogue after World War I. It involved the insertion of slices of chimpanzee testes into the bursae of male patients. Current sex hormone replacement and cell therapies are modern-day versions of this nineteenth and early twentieth century work (Guillerme, 1963).

Throughout evolution, from the supposedly pleasurable, natural sexuality of men and women in prehistory to the belated realization of the connection between coitus and pregnancy and the more modern development of family and differentiated sex roles, there has been the underlying notion of the unity of vigor, youth, beauty, and sexuality. That concept of unity, waxing and waning over the centuries, has continued to relegate middle-aged persons and elders to a "not applicable" category.

Societies, in the past and today, have developed differing sexual practices, with various meanings for the same sexual acts. Sexual expression has been variously perceived as pleasure, natural, evil, reproduction, economic excess, health or illness, and, finally, liberation. More recently, sexuality has been associated with intimacy, love, friendship, and play, and is increasingly an area of personal concern and choice (Gagnon and Simon, 1973). As with so much of human existence, sensual, sexual behavior is learned. The stereotypic image of sexless aging also has been learned, by the society and elders themselves. If more than the biology of reproduction drives human sexual expression, then there is promise of possible intervention. Society can learn about the life span potential for sexual activity, unlearn inappropriate attitudes and behavior, and prepare to understand and enjoy this aspect of human personality and behavior.

SOCIETAL PERCEPTIONS

The mythology of dysfunction, lack of interest, and impotence with the years is still a major folklore. Mores and practices of the American culture related to aging have identified one role as being suitable for the aged—the sick role. This assignation effectively separates older persons from traditional sex-role behaviors, because another myth declares that illness precludes sexual interest and capacity. When elders are removed from the mainstream, the fear of aging and death are also eliminated from easy view.

Denial of ordinary existence enables the denial of sexual expression, and the stereotype continues amid beliefs that die hard: libido begins its diminution in the middle years and is absent during the later years; and if desire, somehow, survives into old age, lovemaking may be hazardous in view of the frailties that accompany aging. In any case, the tale goes on; the aged are sufficiently physically unattractive—no more round, smooth, lithe bodies of yesteryear—to make them sexually undesirable. These negative attitudes and images have serious consequences for people of all ages as they look to lifelong sexuality. More particularly, the message is destructive for many of the middle-aged and elders who fulfill that prophecy, facing their futures in angry, sad resignation.

Although men in their middle and later years generally fare better than older women, they are seen by the public and professionals alike as sexually impaired (Masters and Johnson, 1970). These years are frequently marked by anxiety and restlessness, a dread of aging, a fear of the loss of sexual adequacy, and a preoccupation with sexual vigor, in spite of greater societal acceptance of the aging male over the aging female. A marriage or other liaison of an older man and a young woman is seen as a sign of youthful vigor and vitality. Such an erotic and romantic response of a young woman to a male old enough to be her father is generally applauded as being understandable and normal. However, when job, power, and status are at an end, the customary identity of male vigor with achievement is no longer possible. Confidence and self-image are diminished, and sexual dysfunction, even impotence, may develop.

An old woman is even more at risk. "That old women are repulsive is one of the most profound esthetic and erotic feelings in our culture" (Sontag, 1972, p. 37). Any marital or extramarital pairing of an older woman and a younger man is an emotional, visual improbability for most people. The youth may be seen as a victim of an oedipal complex, the older women as a needful neuter in search of a lost mothering role. A sexual life history that best describes society's view of a woman begins with her as "young and sexy"; she grows to become "mature and exciting," and, by age 50 (and older), she achieves the anonymity of the sexually unseen (Butler and Lewis, 1977).

It is a tribute to some older men and women that they do maintain and enjoy an active sexual life in the face of limited opportunities, lack of privacy, and society's asexual label and expectations that continue as as the modal environment (Laury, 1977).

Various segments of the population demonstrate some differences in their perceptions and attitudes concerning age and sexuality. The negative attitudes of the young toward the sexual activity of their elders have been documented by a number of studies. Golde and Kagan (1959) assessed two groups of college students with a completion-of-a-sentence technique. Group 1 was asked to finish "Sex for most old people...." In this group, 92.9% responded with "negligible or unimportant." Group 2 was asked to complete "Sex for most people...." Only 4.9% used "negligible or unimportant" (LaTorre and Kear, 1977).

In an examination of attitudes toward sexuality in the aged, the staff of a nursing home and university undergraduate students were found by LaTorre and Kear (1977, p. 211) to: (a) have a "lack of negative attitudes toward sex in aged when compared to that toward sex in younger individuals"; and (b) possess a "noncredibility of sexuality" (p. 212) among older persons. Staff members had a more negative attitude toward sex in older persons than students. Merritt and colleagues (1975) concluded that increased age and limited education have been correlated with negative attitudes toward sexual activity among the elderly.

Berezin's (1976, p. 191) observation that the general public has grown more aware of "conditions, statistics, factors, myths, misconceptions and prejudices about sex in general, and specifically about sex in old age" is defensible, as the media and the public begin to respond to changing attitudes and mores. Berezin also notes that articles on sex and old age in popular literature (magazines and newspapers) are increasing and that there is greater attention paid to elders as people in television programs and films (e.g., *Harry and Tonto, Harold and Maude,* and *Tell Me a Riddle*).

At last, elders themselves appear to be slowly shedding some of the destructive imagery. In evidence is the bumper sticker that reads "I am not a dirty old man. I am a sexy senior citizen" (Berezin, 1976), the thousands of older couples who are living together without benefit of a marriage certificate, and the thousands of older women seeking activity, intellectual stimulation, and companionship at senior centers across the country.

SIGNIFICANCE FOR THE INDIVIDUAL

Generally, most human beings are endowed with all the natural physiological equipment needed for reproduction and sexual interaction.

But, human sensuality–sexuality is more than sexual intercourse and orgasm, more than sex hormones and genitalia, and more than the reproductive system and babies. Human sexual expression suggests capacities and activities, essential to the ego and a sense of well-being, that grow from the fact of two sexes. Sexual behavior is not separable, in practice, from the anatomy and physiology involved, nor is it separate from the total and unique personality that participates. Rather than a particular norm for different ages, or each of the two sexes, sexual behavior covers a wide range of possibilities within any group. The survival of the human race depends upon the differentiated sexes and sexuality. Procreation normally requires the engagement of male and female in sexual intercourse. For many generations, the production of progeny has essentially determined the structure and function of the human family.

For the individual, sexual expression is a combination of biology and socialization, and their continual interaction. Sexuality is a function of prenatal development, its biological determination of sex, and postnatal learning experiences, including the complexities of gender identity and role.

The intimacy and warmth often associated with sexual expression have a significance beyond the pleasurable release of sexual tension—an important assertion and commitment of self and a reaffirmation of the connection with life itself (Butler and Lewis, 1976).

RESEARCH

Felt and Expressed Needs

"For human beings, the more powerful need is not for sex per se, but for relationship, intimacy acceptance and affirmation" (May, 1969, p. 311). The facts support the statement: there is no time limit to the sensual, sexual years (Masters and Johnson, 1966, 1970; Weg, 1977, 1978a). Rather than the limits of physiological capacities with age, one of the major deterrants, and the most destructive barrier, to a full expression of human love relationships, is the pervasive attitude toward the sensual and sexual later years. This attitude is held by the community at large (described earlier) by the media, by children of elders (where they exist), by health and social-service professionals, and by older persons them-selves. Expectations often become "parent" to the plunging self-esteem and the withdrawal from social and sexual activities.

Most people in their later middle and older years accept the gradual decline in many bodily systems as the years add up, so that the need to moderate tennis playing, mountain climbing, or late partying is not devastating; often, it is welcome. There is, however, one physiological capacity that stands alone. Any change, any diminution in either reproductive function or activity as a sexual partner conjures up fearsome, ego-damaging consequences. Few changes with age appear to be so threatening to ego identity, to the sense of well-being. This decline suggests the end of productive life. Dysfunction is an awesome image of asexuality, a step closer to death, visiting painful damage upon self-concept, motivation, and the zest for life. Culture still equates sexual performance with manliness or womanliness (and with youthful loveliness and vigor).

Having bought the sexless image, many of those elders who experience sexual want and satisfy such desires, as well as those who want in vain, experience apprehension and guilt. They feel what is perceived as abnormal and know either pain or pleasure in the denial or expression of their sexuality.

The needs for an intimate relationship, for touch, caress, companionship, caring, love, dignity, identity, self-esteem, intellectual growth, and overall human interaction begin very early in human development and continue until death in old age. These needs and their realization may be even more critical in the later years, as other roles and relationships slip away. When participation as worker, community citizen, and active parent generally decreases and a number of friends and relatives die or move away, the one intimate other, the confidant, may be crucial as a connection with human warmth and a deterrent to despair or even suicide (Leviton, 1973; Lowenthal and Berkman, 1967; Weg, 1978a). In 1961, before the significant academic growth in gerontology as an area of inquiry, practice, and education (Weg, 1975b), the late psychologist, L. Frank (1961) saw sexual relations as a major source of psychological reinforcement for some older people. He suggested that, for the older man, sexual activity may be particularly significant, because he often faces the failing prestige and self-confidence consequent to an ebbing work world. The older woman understandably seeks an affirmation of her attractiveness and desirability following menopause; continuing sensual-sexual interaction is an important measure.

Ample documentation exists that sexual interest and activity persist through the ninth decade of life (Comfort, 1974; Kinsey *et al.*, 1948, 1953; Masters and Johnson, 1966, 1970; DeNicola and Peruzza, 1974; Pfeiffer and Davis, 1972). There would appear to be (contrary to the popular image) a remarkable constancy in sexual interest and activity throughout life. Although sexual interest and activity usually decrease gradually with the years, cessation is generally a function of the health status of one or both of the partners. Older men appear to remain more active than older women, but this may be related more to the powerful Victorian sex education of women who are old today and to the limited number of available elder males.

The ratios of older men and women explain the lack of male partners among elders: the average for the total 65 and over population is 146 women per 100 men; between the ages of 65 and 74 there are 130 women per 100 men; for the 75 and over group the ratio reaches 178; and in the 85 and over group, the ratio increases again, to 224 women per 100 men. By the year 2050, among persons 65 and over, a ratio of 152 women to 100 men is projected (Brotman, 1981). Should the trend of women outliving men by an average of 8 years continue, more serious attention will have to be given to the range of sexual behaviors beyond heterosexual intercourse.

The character of the bulk of research in human sexuality has been singular and far too simply identified with the physical act of heterosexual intercourse. There has been a tacit assumption that sexual intercourse and, more specifically, orgasm are the primary facts of the sensual, sexual life. Although intercourse and masturbation are still perceived as the two most significant sexual activities, other variables have been indicated more recently: the degree of erotic feelings, desires, dreams, fantasies, and an evaluation of sexual satisfaction. Increasingly, but sparingly, there is information concerning organic conditions, availability of partners, and other psychological and sociological data, including comparisons between men and women, and, finally, a beginning of serious studies related to homosexuality and age.

What may be most critical, and most absent, are research and comment on sexuality in the elderly that refer to affection, tenderness, love, and relationships. In large part, reports still are concerned with the "physical aspects of sex, statistics, and frequency" (Berezin, 1976, p. 192).

There are signs of change in both printed and visual media. A more accepting societal environment exists concerning the presence of sexual matters in the popular media and in college and university texts and courses. Age-oriented sex counseling and therapeutic programs are in place. It is therefore understandable that literature in human sexuality has begun to include more and varied content on the sexual expression of the elderly (Crooks and Baur, 1980); Hite, 1976; Huyck, 1977; Kaplan, 1974; Lobsenz, 1974; Pearlman, 1972; Pfeiffer, 1975; Reedy, 1978; Seaman and Seaman, 1978; Sviland, 1975; Weg, 1978a).

Behavior

Judith Wax's (1975) interview with 74-year-old Celia in "Sex and the Single Grandparent," describes honestly and lovingly what self-image and sexual expression mean to an older woman.

> Sex isn't as powerful a need as when you're young, but the whole feeling is there; it's as nice as it ever was. He puts his arms around you, kisses you, and it comes to you—satisfaction and orgasm—just like it always did ... don't let anybody tell you different. Maybe it only happens once every 2 weeks, but as you get older, it's such a release from tensions. I'm an old dog who's even tried a few new tricks. Like oral sex, for instance .... We weren't too crazy about it though .... We take baths together, and he washes my body, and I wash his. I know I'm getting old and my skin could use an ironing, but we love each other—so sex is beautiful [p. 43].

Not so long ago (approximately 30 years ago), the level and amount of scientific information on human sexual functioning was minimal, and, in relation to the later years, it was essentially nonexistent. Today, although it is still limited, there is a slow but steady increase in contributions to the psychosocial and biomedical dimensions of human sexual, sensual expression. There have been more articles published on the biology of human sexuality since 1966 than in all previous years combined. Within the past 15 years, observations and studies have dramatically substantiated what had been known but not widely acknowledged—that sensuality, sexuality, and loving relationships among older persons are not the fantasies of sexologists (Berezin, 1976; Comfort, 1974; Huyck, 1977; Masters and Johnson, 1966, 1970; Rubin, 1965; Sheehy, 1976).

Investigators into human sexual behavior early in the twentieth century embarked on an effort to create a favorable environment for sex research. Kinsey and colleagues decided, in their massive interview-and-questionnaire undertaking, to establish quantitative, scientific criteria with which to identify and compare sexual behavior. Therefore, they measured that which could be counted—sexual encounters and orgasms—through a variety of behaviors: masturbation, oral sex, intercourse, and other homosexual, heterosexual, and bisexual activities (Kinsey et al., 1948, 1953).

Although it is true that only 3 of the 1700 pages of the Kinsey reports were devoted to the sexuality of older persons, important realities were brought to light at a time when the talk and/or study of sexuality was still a widespread taboo (Claman, 1966). The work of Kinsey and colleagues, an epidemiological and sociological study of human sexual behavior, reported that there is no loss of satisfaction for the postmenopausal woman. There even may be an increase in pleasure, because concern with conception is at an end. Also noted by Kinsey and colleagues (and confirmed by Pfeiffer and Davis, 1972) was that sexual experience in the earlier years influences libido in the postmenopausal years.

One measure of physical and sexual vigor in the male is the frequency of morning erections, which does not change significantly until age 66 or older (Kinsey *et al.*, 1948). Moreover, Kinsey and colleagues found that, among males over 70, 70% of married men reported a mean sexual frequency of .9 per week, although some men maintained a frequency of 3 times per week.

In 1960, two American physicians, Newman and Nichols, as part of the longitudinal study of the Duke Center for the Study of Aging and Human Development, investigated (by questionnaire and interview) 250 older black and white persons between the ages of 60 and 93 years and found that sexual activity declines sharply after age 75. Of the 149 participants who were married, 54% were still sexually active but, among 101 unmarried (single, divorced, or widowed) persons in the same group, only 7% maintained sexual activity. Blacks remained more active than whites, males reported more activity than females, and the less affluent had greater sexual expression than the rich. Again, as uncovered by the work of Kinsey and colleagues (1948, 1953) and a number of studies since, a full sex life in the early years is an accurate predictor of active sexual expression in the later years—whatever the color, sex, and economic status of the individual.

Masters and Johnson (1966, 1970) were the first to objectively investigate the physiology of sexual expression in a population of 694 subjects, though older persons made up only 4.5% of the total. They confirmed the findings of Kinsey and colleagues (1948, 1953) and Pfeiffer and Davis (1972): "There is no time limit drawn by the advancing years of female sexuality." And, for the male in a supportive physical and emotional situation, they found "a capacity for sexual performance that frequently may extend to and beyond the 80-year-old age level" (Masters and Johnson, 1966, p. 223).

Further, Masters and Johnson demonstrated that sexual disorders (or dysfunction) among older persons are as susceptible to treatment or therapy as those in younger persons. Their concept, that sexual inadequacy is not usually a singular individual malfunction, but rather a problem of the couple, led to the much copied dyadic therapy, which they developed. Older couples responded to such therapy almost as satisfactorily as younger couples, although they often needed more time.

The longitudinal study of the Duke Center for the Study of Aging and Human Development was an interdisciplinary study of physiological, psychological, and social changes among elders (Verwoerdt *et al.*, 1970). It has provided the most documentation concerning the sexuality of older persons available from interviews and questionnaires. Two hundred and sixty community volunteers (60–94 years old), 67% white and 33% black) were involved at the beginning of the study in 1954. None were hospitalized, bedridden, or otherwise immobilized. The data were gathered at three points in time separated by 3–4-year intervals: 1955–1957, 1959–1961, and 1964. Generally, these subjects tended to be married, had moderately good physical and psychological health, and remained sexually and socially active. Other findings were: (a) although the degree of sexual interest declined with age, one-half of the seniors reported a mild or moderate degree of interest into their 80s and 90s; (b) in both females and males, interest exceeded activity; (c) married women had a higher incidence of sexual activity than single females; (d) among men surviving into their 80s and 90s, one-fifth remained active; (e) in women, the incidence of continuous absence of activity increased steadily with age, and men showed patterns of continuous abstinence with the years; (f) differences between older men and women decreased with age, and women had a higher incidence of interest after 78 years of age; (g) although the overall picture is one of decline, one-quarter of the male seniors displayed an increase in degree of activity and interest; (h) for both men and women, the pattern of sexual interest, enjoyment, and behavior of the earlier years could predict the level of interest and activity in the later years; (i) for the older female, another important factor regarding interest and activity was a sanctioned (or marriage) partner, whereas for the male, diminished health presented a barrier, and (j) when the female reported a decrease or cessation of sexual activity, it was more apparent than real. Cessation was reported by 14% of the males and 40% of the females. Generally, women attribute cessation to their male mates, and the men confirmed that statement (Pfeiffer and Davis, 1972).

Twelve years of experience as the attending physician for a rural nursing home demonstrated to West (1975) that sexual desire, physical love, and sex existed in a significant number of the elderly as "an important, integral part of their lives. (p. 551)" He added two other interesting findings. First, there was a considerable degree of variation in the mode of sexual activity (including intercourse, fondling, caressing, and oral contact). Second, although orgasm was not always a result of sexual activity, the residents interviewed (men and women) experienced "much pleasure and release from tension. (p. 552)" They described the activity as contributing to the fulfillment and gratification of a relationship. In this population there also appeared to be a "feeling that sex and love go together. (p. 552)"[2]

The importance of sexual daydreams in the enhancement of potency was put to use in a study of sexual responsiveness among older and younger males by Solnick (1977). Giambra and Martin (1977, p. 497), in a study of 277 men, found that "the frequency and intensity of sexual daydreams declined with increasing age, and after age 65 virtually disappeared." There was a direct correlation between the occurrence of sexual daydreams with "each of the three behavioral indicators of sexual vigor for all age groups through age 64. (p. 497)" Among women, sexual fantasies and daydreams have also been found to be common during intercourse and to heighten desire and pleasure (Hariton and Singer, 1974).

Differences between male and female sexual expression have been addressed by Kaplan (1974). She has found that female sexual responsiveness (in the American culture) peaks in the late 30s and early 40s and is usually maintained into the 60s and beyond. Male sexuality generally declines from a maximum responsiveness at 18 years. Elderly women continue to have the capacity for multiple orgasms. Contrary to the menopause mythology, many postmenopausal women experience increased libido and interest, which may relate, in part, to the now minimally opposed androgen action due to diminished estrogen (Kaplan, 1974). The strong sexual drive in women (even without a male partner) has been demonstrated by masturbation data: there is a higher incidence of masturbation in widowed and divorced females, and 25% of single 70-year-old females masturbate (Christenson and Gagnon, 1965).

Although it is useful to identify the sex differences in sexual physiology and expression—in capacities, needs, interests, and enjoyment—it also is important to recognize the commonalities between men and women as reproductive and sexual human beings. The decreasing sex hormones in both sexes affect older men and women similarly in weight gain, receding hair lines, loss of hair color and genital tissue, and the alteration of sleep patterns. In "the primary sexual response of the adult male and female, there is no differentiation between man and woman"(Roszak, 1969, p. 305). The basic qualities of orgasm are the same for male and female. Nevertheless, the available data do indicate that particular physiological changes and capacities among men and women

------

[2]Elsewhere in this volume (Kassel and Schlesinger), the actuality and the potential for sexual expression among institutionalized elderly are treated more fully.

affect individual self-esteem and illuminate the potential for meaningful dyadic relationships.

CLIMACTERIC

The double standard of aging (Sontag, 1972) is extant, and it is exaggerated in the consideration of sexual expression. Growing middle-aged and old is still experienced as a more threatening reality for women than it is for men. Men are perceived as desirable, distinguished, and mature in their 50s, 60s, and 70s, in spite of gray hair, mid-body paunch, and flabby muscles. Women in their middle and older years, on the other hand, are perceived as neutered, colorless, wrinkled hags—no longer the decoration of society.

A very early description of the menopausal woman and the sexually vigorous, performing middle-aged and older male can be found in the Bible: "It ceased to be with Sarah after the manner of women" (Greenblatt et al., 1979, p. 481). Then a description of Sarah's personality changes is presented; she became irritable and cantankerous. Sarah commanded Hagar (her bondswoman) to leave her home, because she was "with child by Sarah's husband, Abraham," whereas Sarah remained barren into her middle and later years. God was good, and Sarah did conceive a so-called "change of life" baby. Moses, however, was described at his death (at the age of 120 years) in these words: "His eye was not full nor his natural forces abated" (p. 482).

Most medical dictionary definitions describe the climateric as a period beginning between the ages of 40 and 50 years, with manifestations of endocrine, somatic bodily changes and an overlay of emotional and psychological symptoms applicable to both men and women. The period can span 10 or more years, but it frequently is essentially resolved in 5 years.

The Male

Although many physicians and psychiatrists ignore or deny the reality of a male climacterium, increasing attention in the medical literature is being given to those men in the fifth and sixth decades who experience a "climacteric syndrome" (Greenblatt, et al., 1979; Albeaux-Fernet et al., 1978; Vermeulen et al., 1972). They appear to experience "a rather abrupt loss of general well-being involving physical, emotional and sexual disturbances" (Henker, 1977, p. 23). Studies document instances of each of these experiences.

Both Jaszmann (1978) and Vermeulen and colleagues (1972) found that testosterone levels usually diminish gradually after 50 years of age. In contrast with perimenopausal and menopausal women; levels of follicle-stimulating hormone (FSH) and luteinizing hormone (LH) increase very little, because the level of estradiol, which appears to keep the FSH and the LH in balance, rarely diminishes in the older male. It also is suggested that the estrogen present in the climacteric male may help to keep the autonomic nervous system in balance and to prevent any vasomotor changes (hot flashes) (Greenblatt et al., 1979).

Henker (1977) reports on a study of men between ages 40 and 60 who were seen by a psychosomatic consultation service in a university medical center. Of 486 men, 50 presented symptoms including physical complaints, psychic disturbance, and sexual impairment. The sexual inadequacies ranged from "reduced libido to total impotence," with a reduction in sexual activity to less than one-half of former levels. Thirty-eight of the 50 men indicated occasional to frequent impotence. The most reported pattern began as a noticeable drop in libido, with an occasional impotent incident that engendered embarrassment. Anxiety increased about the possible rate of decline in potency. As the men made an effort to put aside these feelings and achieve an adaptive state, heavy smoking, sleep disturbances, and working hours increased. Frequent clinical manifestations of depression were noted. All these consequences feed the diminished libido and occasional impotence, stimulate hypochondriasis, and may result in almost total absence of sexual interest and expression.

Vague physical complaints are heightened, so that for the first time, weakness, fatigability, poor appetite, and constipation are perceived as signs of serious disability. On the other hand, there are those men who use this time and these experiences to seek validation for former sexual drives and capacities with younger women.

Treatments to moderate these apparently climacteric-related symptoms have been variously reported as successful or unsuccessful since the 1940s. In 1945 Werner cited success in 54 cases with testosterone injections 3 times per week, and reported impressive results with 273 cases in 1946. Others (Bauer, 1944; McCullagh, 1946; Wershub, 1962) disagreed with the reports of positive effects of male hormone therapy. Rutherford (1956) suggested that the husband's climacteric was caused by the troublesome, problematic menopause of the wife, along with other environmental aspects of work and family, all of which are unresponsive to exogenous testosterone.

More recent clinical studies report fair to excellent results in approximately 67% of the patients using injectable testosterone esters or subcutaneously implanted pellets of pure testosterone. Depression, headaches, fatigue, and insomnia frequently are measurably diminished, libido is increased, and well-being is enhanced (Witherington, 1974). Double-blind studies would appear to minimize the placebo effect of hormones, and Albeaux-Fernet and colleagues (1978) report unambiguous superiority for the androgens.

In summary, the male climacteric is not uniform or subjectively experienced by all men. A similar individuation occurs among climacteric women. Recent clinical investigations would suggest that some men could benefit from appropriate androgen therapy to restore adequate function and well-being. Certain changes in anatomy and physiology that begin in the middle years become pronounced in the later years. There is no menopause in the male, in spite of magazine and newspaper articles to the contrary, but particular climacteric alterations in the male are comparable to those in the middle-aged and older female.

1. Lower levels of testosterone are accompanied by diminished spermatogenesis—fewer sperm, and fewer sperm that are viable.

2. Male hormones are involved with nonreproductive, nonsexual processes and functions: protein synthesis, salt and water balance, cardiovascular function, and immune surveillance. Muscle tone and strength are negatively affected by the decrease in sex steroids.

3. Testes are smaller and more flaccid. Testicular tubules that store and carry sperm become increasingly narrowed by layers of nonproductive cells. Finally, the degenerative process inhibits spermatogenesis.

4. The prostate gland enlarges, its contractions grow weaker, and it contributes to the changes in the ejaculate. Prostatitis, related to chronic congestion, though not considered a function of diminished testosterone, can result in dyspareunia: "aching testes or a sharp discomfort at the distal end of the penis" (Biggs and Spitz, 1975, p. 232).

5. There is a reduction in the viscosity and volume of seminal fluid; as a result, the force of the ejaculation is decreased.

The Female

Many women in their middle years exhibit changing body contours: round, firm breasts begin to sag, muscle tone and skin elasticity of arms, legs, and abdomen decrease visibly, and misplaced fatty bulges may appear. The specific phases of the climacteric vary in extent and degree among women, which is indicative of the individual nature of this total period and the menopause within it.

There is not the same kind of controversy concerning the female climacterium as exists around the male climacteric. In the female this period generally begins in the middle 40s but may start earlier—in any case, it begins some time before the cessation of menses, or menopause. It is characterized by a sequence of phases: reduced fertility, irregular menses, final cessation of menses, blood vessel instability, anatomic atrophy, and other physiological changes.

1. Fertility decreases. Ovarian follicles become less susceptible to stimulation by pituitary gonadotropins. This moderate alteration in the hypothalamic–pituitary interaction and diminished follicular responsivity leads to temporary normal or elevated estrogen levels (Dilman, 1971; Sherman and Korenman, 1975).

2. Irregular cycles increase. As the regular menstrual rise and fall of estrogen begins to fail, FSH levels rise.

3. Estrogen concentration and activity continue to fall; this is directly related to decreased follicular responsivity and maturation and the consequent decrease in corpora lutea formation. The premenstrual uterine proliferation decreases and is finally minimal.

4. Other estrogen-related, nonreproductive reactions (similar to testosterone-related nonreproductive processes) are reduced but maintained at a low homeostatic level until the late 60s. Among these processes are protein synthesis, bone formation, salt and water balance, immune response, and reciprocal hormonal interaction with other glands.

5. Menopause, the final cessation of menses, ushers in significantly lower levels of estrogen. FSH and LH concentration are from 8 to 14 times greater than in the premenopausal period (Greenblatt et al., 1979).

Irregular bleeding may be present for 2 to 3 years before menses cease. Such bleeding is frequently corrected by dilation and curettage. Between 70 and 75% of all bleeding ceases without medical or surgical intervention, but 25 to 30% may be due to malignancy and usually continues until surgically treated (Procope, 1971).

Other complaints or symptoms that may be heightened during this time include anxiety, irritability, palpitation, loss of appetite, insomnia, headaches, and depression. These general symptoms do not occur in all women, or in a majority of women; therefore, it is inappropriate to consider them inevitable with menopause. In some women, the hot flash is fairly common. It is experienced as a spreading, hot sensation, often accompanied by profuse sweating. The hot, patchy redness usually starts on the chest, extending rapidly to the neck and face. There remains a difference of opinion concerning the vascular instability marked by periodic dilation of small blood vessels. The consensus suggests that the increased levels of pituitary gonadotropins FSH and LH, without the opposing, reciprocal effect of significant amounts of estrogen–progesterone, may be a major contributing factor. The individuality of this physiological symptom is emphasized by the fact that many females complete the climacteric without a single flash.

6. Involutional changes in genital and other systemic tissues are a direct result of sex steroid starvation. These atrophic changes in genital, muscular, and skeletal systems develop gradually and are more pronounced by the seventh decade, particularly if there has been no hormonal replacement therapy. They cannot be modified by sedatives or psychotherapy, but they can be partially prevented, reversed, or slowed by hormone replacement therapy.

a. Skin elasticity is reduced, glandular tissue and muscle tone decrease, the ligaments relax, fatty tissue is redistributed from periphery to viscera, leading to the diminished fullness in the breasts and other body area contours mentioned earlier.

b. Vulvar substance is lost, the mons flattens, and the major labia are less full.

c. The cervix, the body of the uterus, and the ovaries grow smaller and may reach prepubertal size in some women.

d. The vaginal canal undergoes important changes: the mucosa thins, length is reduced, and the rugal pattern slowly disappears. The capacity for expansion is reduced, and elasticity diminishes. Estrogen-deficient vaginitis also may be present. Bartholin glands (external to and located in the first one-third of the vagina), which may assist in the lubrication of the canal, decrease in number and activity with age. The "sweating," an exudation phenomenon from the mucosal walls of the vagina during arousal is the primary source of vaginal lubrication. If the tissue is maintained in a moderately healthy state (coital or masturbatory activity), this lubrication should remain relatively intact.

e. Although the clitoris undergoes a modest reduction in size, there is "no objective evidence to date to suggest any appreciable loss in sensate focus" (Masters and Johnson, 1970, pp. 337–338).

f. Portions of the urinary system, the urethra and bladder, frequently undergo moderate atrophy and compound urogenital symptoms.

7. "Change of life" physiology–psyche interaction has been investigated, and recent information suggests that vasomotor instability (hot flash, or sweats) and atrophic vaginitis may not be the only major symptoms of estrogen deficiency. Affective, psychological problems, heretofore largely assigned as coincidental or reactive behavior to society's negative stereotype of the menopausal and postmenopausal female, may be functions of estrogen depletion. Double-blind studies with estrogen and placebo have shown that anxiety, depression, and headaches are responsive to hormones (Greenblatt et al., 1970; Dennerstein et al., 1978; Moaz and Durst, 1979; Lauritzen, 1973). Alyward (1973) suggests that the biochemical basis for these symptoms may be found in the low plasma levels of free tryptophan in depressed menopausal women. These low levels can be improved by estrogen replacement. (Greenblatt et al., 1979). Since low brain serotonin is correlated with depressive states, and serotonin is synthesized from tryptophan, this explanation is reasonable. Greenblatt and colleagues (1979) also note that instability of adrenergic (norepinephrine) and cholinergic (acetylcholine) hormones may be stimulated by low estrogen concentrations.

However, there are other students of menopausal (and postmenopausal) women who disagree with the foregoing biological base of what have been identified as emotional and psychological correlates of menopause. These clinicians and researchers maintain that such symptoms as irritability, headaches, fatigability, depression, palpitations, and loss of libido are more appropriately a function of the psychosocial realities in contemporary culture (Utian, 1975; Bart and Grossman, 1978; Neugarten and Datan, 1976; Detre et al., 1978; Weg, 1978a). These symptoms do occur in some women, but rarely all together, and, in general, only occasionally. In those instances in which this symptomology is present, it may be more closely correlated with societal feedback concerning the importance of youth, physical beauty, reproductive potential, and the unfortunate realities of aging rather than with the biology of menopause (Gruis and Wagner, 1979; Weg, 1977, 1978a).

Cultural influences on the perception of menopause have been addressed. There are societies that reward women when they reach the end of fertility; these women experience few symptoms (Flint, 1976). Other cultures punish women for leaving their youth and productive years (Van Keep, 1976); these women appear to experience more severe symptomology. The woman whose identification was invested primarily in household and mother roles tends to have a more difficult time (physically and psychologically). Those women who work outside the home or have additional purposive roles are aware of minimal or no symptomology (Neugarten, 1970; Neugarten and Datan, 1976; Bart and Grossman, 1976). A recent report from a multiphasic screening program conducted by the Pacific Health Research Institute of Hawaii that studied females of Caucasian and Japanese origin indicated that 75% of the middle-aged and older women sampled reported no menopausal symptoms (Goodman *et al.*, 1977).

8. Sex steroid depletion continues to be linked to some pathology associated with aging.

 a. *Vaginitis and urologic disorders.* Vaginitis is an infection generally caused by yeast organisms and can include trichomonas, or bacterial invasion, as well. It becomes more prevalent during or after menopause, and it can result in dyspareunia, or painful intercourse. The symptoms include a white, cheesy discharge, and burning and itching deep in the vagina as well as around the introitus (entrance to the vagina). The consensus is that yeast is part of the normal flora of the vagina, and that it becomes symptomatic when the physiology of the vagina changes, as with steroid starvation or antibiotic therapy. Control by weak acid-solution douches and other vaginal medical treatment is usually successful. The protozoan trichomonads are a less common cause of vaginitis that produce similar symptoms, but with a foamy yellow discharge. Trichomonad vaginitis is, by classical definition, a venereal disease, transmitted by intercourse, often with an unsymptomatic male. There are vaginal and oral medications that can control this disorder.

 In both instances of vaginitis, intercourse will prolong the course of the infection and result in continued inflammation of the genital tissues and painful, unpleasant sexual activity. Generally, if abstinence is advised by a health professional and is followed, with treatment faithfully carried out, recovery is rapid.

 Urologic disorders—inflammations and infections of the urethra, bladder, and prostate—are possible, uncomfortable, and dysfunctional in relation to sexual expression. With age, and in the face of decreased immune efficiency, it is particularly important to seek medical treatment. Prolonged infection of any part of the urogenital system presents an unneeded barrier to healthy, physical sexual communication and satisfaction.

b. *Cardiovascular (CV) disease.* The equalization with male mortality from CV disease among postmenopausal females led to the suggestion some time ago that female sex steroids probably protect women during their reproductive years.

A rise in atherosclerotic changes had been reported in coronary blood vessels in ovarectomized younger women and postmenopausal women (Higano *et al.*, 1963). Estrogen-treated ovarectomized women have fewer coronary accidents. On the other hand, cardiovascular disease is very low in women during the reproductive, menstruating stage. This apparent protection is lost during menopause. The Framingham Study (Kannel *et al.*, 1976) supports this thesis: only 20 cardiovascular events were reported among premenopausal women, whereas 70 events were recorded from among postmenopausal women. A twofold relative risk has been calculated in postmenopausal women as compared with premenopausal women. However, this increased incidence was not explainable by validated, biochemical data concerning the menopausal effect on the risk factors associated with cardiovascular disease.

A very different current opinion suggests that the higher rate of severe heart disease in American men as compared with American women may be primarily a function of a subgroup of very susceptible men "rather than the protective effects of ovarian secretion of hormones" (Detre *et al.*, 1978, p. 375). Several studies support this notion.

There was no increase in coronary artery disease in women who were surgically castrated (Manchester *et al*, 1971).

The increase in serum cholesterol levels is not a uniform finding (Hamman *et al.*, 1975).

Although estrogens reduce the concentration of cholesterol and low-density lipoproteins, the concentration of very low-density serum lipoproteins increases (Coronary Drug Project, 1972).

During the Coronary Drug Project, high doses of estrogen were used with men to reduce the risk of myocardinal infarct, but this resulted in thromboembolic complications. Hyperlipidemia appears resistant to such treatment, which incurs the attendant, identified risk (Coronary Drug Project Research Group, 1973; Davidoff *et al.*, 1973).

Since female sex hormones are involved in the metabolism of fats and proteins, there may be some correlation between atherosclerosis, coronary accidents, and estrogens. Susceptibility to cardiovascular diseases does in fact involve many risk factors, such as diet, smoking, exercise, and stress. Continued research is necessary to identify any definitive causative factor(s) of menopause in atherosclerosis and coronary heart disease.

c. *Osteoporosis.* For a long time osteoporosis was thought to be a specific response to estrogen depletion and, therefore, widespread only among postmenopausal women. But, this disorder is found in approximately 30% of people (men and women) over 65. Although it is four times more common in women than in men, it can no longer be considered solely estrogen dependent.

Osteoporosis, characterized by a measurable loss of bone mass, results in diminished height, instability of normal posture, increased susceptibility to fracture, and, often, acute pain. Postmenopausal osteoporosis is now recognized as a significant health problem associated with aging. Approximately 26% of white women who reach the age of 50 demonstrate vertebral fractures induced by osteoporosis. This figure increases to 50% by age 75 (Greenblatt *et al.*, 1979).

The current treatment of choice includes high calcium intake, fluoride, vitamin D metabolite, vitamin K, estrogen at times (Jowsey, 1976), and, if possible, a regimen of regular, mild exercise. Early therapeutic studies provided equivocal results concerning the efficacy of estrogen in maintaining or restoring bone mass: some estrogen-treated women and men were stabilized, but others did not respond (Bartter, 1973). Some research indicates that estrogen replacement can play a more major role. A 10-year double-blind study, using a sequential estrogen–progestogen regimen and a placebo, found significant benefits associated with the hormonal therapy (Nachtigall *et al.*, 1979).

Lutwak (1976, p. 145) suggests that bone demineralization is a function of a "chronic dietary deficiency of calcium associated with excess dietary phosphorus." Diagnosis remains problematic due to a frequent lack of symptomology, even in those persons with considerable bone loss. Etiology remains uncertain, but it appears to involve the interaction of multiple factors: diet, heredity, exercise, and neurohormonal coordination.

SENSUAL, SEXUAL PERSONS

Although a number of anatomical and physiological changes do take place in the genital and related organ systems, there is nothing in the changing biology that warrants the prevalent image of sexless, neutered, loveless aging.

The research reported earlier has set the record straight repeatedly— interest, activity, and pleasure continue with age. It was however, the work of Masters and Johnson that addressed the physiological age changes of the sex act. They found that the majority of older persons in their study retained the physical capacity for sexual intercourse. At the Reproductive Biology Research Foundation in St. Louis, Masters and Johnson (1970) used interviews and clinical observations to gather data. Each of the four phases of intercourse shows some departure from youthful patterns, although important individual differences also exist (Masters and Johnson, 1966, 1970). Both men and women exhibit measurable changes in time and intensity of the physiological response to effective stimulation.

The Male

Frequency of intercourse, intensity of sensation, speed of attaining an erection, and the force of the ejaculation are diminished. However, the capacity to enjoy the physical aspect of a relationship remains even more often than is suggested by the mean frequency statistic of 1.3 for total sexual outlet per week for the 60-year-old married male (Kinsey *et al.*, 1948). Men between ages 50 and 60 were reported by Kaplan (1974) as generally satisfied with experiencing one or two orgasms in a week. The changes noted imply a decline from earlier years, but not the end of sexual activity. More direct stimulation to the penis is generally required to reach an erection. Although more time is needed to achieve the erective state, there is also an extension of the time that the erection can be maintained. This reduction in ejaculatory demand meshes well with the slower excitation response of the older woman and enhances the potential for increased arousal and orgasm to the greater satisfaction of both partners.

Some middle-aged and older males increase extramarital sexual encounters, and others merely reduce sexual activity with a mate. Many nongenital factors appear to alter the sexual behavior of older men; for example, a long-term marriage partner is often described as boring, unattractive, and unwilling to consciously plan for the reawakening of libido—all of which is related to the quality of the relationship.

Each of the four phases of intercourse reflects some of the anatomical and physiological differences of sexual intercourse from earlier years.

1. *Excitement.* Excitement builds slowly and generally requires longer direct stimulation to the penis. The intensity and duration of the sex flush and involuntary spasms are diminished. Erection requires more time and stimulates little scrotal vasocongestion and testicular elevation.

2. *Plateau.* This phase is longer than it was in youth. The minimal vascular engorgement of the testes continues. Penile circumference increases but is marked by the reduction or absence of preejaculatory fluid emission common in the younger years.

3. *Orgasm.* This phase is of shorter duration, and generally the first stage of ejaculatory demand is reduced or absent. The entire ejaculatory process is divided into two stages in the younger male: the first, ejaculatory inevitability, is brief (2–4 seconds) and difficult to control; the second involves the expulsion of the seminal fluid bolus through the penis and is completed within four or more contractions. This contrasts with one or two contractions in the older male.

4. *Resolution.* In the older male, the loss of erection and the return of the penis to a flaccid state may take only a few seconds, whereas this requires minutes, or an hour in the younger male. The subsequent refractory period may be extended from 2 minutes in the younger male to 12 to 24 hours in the older male.

The Female

As with older men, hormonal (estrogen depletion) and neuronal (diminished responsivity) factors interact to create functional changes in older women as sexual partners.

For some postmenopausal women, coitus is not satisfying and may even be painful. Decreased lubrication and thinning vaginal walls may make penetration difficult and cause bleeding. Rhythmic uterine contractions that are typical of the earlier years may give way, under hormonal deprivation, to spasmodic, painful cramping. The atrophic bladder and urethra are increasingly susceptible to irritation and inflammation; as a result, intercourse may trigger burning and frequent urination. Just as with the aging male, the intensity of physiological responses to effective stimulation is decreased through all four phases of intercourse (Masters and Johnson, 1966, 1970).

1. *Excitement.* Vasocongestion of the genital tissues is diminished, and the purplish hue of the younger years has changed to pink. Time required for lubrication is increased from 15 to 30 seconds to as much as 5 minutes, but it is comparable to the erective delay in the aging male.

2. *Plateau.* Uterine elevation is diminished. The major labia do not elevate but may hang in limp folds around the vaginal opening. The deep skin coloration of the minor labia of younger women is lacking. However, the clitoral response remains fairly intact and includes the elevation and flattening of the anterior border of the symphysis, as is usual in earlier years.

3. *Orgasm.* Duration of orgasm is measurably reduced between ages 50 and 70. The spread of uterine contractions from fundus to midzone to lower segment may be similar to that of younger women, but, as noted earlier, the contractions may be spastic rather than rhythmic and reduced from 3 to 5 down to 1 or 2. Although the contractions of the vaginal orgasmic platform are still initiated within .8-second intervals, the contractions are reduced from 8 to 12 down to 4 or 5 times during this phase.

Confusion and ignorance regarding the nature of female orgasm have triggered guilt and feelings of inadequacy in many women at various ages. Since the days of Sigmund Freud, and until 10 or 15 years ago, psychoanalysts and others accepted and reinforced the notion that there were two kinds of female climax: the vaginal orgasm of "mature" women, and the clitoral orgasm, a sign of narcissism and sexual inadequacy (Freud, 1960).

Physiologists continued to note that vaginal walls contain few erogenous nerve endings and that direct and/or indirect stimulation of the clitoris initiates orgasmic contractions, which then spread through the vagina and uterus. Nevertheless, the myth of two kinds of female orgasm continued. Convinced that orgasm through coition (indirect stimulation of the clitoris) was the only mature behavior, most women suffered silently.

However, the Masters and Johnson (1966, 1970) research should dispel this myth. They found, both from the anatomical and the physiological perspective, little or no difference in the response of the pelvic viscera to effective stimulation of the breast, the clitoris, or coition. In spite of the somewhat stronger response to direct clitoral stimulation than to indirect stimulation in vaginal penetration, many women prefer coition for various psychological reasons.

4. *Resolution.* Rapid resolution, as with older men, is characteristic of female sex steroid imbalance. If any minor labia color change is present, it is faint, and its fading is initiated even before orgasm is reached. Pelvic viscera return to the prestimulatory state, the uterus returns to its

nonelevated position, and the vaginal canal collapses from its moderately expanded state.

Menopausal and postmenopausal women have a physiological advantage, because the multiorgasmic capacity of their younger years is retained (Kinsey *et al.*, 1953; Masters and Johnson, 1970; Roszak, 1969). Fertility and libido (desire) are functionally separable; sexual desire and activity are reported intact after hysterectomies (Post, 1967). Frequently, naturally (nonsurgically) menopausal and postmenopausal women, released from the fear of pregnancy and freed from some of the inhibitions learned during youth and mothering, experience a heightened period of arousability and greater interest in sexual expression. Only infrequent opportunity, an early-Victorian sex education, and negative feedback from society frustrate their expression.

Nature of Sexual Interaction

With the years, the physical act of intercourse generally becomes less primary; the goal orientation of youth to orgasm has diminished. Lovemaking tends to be more gentle and caring. The body warmth and closeness of another human being, the touching and affection, the quality of caring in the arms of another become more important than the intense pleasure of climax. There is then the move away from the compelling passion of youth to the person-oriented intimacy of the mature and later years. Butler and Lewis (1976) speak of a "second language of sex" more characteristic of the later years, in which sexual expression is "emotional, communicative and physical"—a slowly developing understanding and behavior. Time and experience are essential to moving beyond the urgent and explosive sexual encounters of the younger years.

Homosexuality

The discussion so far has addressed heterosexual behavior. Verifiable data on homosexuality are still meager, but they are growing. It is clear, however, that homosexual and bisexual activity are a part of the range of human sexual behavior.

Some investigations have looked into the amount of homosexuality in the majority heterosexual world and others have studied age-related effects on members of homosexual groups (Kelly, 1977; Christenson and Johnson, 1973).

In a research study recently published, Bell and Weinberg (1978) agree. They stated (p. 23), "It will become increasingly clear to the reader that there is no such thing as *the* homosexual (or *the* heterosexual, for that matter." Bell does see a major specific sex problem for homosexuals—finding suitable partners. In that sense, the problem differs little from the difficulties faced by older heterosexual men and women.

In his study of the aging male homosexual in Los Angeles, Kelly (1977) found that older men desired contact with men of their own age cohort, though they were less likely to be involved in permanent relationships than were younger males. In this study, 50% of those 50–65 years of age reported satisfactory sex lives and 83% of those over 65 noted satisfaction with their sexual lives.

Widespread ignorance about homosexuality has helped to create a variety of stereotypes. Usually, subjects for studies of gay males have been drawn from gay bars, which restricts results regarding the dynamics of any long-term liaison because the data are limited to "on sight" short-term, sexual attraction. Harry and DeVall (1978) argue that it is an overgeneralization to say that the homosexual male is "heavily youth oriented" or that all homosexual males are alike. Rather, partner age-preference depends on social class and age. Working-class and young gay men are interested in older or same-age partners, whereas middle-class, older gays, and those who frequent gay bars, are youth oriented.

Bell (1971) considers aging for the lesbian less problematic than it is for the gay male. This may relate to the greater commitment of the lesbian to aspects of the interpersonal relationship. There is a suggestion by Laner (1979) that lesbians may be advantaged over nonlesbians with regard to aging. The number of eligible partners available to older lesbians may, in fact, be larger than that available to older heterosexual women who continue to search for the traditional older male–younger female liaison.

There are implications for the aging population (over 65) in which there are only 68 men per 100 women. It may be that, when Victorian sexual mores can be put aside, older women may find it possible to seek and share not only support, friendship, and warmth with other women but also physical love.

Masturbation

Although it is not precisely a major activity, masturbation is another way in which persons experience their sexual, sensual selves. The taboos regarding masturbation have decreased, and, particularly with the growth of the women's movement, self-pleasuring has become more acceptable.

Hite (1976, p. 231) asked her interviewees, "What is wrong with using your own hand, for example, to stimulate yourself?" She emphasizes the taboo learned early by men and women about touching themselves. This question becomes particularly poignant in the face of widowhood and singleness for many older women.

Kinsey's study of female sexuality notes that women, more than men, accepted the Victorian horror of masturbation (Kinsey et al., 1953; Offir, 1982). He found that masturbation represented the highest percentage of total sexual outlet for single women; for married women, it accounted for 10% of the total outlet" (Silny, 1980, p. 132). Single women demonstrated little change in frequency from the late teens through the 50s—about once per week. At all ages, masturbation represented a three to seven times higher percentage of sexual outlet in single women than in married women. In younger women, Kinsey found that 20% were masturbating, but 58% of older groups were using this outlet. He suggested that the increase might be due to (a) a decrease in the number of sociosexual outlets, and (b) the discovery through experience that masturbation was as physically satisfying as intercourse.

Masters and Johnson (1966) indicate that in single and married women who masturbate in old age (though with diminishing frequency), masturbation was a part of sexual activity in the earlier adult years. Christenson and Gagnon (1965) found that 25% of a group of postmarital women in their 70s masturbated.

Reports of masturbation among older men contrast with those regarding older women, because masturbation among men peaks in the midteens and decreases thereafter (Berezin, 1975). Rubin (1965) discusses a study carried out in 1959 by the magazine *Sexology*. A questionnaire was sent to men listed in "Who's Who in America." Approximately 25% reported masturbating after 60 years of age.

It is clear that sexual self-pleasuring starts very early in childhood and can continue all through adult life into old age. Like caressing, fondling, oral and genital stimulation, and other forms of heterosexual, homosexual, and bisexual expression, masturbation is a sexual outlet. Rather than engendering guilt, it may be an important technique in maintaining the responsivity of aging genitalia—potency in men and lubrication in women. Moreover, masturbation can "release tensions, stimulate sexual appetite and contribute to well being" (Weg, 1975a, p. 221).

PATHOLOGY: CONSEQUENCES FOR SEXUAL, SENSUAL ACTIVITY

Normal aging of the reproductive system leaves more than adequate capacity for the physical components of sexual expression. What, then, accounts for the stereotype of the impotent, sexless later years? Some illness and disease with age are a current reality, but there is normal aging—pathology is not inevitable (Weg, 1980). Nevertheless, the "sick role" has been imposed on many elders. When the aged are dependent and out of mainstream living patterns, their human needs and wants become easier to ignore. Older persons are separated not only by the years, but also by the denial of participation in activities considered the province of the young and the well. The myth of asexuality is difficult to defuse.

Other sources of the label "sexually uninterested and dysfunctional", stem from the effects of more specific disease entities and the overall health status of elders. Systemic disease, drug abuse, surgery, excesses in eating and drinking, and the most common affective disorder among elders—depression—can affect sexual interest and expression at any age, though their incidence increases with the years. Anemia, diabetes, fatigue, and malnutrition can, when untreated, inhibit desire, abort arousal and sexual climax, and seriously modify the overall physical and affective quality of life.

Chronic disease, either alone or in combination with other natural age changes in physiological efficiency, may have secondary effects on the reproductive system, thereby modifying sexual expression. A related source of difficulty is the fear that many elders have that any sexual involvement will exacerbate an illness and possibly result in death (Masters and Johnson, 1970; Rubin, 1966a, b). Fortunately, this fear is unfounded. The resultant enhanced sense of well-being, the improved circulation, and the shared pleasures not only have a generally salutary effect on health; but they also more than outweigh the rate of sudden coital coronary deaths, which is .3–1% of the rate of all sudden coronary deaths (Butler and Lewis, 1976, 1982).

Drug Abuse

The common medical practice of excessive drug prescription for any complaint or dysfunction in the older population has contributed significantly to the suppression of libido, arousal, and erective ability (Lamy and Kitler, 1971; Kayne, 1976; Weg, 1978b). Alcohol, marijuana, and a number of tranquilizers in common usage among elders (e.g., chlorpromazine, Librium®, Mellaril®, and reserpine) weaken erection and delay ejaculation. Continued use of these drugs may lead to impotence.

Hypertension

Sexual activity among severely hypertensive males was found to be decreased or absent in a study completed in Australia (Laver, 1974). Loss of libido may occur as a result of the sedative effect on the central nervous system of many drugs used. The most frequent complaint associated with antihypertensive drug therapy is the loss of erective ability, though libido and sexual arousal remain intact. Especially revealing was a self-report completed by patients—they were convinced that the pills were the cause of problems with sexual potency. Before the age of 80 or 90, a large proportion of cases of impotence is considered to be psychogenic; fear and expectation of impotence will frequently ensure its occurrence (Butler and Lewis, 1976). Other patients became self-imposed celibates, believing that sexual activity was dangerous with illness. Surely one of the challenges in the pharmacology of aging is to identify new antihypertensive agents that will have few, if any, side effects.

Diabetes

Despite continued libido, sexual dysfunction is a common complaint among diabetic men and women. In women, vaginal lubrication is delayed and scant, though vaginal mucosa and cytology indicate adequate estrogen. No specific etiology can be implicated, but a number of factors may be involved: neuropathy, susceptibility to infection, microvascular changes, and the chronicity of diabetes (Kolodny, 1971).

Retrograde ejaculation and/or premature ejaculation may also be present in the diabetic male. A number of investigators indicate that as many as 50% of impotent, diabetic males are unable to masturbate or stimulate erection in any way (Kolodny et al., 1974). Some studies suggest that a low level of testosterone is responsible, but frequently, concentration is within normal limits. Moreover, hormone therapy has not been successful in the treatment of diabetes-related impotence (Kolodny et al., 1974). Possible adverse effects of testosterone therapy, such as sodium retention, hepatic dysfunction, and prostatic hypertrophy, suggest that prior careful evaluation and deliberation are necessary. The potential increase in libido is particularly problematic and would frustrate the patient further if the capacity for erection continued to fail.

Morphological changes in the arterial bed of the penis in older men were identified in postmortem material from 30 males 19 to 85 years of age, 15 of whom had diabetes. By 38 years of age, fibrous connective tissue had taken the place of the longitudinal smooth muscle, followed in later years by additional fibrosis and calcification that narrowed the vessel lumen. Such pathology was considered to be related to both age and diabetes and was considered sufficient to cause or contribute to impotence (Ruzbarsky and Michal, 1977).

Neuropathy has also been suggested as a reason for erective failure. The polsters, valvelike structures containing smooth muscle (under the control of the autonomic nervous system), have been described near the corpora cavernosa (two cylindrical bodies), which fill up with blood during erection. Difficulty or interruption in neural transmission may diminish the steady, increased blood flow to the erectile tissue (Weiss, 1972).

Cardiovascular Disease

There is little medical justification for any recovered coronary disease patient to avoid sexual intercourse. The increases in heart rate, blood pressure, and oxygen consumption that occur during intercourse are comparable to moderate, rather than strenuous, exercise. In a study of 91 middle-aged, middle-class men, it was found that sexual intercourse was resumed on an average of 13.7 weeks after a coronary accident; it was resumed earlier in more sexually active people (Hellerstein and Friedman, 1970). The important benefits of human warmth and sexuality have been lost to many because of an estimated maximum 1% sudden coronary death during or after intercourse (Butler and Lewis, 1976). Rather than a threat to health maintenance, sexual activity may be both preventive and and therapeutic. For instance, an increase in the adrenal corticoids during intercourse may relieve arthritic symptoms; and the sense of well-being that comes from shared intimacy reduces physical and emotional tensions.

Surgery

Pelvic surgery has marked an end to effective sexual activity for large numbers of older men and women. In some instances, people who have a low sex drive use the surgery as an excuse for welcomed abstinence.

Clinical data suggest that although prostatectomies (removal of prostrate tumors) and hysterectomies (removal of all or part of uterus, and, at times, more of internal genitalia) appear to depress desire and interfere with the capacity for climax, these are not inevitable consequences (Finkle and Moyers, 1960). A recent study by Dennerstein and colleagues (1977) of 89 patients who had experienced an hysterectomy and oophorectomy found that 34% reported heightened sexual responsiveness and 37% felt their sexual relationships had deteriorated. More than 80% of the patients who have prostatectomies retain potency; and more than 70% of women retain orgasmic capacity following hysterectomies (Patterson and Craig, 1963).

Recent studies into transurethral prostatectomy suggest that the postsurgical experience is very individual and is affected by psychosocial factors. From 5 to 40% of the patients experienced a decrease or loss of potency (Maoz and Durst, 1976), and 80 to 90% developed retrograde ejaculation, which was disturbing to most patients. Two other procedures—suprapubic (using an abdominal approach) and perineal exposure for removal of the prostate—lead to a loss of potency more frequently, due to nerve damage.

In the past, little attention was given by health professionals to the preservation of the pudendal nerves (and the capacity for erection) when surgery was indicated. Potency was supposed to be of negligible concern to those over 60 years of age. With increased public awareness of the growing older population, and academic involvement with gerontology, the man of years is less willing to remain outside the decisions related to surgery, and the surgeon is more willing to be concerned. Adequate presurgery discussions with the patient should be held to describe the procedure and any expected effects.

Many females who have undergone hysterectomies and/or oophorectomies (removal of one or both ovaries) feel defeminized—less than a whole woman, unlovable and unloved. A number of studies indicate a wide range of decreased sexual function after surgery, from 10 to 38%. Dennerstein and colleagues (1977) concluded from their restrospective investigation of women who had had surgical menopause that psychological factors rather than any physiological consequences of the surgery, played a major role in the changing pattern of sexual relationsips.

As with prostatectomy, some informative discussions with the woman (and her sexual partner) prior to surgery can help to avoid some defeating fears and myths. Recent criticism of excessive, unnecessary pelvic surgery among women, along with greater choice exercised by women, may reduce the psychic and physical damage that can occur as a result of unwarranted surgery.

Mastectomy

Approximately 1 of every 11 American women develop breast cancer, the major cause of cancer death among women (American Cancer Society, 1981). An estimated 111,200 new cases were reported in 1981. The treatment of choice has been radical mastectomy, surgery that removes the breast, some underlying chest muscles, and all axillary lymph nodes and intervening lymphatics. Currently, less drastic surgery—lumpectomy or modified radical mastectomy—is being combined with radiation and/or chemotheraphy.[3]

For many women who have lost one or both breasts, personal devaluation is considerable; the assault on their body integrity becomes a major threat to self-image and acceptance as a woman. In addition to the fear of cancer and death, there is the panic over the potential loss of a love relationship with a husband or partner who can, in turn, be affected by the negative attitudes and feelings that burden the breast cancer patient. Loving, being lovable and relaxed, and maintaining spontaneous sexual relations become difficult and limited.

Corby and Solnick (1980, p. 899) note recommendations made by researchers: "presurgical counseling, involvement of the husband in the entire process, and the need for the surgeon to be responsive to evidence of depression in the patient." Jamison and colleagues (1978, p. 435) found that "emotional suffering appears to far outweigh the physical pain in women who have undergone mastectomy."

Future breast cancer patients may have to deal less with the emotional and sexual consequences of the radical mastectomy if researchers validate data suggesting that the course of the disease and survival are the same with lumpectomy and adjuvant therapy as they are with radical mastectomy.

In summary, whatever the pathology, there is rarely a physiological reason to avoid loving, sexual relationships. On the contrary, support, energy, satisfaction, and physical pleasure can boost the motivation to cope. Being ill does not mean being devoid of human needs and wants. Although self-image and confidence may be fragile and fear of rejection in a physical relationship may exist, a number of researchers and clinicians report the continuation of sex desires and feelings (Masters *et al.*, 1982). These data contradict earlier mythology concerning sexuality

---

[3]Lumpectomy is surgery in which only the cancerous tumor is excised. A modified radical mastectomy leaves some axillary lymph nodes.

and chronic disease/terminal illness, and more concern by the professional community is in evidence (Derogatis and Kourlesis, 1981).

POTENTIATION OF SEXUAL CAPACITIES AND INTERESTS

There are short-range and long-range activities and recommendations that can contribute to the realization of the physiological and affective sensual, sexual needs of the later years. Changes in all the areas that follow would better prepare the individual and society.

Hormone Replacement Therapy

Only hormone therapy can effectively relieve and correct some of the symptomology in the middle-aged and older female: vasomotor instability, vaginitis, and inadequate lubrication (Masters and Johnson, 1970; Schleyer-Saunders, 1971). The increased risk of endometrial cancer among users of conjugated estrogen (in estrogen replacement therapy) was reported in four retrospective studies by Ziel and Finkle (1975). These data created caution, concern, and fear among lay persons and health professionals. An alternative therapy that combines estrogen and progestogen has been used by a number of clinicians for the long term (30, 16, and 10 years), with safe results for patients and no excess of endometrial cancer over the incidence in the control group, which received no hormone therapy (Greenblatt, 1977; Jern, 1973; Nachtigall, 1976). This latter approach has received wider acceptance only very recently.

A number of researchers of menopause and osteoporosis have theorized that estrogens protect against the thinning out of the bone, thereby minimizing the possibility of fractures. (This was mentioned earlier in the comments on osteoporosis.) Hutchinson and colleagues (1979) studied a group of patients between 40 and 80 years of age with new fractures of the hip and/or distal radius, and they concluded that estrogen does protect people from the likelihood of these fractures occurring. Matched controls also were developed. Subjects who were using estrogens had a protection index of 1.5 times that of nonusers with these two fractures. Osteoporosis was present in 32% of the fracture cases and in only 15% of the controls.

Testosterone replacement therapy for the older male who has experienced impotence or other troublesome climacteric symptoms has met with mixed evaluation and application. Some studies reported earlier in this chapter were related to the male climacteric. Fellman (1975) is of the opinion that any improvement in erective ability is not a direct result of androgen treatment. Any success that is achieved, he believes, is probably related to a reduction in anxiety during treatment, confidence in the physician, and the general feeling of well-being that anabolic androgens can stimulate. Much research remains to be done before androgens can automatically be prescribed prior to, during, and after the male climacteric.

Sexual Therapy

If lifelong sexuality is the accurate norm, then elders, as well as youth, should be able to receive help when they seek it out. Increasingly, professionals have found the elders responsive and interested.

Perhaps the single most important technique in sexual therapy that has worked for the old as well as the young was pioneered by Masters and Johnson (1966, 1970). A couple working through sexual difficulties who are told they do not have to succeed coitally learn various kinds of desensitizing methods, the squeeze technique, and means of giving pleasure to each other before, during, and after intercourse. Masters and Johnson believe that this approach encourages people to get off the "performance kick" and concentrate on the person-to-person relationship. They estimate that the success rate of 50% with older clients could be higher if the problem had not existed for a long period of time. Sviland's (1978) emphasis is on sexual liberation for the older couples over the age of 60 whom she counsels. She is convinced that sexual behavior among older persons can be expanded and that positive growth takes place in attitudes when sexual inhibitions are removed and sexual expression is increased with her counseling and therapy program.

Education for Sexuality throughout the Life Span

Attitudes toward sensuality, sexuality, and sexual behaviors are learned. Reality-oriented information about life-span changes in sexuality, rather than mythology, could make a difference in self-image and confidence among older persons and could allay anxieties and fears.

This learning should start in childhood and extend through old age. The later years would not need to be seen as years of deprivation in affection, love, and intimacies—a sexless future. Included in the concepts of sexuality and age for middle-aged and older people should be the encouragement to enjoy each other, release from tradition and the time-bound practice of sexual expression only in the dark and only at night and acceptance of the reality of individual differences and the variability of sexual activities.

Implications for the Helping and Health Professions

Gynecological and other medical texts require a careful review. It is time that those books or sections that continue to incorporate the mythologies of aging and sexuality (Scully and Bart, 1973) be discarded or rewritten. Few texts mention the multiorgasmic nature of women and most describe the sexual pace for marital coitus as set by men.

1. In keeping with the reality of sexual expression, especially for the middle years, it is time that emphasis be placed on the quality of the relationship, with focus on the person, not on performance.

2. With the increasing number of older persons (mostly women) who are alone, single, and alienated, efforts for greater acceptance of alternate life-styles appear reasonable.

3. It is essential that professionals recognize the need for affect and sexual expression as part of feeling and being alive at any age—even old age.

4. Health professionals (doctors and nurses) and allied personnel have a responsibility to be well informed and to be comfortable with their own sexuality so that they may serve as informative guides to those elders who do seek advice. Professional school curricula are beginning to institute some geriatric concepts, but the effort needs acceleration and broadening.

Societal Attitudes and Policies

In order to alter attitudes toward aging and the needs of older men and women, basic positions regarding sex roles and aging need to be public and positive. Specifically, they should

provide women and men with equal opportunities and recognition, equalize sex roles,
encourage dating, liaison, and/or marriage of younger men with older women,
develop greater comprehension and constructive attitudes toward homosexuality and polygamy,

project and present elders as whole persons worthy of respect and support; and

structure, in conṡultation with elders, a legitimate role for their particular contributions.

Research Goals

A continuing source of new information is essential to ensure fact over fiction and reality over mythology and stereotypes. Researchers should strive to do the following:

1. Develop a health promotion–disease prevention approach and support for its implementation. Only in this way can health professionals hope to modify the ravages of chronic diseases in the late middle and older years. Health maintenance and promotion enhance the sexual potential.

2. Continue studies that elucidate aging mechanisms so that the changing, decreasingly efficient physiology could be restored to optimum efficiency, or, at the least, so that the decrease in efficiency could be minimized.

3. Diligently pursue the identification of those factors that provide women with approximately an 8-year advantage over men in life expectancy. On this basis, it is conceivable that some methods of intervention could be assembled to enhance the vigor and health of men and perhaps extend, on the average, the male's active life span.

4. Develop a family of efficacious drugs useful in the treatment of chronic diseases that would have the fewest side effects (none, if possible) in relation to potency, cognition, and energy.

5. Undertake varied, multilevel (from childhood to old age) and nationwide model educational and promotional campaigns for attitude and behavior changes regarding aging and older persons.

6. Test and evaluate each of the carefully constructed programs in terms of desired outcomes.

SUMMARY

Evidence is clear and considerable that the need for intimate, affective relationships exists for most men and women throughout life. Sexual expression may be even more important in the later years than it is in the earlier years. For the elderly, many of life's roles are diminished or lost, friends and close, beloved relatives die, neighborhoods become hostile, work is generally denied, and often health is at risk.

Contrary to the unfounded, unfortunate stereotype of the elderly as asexual or sexless "nonpersons," older men and women have a continued interest and capacity for sensual–sexual expression. Illness does not have to result in abstinence; the energy expended during intercourse is modest, and the rewards for sexual activity can be great. The loving liaison shares touching, warmth, and caring, reinforces a tenuous self-image, restores energy and a sense of well-being, and celebrates being alive and connected.

The destructive reality for the sensuality and sexuality of older persons is not the gradual, small changes in the anatomy and physiology, but rather the societal mythology of impotence and disinterest. On the other hand, there is no charity, honesty, or science in a new image that declares that all elders must either be sexually active or labeled "abnormal." That can only create a new damaging stereotype. There are many reasons for putting aside the physical act of dyadic intercourse: some elders live in loneliness (not by choice), others have given up sexual interests (in distaste or defense), and still others, educated in the Victorian past, are unable to be sexually pleasured or to give such pleasure. Sexual needs and expression, as with all other aspects of older persons, are as varied as the age group is heterogenous.

There is no one way to love or to be loved; there is no one liaison that is superior to another. No one life-style in singlehood or marriage, heterosexual or homosexual, will suit all persons. Self-pleasuring, homosexuality, bisexuality, celibacy, and heterosexuality are all in the human sexual repertoire.

Sensual–sexual expression is generally not the same in old age as it is in youth. The years bring pressure to see beyond the sex act and beyond orgasm, to the total personalities involved. In a social climate that is more open and accepting, the reality of numbers is helping to return the "old" to the mainstream of living and sexuality to the elderly.

"Nothing, so it seems to me," said the stranger "is more beautiful than the love that has weathered the storms of life . . . . The love of the young for the young, that is the beginning of life. But the love of the old for the old, that is the beginning of—of things longer."[4]

[4]From "The Passing of the Third Floor Back," 1908, by Jerome Klapka Jerome (1859–1927), English humorist and dramatist.

REFERENCES

Albeaux-Fernet, M., Bohler, C. S. S., and Karpas, A. E. (1978). *In* "Geriatric Endocrinology" (Vol. 5, "Aging") (R. B. Greenblatt, ed.), pp. 201–216. Raven, New York.

Alyward, M. (1973). *Med. Sci*, **1**, 30.

American Cancer Society (1981). "Cancer Facts and Figures, 1980." Am. Cancer Soc., New York.

Bart, P., and Grossman, M. (1976). *Women and Health* **1**, 3. (ed.), pp. 337–354. Science Research Associates Inc., Chicago.

Bartter, F. C. (1973). *Perspect. Biol. Med.* **16**, 215.

Bauer, J. (1944). *J. Am. Med. Assoc.* **126**, 914.

Bell, A. P., and Weinberg, M. S. (1978). "Homosexualities: A Study of Diversity Among Men and Women." Simon & Schuster, New York.

Bell, R. R. (1971). "Social Deviance." Dorsey Press, Homewood, Illinois.

Berezin, M. A. (1975). *In* "Masturbation from Infancy to Senescence" (I. M. Marcus and J. J. Francis, eds.), pp. 329–347. International Universities Press, Inc., New York.

Berezin, M. A. (1976). *J. Geriatr. Psychiatry* **9**, 189.

Biggs, M., and Spitz, R. (1975). *In* "Human Sexuality: A Health Practitioner's Text" (R. Green, ed.), pp. 223–232. Williams & Wilkins, Baltimore.

Brotman, H. B. (1981). "Every Ninth American," prepared for "Developments in Aging." Special Committee on Aging, U. S. Senate, Washington, D. C.

Butler, R. N., and Lewis, M. I. (1976). "Sex After 60: A Guide for Men and Women for Their Later Years." Harper & Row, New York.

Butler, R. N., and Lewis, M. I. (1982). "Aging and Mental Health," 3rd ed. Mosby, St. Louis.

Christenson, C. V., and Gagnon, J. H. (1965). *J. Gerontol.* **20**, 351.

Christenson, C. V., and Johnson, A. B. (1973). *J. Geriatr. Psychiatry* **6**, 80.

Claman, A. D. (1966). *Can. Med. Assoc. J.* **94**, 207.

Comfort, A. (1974). *J. Am Geriatr. Soc.* **22**, 440.

Corby, N., and Solnick, R. L. (1980). *In* "Handbook of Mental Health and Aging" (J. E. Birren and R. B. Sloane, eds.), pp. 893–921. Prentice-hall, Englewood Cliffs, New Jersey.

Coronary Drug Project Research Group (1972). *J. Am. Med. Assoc.* **220**, 996.

Coronary Drug Project Research Group (1973). *J. Am. Med. Assoc.* **226**, 652.

Crooks, R., and Baur, K. (1980). "Our Sexuality." Benjamin-Cummings, Menlo Park, California.

Davidoff, F., Tishler, S., and Rosoff, C. (1973). *N. Engl. J. Med.* **289**, 552.

DeNicola, P., and Peruzza, M. (1974). *J. Am Geriatr. Soc.* **22**, 380.

Dennerstein, L., Wood, C., and Burrows, G. D. (1977). *Obstet. Gynecol.* **49**, 92.

Dennerstein, L., Laby, B., Burrows, G. D., and Hyman, G. J. (1978). *Headache* **18**, 146.

Derogatis, L. R., and Kourlesis, S. M. (1981). *Ca: Cancer J. Clinicians* **31**, 46.

Detre, T., Hayashi, T., and Archer, D. F. (1978). *Ann. Intern. Med.* **88**, 373.

Dilman, V. M. (1971). *Lancet* **1**, 1211.

Fellman, S. L. (1975). *Med. Aspects Hum. Sex.* **9**, 32.

Finkle, A., and Moyers, T. (1960). *J. Urol.* **84**, 152.

Flint, M. (1976). *In* "Consensus on Menopause Research" (P. A. Van Keep, R. B. Greenblatt, and M. Albeaux-Fernet, eds.), pp. 73–83. Univ. Park Press, Baltimore.

Ford, C. S., and Beach, F. A. (1951). "Patterns of Sexual Behavior." Harper & Row, New York.

Frank, L. (1961). "The Conduct of Sex." Morrow, New York.

Freud, S. (1960). "The Letters of Sigmund Freud" (E. L. Freud, ed.). Basic Books, New York.

Gagnon, J., and Simon, W. (1973). "Sexual Conduct: The Social Sources of Human Sexuality." Aldine, Chicago.
Giambra, L. N., and Martin, C. E. 91977). *Arch. Sex. Behav.* **6**, 497.
Golde, P., and Kogan, N. (1959). *J. Gerontol.* **14**, 355.
Goodman, M., Stewart, C. J., and Gilbert, F. (1977). *J. Gerontol.* **32**, 291.
Greenblatt, R. B. (1977). *Mod. Med. (Minneapolis)* **45**, 47.
Greenblatt, R. B., Nezhat, C., Roesel, R. A., and Natrajan, P. K. (1979). *J. Am. Geriatr. Soc.* **27**, 481.
Gruis, M. L., and Wagner, N. M. (1979). *Postgrad. Med.* **65**, 197.
Gruman, G. J. (1966). *Trans. Am. Philos. Soc.* **56**, Part 9.
Guillerme, J. (1963). "Longevity." Walker Publ. Co., Inc., New York.
Hamman, R. F., Bennett, P. H., and Miller, M. (1975). *Am. J. Epidemiol.* **102**, 164.
Hariton, E. B., and Singer, J. L. (1974). *J. Consult. Clin. Psychol.* **42**, 313.
Harry, J., and DeVall, W. (1978). *Arch. Sex. Behav.* **7**, 199.
Hecaton of Rhodes (1966). Quoted in "Springs of Greek Wisdom." Herder Book Center, New York.
Hellerstein, H., and Friedman, E. (1970). *Scand. J. Rehab. Med.* **2-3**, 109.
Henker, F. O., III (1977). *Psychosomatics* **18**, 23.
Higano, N., Robinson, R., and Cohen, W. (1963). *N. Engl. J. Med.* **268**, 1123.
Hite, S. (1976). "The Hite Report: A Nationwide Study of Female Sexuality." Macmillan Co., New York.
Hutchinson, T. A., Polansky, S. M., and Feinstein, A. R. (1979). *Lancet* **2**, 705.
Huyck, M. H. (1977). In "Looking Ahead" (L. E. Troll, J. Israel, and K. Israel, eds.), pp. 43-58. Prentice-Hall, Englewood Cliffs, New Jersey.
Jaffe, D. D. (1976). *Los Angeles Times* 21 March, 8.
Jamison, K. R., Wellisch, D. K., and Pasnau, R. O. (1978). *Am. J. Psychiatry* **135**, 432.
Jaszmann, L. (1978). "De Middelbare Luftijd van de man." Van Loghum Slaterus, Dwenter, Holland.
Jern, H. Z. (1973). "Hormone Therapy of Menopause and Aging." Thomas, Springfield, Illinois.
Jowsey, J. (1976). In "Nutrition and Aging" (M. Winick, ed.), pp. 131-144. Wiley, New York.
Kannel, W. B., Hjortland, M. C., McNamara, P. M., and Gordon, T. (1976). *Ann. Intern. Med.* **85**, 447.
Kaplan, H. S. (1974). "The New Sex Therapy." Brunner/Mazel, New York.
Kayne, R. C. (1976). In "Nursing and the Aged" (I. M. Burnside, ed.), pp. 436-451. McGraw-Hill, New York.
Kelly, J. (1977). *Gerontologist* **17**, 328.
Kinsey, A. C., Pomeroy, W. B., and Martin, C. I. (1948). "Sexual Behavior in the Human Male." Saunders, Philadelphia.
Kinsey, A. C., Pomeroy, W. B., Martin, C. I., and Gebhard, P. H. (1953). "Sexual Behavior in the Human Female." Saunders, Philadelphia.
Kolodny, R. C. (1971). *Diabetes* **20**, 557.
Kolodny, R. C., Kahn, C., Goldstein, H., and Barnett, D. (1974). *Diabetes* **23**, 306.
Lamy, P. P., and Kitler, M. E. (1971). *J. Am. Geriatr. Soc.* **19**, 23.
Laner, M. R. (1979). *J. Homosexuality* **4**, 267.
LaTorre, R. A., and Kear, K. (1977). *Arch. Sex. Behav.* **6**, 203.
Lauritzen, C. (1973). *Front. Horm. Res.* **2**, 2.
Laury, G. V. (1977). *Med. Aspects Hum. Sex.* **11**, 31.
Laver, M. C. (1974). *Aust. N. Z. J. Med.* **4**, 29.

Leviton, D. (1973). *Omega* **4**, 163.

Lobsenz, N. M. (1974). *N. Y. Times Mag.* January 20.

Lowenthal, M., and Berkman, P. L. (1967). "Aging and Mental Disorder in San Francisco." Jossey-Bass, San Francisco.

Lutwak, L. (1976). *In* "Nutrition and Aging" (M. Winick, ed.), pp. 145-153. Wiley, New York.

Manchester, J. H., Herman, M. V., and Gorlin, R. (1971). *Am J. Cardiol.* **28**, 33.

Maoz, B., and Durst, N. (1979). *In* "Female and Male Climacteric" (P. A. Van Keep, D. M. Serr, and R. B. Greenblatt, eds.), pp. 9-16. MTP Press, Ltd., Lancester, England.

Masters, W. H., Johnson, V., and Kolodny, R. C. (1982). "Human Sexuality." Little, Brown, Boston.

Masters, W. H., and Johnson, V. (1970). "Human Sexual Inadequacy," p. 337. Little, Brown, Boston.

Masters, W. H., Johnson, V., and Kolodny, R. C. (1982). "Human Sexuality." Little, Brown, Boston.

May, R. (1969). "Love and Will." Norton, New York.

McCullagh, E. P. (1946). *Bull. Chicago Med. Soc.* **49**, 193.

Merritt, C. G., Gerstl, J. E., and LoScuito, L. A. (1975). *Arch. Sex. Behav.* **4**, 605.

Nachtigall, L. E. (1976). *Med. World News* **17**, 39.

Nachtigall, L. E., Nachtigall, R. H., Nachtigall, R. D. and Beckman, E. M. (1979). *Obstet. Gynecol.* **53**, 277.

Neugarten, B. (1970). *J. Geriatr. Psychiatry* **4**, 71.

Neugarten, B., and Datan, N. (1976). *J. Geriatr. Psychiatry* **9**, 1.

Newman, G., and Nichols, C. R. (1960). *J. Am. Med. Assoc.* **173**, 33.

Offir, C. W. (1982). "Human Sexuality." Harcourt Brace Jovanovich, New York.

Patterson, R. M., and Craig, J. B. (1963). *Am. J. Obstet. Gynecol.* **85**, 105.

Pearlman, C. K. (1972). *Med. Aspects Human Sexuality* **11**, 31.

Pfeiffer, E. (1975). *In* "Sexual Issues on Marriage" (L. Gross, ed.), pp. 151-158. Spectrum, New York.

Pfeiffer, E., and Davis, G. C. (1972). *J. Am. Geriatr. Soc.* **20**, 151.

Post, F. (1967). *Practitioner* **199**, 377.

Procope, B. (1971). *Acta Obstet. Gynecol. Scand.* **50**, 311.

Reedy, M. N. (1978). *In* "Sexuality and Aging" (R. L. Solnick, ed.), rev., pp. 184-195. Andrus Gerontology Center, Univ. of Southern California Press, Los Angeles.

Roszak, B. (1969). *In* "Masculine/Feminine" (B. Roszak and T. Roszak, eds.), pp. 297-306. Harper & Row, New York.

Rubin, I. (1965). "Sexual Life After Sixty." Basic Books, New York.

Rubin, I. (1966a). *In* "An Analysis of Human Sexual Response" (R. Brecher and E. Brecher, eds.), pp. 251-266. New American Library, Inc., New York.

Rubin, I. (1966b). *Sexology* **32**, 512.

Rutherford, R. N. (1956). *Postgrad. Med.* **50**, 125.

Ruzbarsky, V., and Michal, V. (1977). *Invest. Urol.* **15**, 194.

Schleyer-Saunders, E. (1971). *J. Am. Geriatr. Soc.* **19**, 114.

Scully, D., and Bart, P. (1973). *Am. J. Sociol.* **78**, 1045.

Seaman, B., and Seaman, G. (1978). "Women and the Crisis in Sex Hormones." Bantam Books, New York.

Sheehy, G. (1976). "Passages: Predictable Crises of Adult Life." Dutton, New York.

Sherman, B. M., and Korenman, S. G. (1975). *J. Clin. Invest.* **55**, 699.

Silny, A. J. (1980). *In* "Handbook of Human Sexuality" (B. B. Wolman and J. Money, eds.), pp. 123-146. Prentice-Hall, Englewood Cliffs, New Jersey.

Solnick, R. L. (1977). Doctoral Dissertation, University of Southern California, Los Angeles.

Sontag, S. (1972). *Saturday Rev.* **55**, 29–38.

Sviland, M. A. (1975). *Couns. Psychol.* **5**, 67.

Sviland, M. A. (1978). *In* "Sexuality and Aging" (R. L. Solnick, ed.), rev., pp. 96–114. Andrus Gerontology Center, Univ. of Southern California Press, Los Angeles.

Tannahill, R. (1980). "Sex in History." Stein & Day, New York.

Trimmer, E. J. (1970). "Rejuvenation: The History of an Idea." A. S. Barnes and Co., Inc., Cranberry, New Jersey.

Utian, W. H., (1975). *Front. Horm. Res.* **3**, 74.

Van Keep, P. A. (1976). *In* "Consensus on Menopause Research" (P. A. Van Keep, R. B. Greenblatt, and M. Albeaux-Fernet, eds.), pp. 5–8. Univ. Park Press, Baltimore.

Vermeulen, A., Rubens, R., and Verdonck, L. (1972). *J. Clin. Endocrinol. Metab.* **34**, 730.

Verwoerdt, A., Pfeiffer, E., Wang, H. S. (1970). *In* "Normal Aging: Reports from Duke Longitudinal Study, 1955–1969" (E. Palmore, ed.), pp. 282–299. Duke Univ. Press, Durham, North Carolina.

Wax, J. (1975). *New Times* **5**(6) 43.

Weg, R. B. (1975a). *In* "The Physiology and Pathology of Human Aging" (R. Goldman and M. Rockstein, eds.), pp. 203–227. Academic Press, New York.

Weg, R. B. (1975b). *Symp. Abstr., Proc. Int. Congr. Gerontol., 10th, 1975* p. 340.

Weg, R. B. (1977). *In* "Looking Ahead" (L. Troll, J. Israel, and K. Israel, eds.), pp. 22–42. Prentice-hall, Englewood Cliffs, New Jersey.

Weg, R. B. (1978a). *In* "Sexuality and Aging" (R. L. Solnick, ed.), rev., pp. 48–65. Andrus Gerontology Center, Univ of Southern California Press, Los Angeles.

Weg, R. B. (1978b). *In* "Drugs and the Elderly" (R. C. Kayne, ed.), pp. 103–142. Andrus Gerontology Center, Univ. of Southern California Press, Los Angeles.

Weg, R. B. (1980). *In* "Nursing and the Aged" (2nd ed.) (I. M. Burnside, ed.), pp. 362–373. McGraw-Hill, New York.

Weiss, H. D. (1972). *Ann. Intern. Med.* **76**, 793.

Werner, A. A. (1945). *J. Am. Med. Assoc.* **127**, 705.

Wershub, L. P. (1962). "The Human Testis—A Clinical Treatise," p. 197. Thomas, Springfield, Illinois.

West, N. D. (1975). *J. Am. Geriatr. Soc.* **23**, 551.

Witherington, R. (1974). *In* "Clinician: Male and Female: An Endocrine Update" (L. Mastroiani, ed.), pp. 51–55. Medcom Press, New York.

Ziel, H. K., and Finkle, W. D. (1975). *N. Engl. J. Med.* **293**, 1167.

4

The Sociological Perspective

Pauline K. Robinson

SEXUALITY IN THE
LATER YEARS

81

INTRODUCTION

We pay more attention to sexuality among older persons these days, but then we give more public attention to sex per se. "Why even discuss the sexuality of the aged?" some of my dismayed older friends ask. For one thing, there are more of the aged among us. At the turn of the century only 4% of the population were 65 years and over, and now that proportion is 11.3%. When population data are translated into subjective expectations, more of us realistically look ahead to our own old age, and the question of sexuality is no small part of our anticipations or apprehensions. At age 65 men have an average of 14 years left to live, and women have 18.4 years. Some of those persons who are now old express great interest in maintaining and enhancing the sexual aspects of their lives.

How much do we know about the potential for sexual expression in the later years? Our knowledge is dependent on the occasional research that has been conducted and on the inherent limitations of such research. The Masters and Johnson (1966) study has been hailed as a breakthrough in our understanding of sexual functioning and the role of aging, but only 31 of their 694 subjects were 60 years old or older. We also have the benefit of a few cross-sectional and logitudinal surveys of older populations, with specific attention paid to sexual interests and behavior.

Several studies have described levels of sexual behavior that older persons actually engage in, but the described levels of activity are low; it is therefore difficult to infer from these descriptions what the *potential* is for sexual activity in old age (Christenson and Gagnon, 1965; Kinsey *et al.*, 1948, 1953; Palmore, 1970; Verwoerdt *et al.*, 1970). The reason for this, of course, is that actual behavior is limited by social constraints such as the availability of acceptable partners and the norms and social values held by a particular generation of older persons. To understand the potential for sexual expression, we need to focus on research that describes sexual behavior under the best of circumstances.

LIMITATIONS OF BEHAVIORAL RESEARCH

It is easier to list problems of available and feasible research methods than it is to suggest an ideal research model for studying sexuality among the aged. Research into this important aspect of our lives—sexual behavior—is inevitably restricted by the lack of experimental control that can be exercised. Nevertheless, we proceed to use the knowledge available to us, after we acknowledge its limitations (Kleemeier and Kantor, 1962; Wales, 1974; Ludeman, 1981). Ludeman has summarized some of the methodological weaknesses in the research literature on sexuality and older persons.

Research Design

Cross-sectional surveys, for example, are problematic because they are conducted at a single point in time with individuals of differing ages (Cameron and Biber, 1973; Christenson and Gagnon, 1965; Kinsey *et al.*, 1948, 1953; Lowenthal *et al.*, 1975). Differences between young and old individuals are often interpreted as being due to changes over time as persons grow old; the differences might instead be due to the fact that the older individuals grew up in a different social period and thus display generational differences in values, attitudes, and behavior.

Longitudinal research, in which individuals are observed at various points of their lifetimes, would seem to be ideal for the study of age changes in sexual behavior. Such studies coming out of Duke University, for example, provide some of the best factual information regarding changes in individuals as they age (Palmore, 1970; Pfeiffer and Davis, 1972). Unless, however, longitudinal studies include a broad age range of subjects initially and follow each age group through critical stages of the life cycle (a long-drawn-out and hardly feasible process), the studies are limited to descriptions of the aging experiences of a particular generation in a specific historical period. These time-related experiences cannot be expected to be typical of generations and social periods in the future.

Both cross-sectional and longitudinal surveys regarding sexual behavior have been conducted with samples that are limited by a combination of factors. The samples may be small, because such surveys are time-consuming and expensive, and unrepresentative, because convenience, volunteer, or even clinical samples are depended upon. In the case of longitudinal samples, there is bias, because those who survive as subjects through the successive stages of the survey are more representative of the healthy, long-lived, geographically stable, cooperative, and self-disclosing population.

Generalizations, Validity, Interpretation

Studies of the sexual behavior of the aged population share with other studies of aging the hazard of exaggerating the homogeneity of the older population in the search for generalizations. As mentioned in earlier chapters, individuals become more differentiated and individualized as they grow older. Therefore, interpretations of the aging process must be placed in the context of the great diversity of the aged population (Ragan and Davis, 1978).

Studies of sexual behavior raise questions about the validity of self-reports of activity that is surrounded by secrecy, taboo, and negative sanctions on the one hand, and bravado on the other (Wales, 1974). Sexual frustrations or disappointments may not even be accessible to the conscious awareness of many of us. How can we infer that they exist or do not exist on the basis of interview surveys? Nevertheless, as with any methodological problem, investigators test for validity to the extent possible (for example, by interviewing both spouses independently, as in Pfeiffer *et al.* [1970]) and accept with caution the results of interview and questionnaire surveys.

Another problem with surveys of sexual behavior is the tendency to *count* occasions of sexual activity, such as coitus. The particular problem with counting sexual activity in the later years is that young and middle-age standards, such as evaluating sexual success in terms of coitus or climax, will be inappropriately applied to the elderly. Sexual behavior other than coitus (e.g., masturbation, noncoital expressions of affection, such as snuggling, and intercourse without climax) may provide rewarding and satisfying experiences in the later years, but these satisfactions are overlooked in a narrow interpretation of sexual activity. The survey researcher who counts often, therefore, misses essential information.

SOCIOLOGICAL PERSPECTIVE
ON THE SEXUALITY OF OLDER PERSONS

In our society, and indeed in most societies, almost all important roles are assigned according to age strata (categories) (Ragan and Wales, 1980); sexual roles are no exception. Shared expectations, norms, rules, and values determine both for young people and for old people what is acceptable in the way of their sexual thoughts, interests, activities, and the age, race, appearance, and gender of their partners. Individuals usually experience these normative sanctions not only as external contraints on their behavior, but also as their own natural inclinations and preferences.

This chapter explores the effects of the social environment on the sexual expression of older persons. Although we are not dealing here with the biological aspects of sexuality (see Chapters 3, 10, and 11), the biological and social aspects are really inseparable (Weg, 1978). From our point of view, intrinsic physiological aging effects provide the parameters within which the social variations of sexual expression can be played out. From the point of view of physiological studies, social factors are often direct contributing causes of phenomena such as impotence in the older male (Masters and Johnson, 1966).

In limiting our approach to a sociological perspective, we will leave to psychology (Chapters 9, 12, 14, and 15) such puzzles as the "long dormant fears and incest taboos associated with the idea of sexual expression on the part of parental figures" (Lobsenz, 1981, p. 201; see also Pfeiffer, 1975; Silverstone and Hyman, 1976). The challenge of dealing with all the material that is accessible to conscious awareness on the part of older persons, their children, and other members of society is great enough for the scope of this chapter.

The discussion that follows deals first with the social constraints that limit the sexual expression of many older people (for both sexes, and then for men and women separately). In contrast, some of the promising evidence for the potential of sexual expression in the later years is then reviewed. Next, the implications of this discussion for younger and older individuals and for social organizations are explored.

CONSTRAINTS ON SEXUALITY IN THE LATER YEARS

Alex Comfort has often been quoted regarding sexuality in old age as follows: "In our experience, old folks stop having sex for the same reason they stop riding a bicycle—general infirmity, thinking it looks ridiculous, no bicycle" (1974, p. 440). There are many substantial reasons that explain why sexual activity is difficult for older persons. The difficulties are especially prominent when we start out with certain common assumptions, namely, that we are discussing:

sexual behavior defined as sexual intercourse,

a heterosexual relationship,

generally, a married relationship,

a marriage in which the wife is younger or about the same age as the husband,

the attitudes and values of the current cohort of older persons, and

the current social environment of negative sanctions against sexuality in old age.

With these assumptions, the deck is stacked against the fulfillment of sexuality among older persons, and especially among older women, the single elderly, and homosexuals. Constraints against sexuality in the later years include ill health, the social environment of values and norms, the resistance of children to parents' sexual activity, institutional barriers, population factors, conventional sex roles, and the double standard of aging. These constraints are discussed next.

Health

According to Masters and Johnson (1966), the two major requirements for enjoyable sexual activity until late in life are reasonably good health and an interested and interesting partner. Those are two serious qualifications. As in Comfort's bicycle metaphor, general infirmity is a serious impediment to sexual activity for some older persons; and the older the persons we are considering, the more frequent are the impediments. Nevertheless, for the "young–old," the prevalence of serious incapacitation is relatively low. For some older persons with cardiac disease, fears associated with sexual activity are unnecessarily limiting and could be allayed by careful counseling. For some older persons with disabilities, inhibitions work against the exploration of a range of alternative sexual expressions, such as variations in position in intercourse. Thus, even in this area of health limitations, which are, strictly speaking, outside a sociological perspective on sexuality, we can find some interaction with social factors. Examples include patients' and physicians' misperceptions of the relative importance of sexuality in the later years, and resistance to open communication and innovation in sexual matters in an age cohort that is, by and large, sexually restrained.

Stigmas Attached to Old Age

It has been observed to the point of being trite that ours is a youth-oriented society in which being young and/or youthfully attractive is highly valued. In no domain is this more apparent than in sexual roles. As Comfort says, some people think that older people look ridiculous riding a bicycle or having sex. Sontag (1972) has observed that the superficial aspects of aging do not interfere with physical functioning, but they are powerful in that they are incorporated into the self-image. A cartoon depicts two wrinkled and sagging old women on the beach surrounded by wrinkled old men and women; one of the women is commenting "I'm glad they don't allow nudity on *this* beach." Kuypers and Bengtson (1973) use the concept of "social breakdown syndrome" to analyze the process by which the societal view of the elderly in negative terms leads to negative self-labeling.

Older persons internalize society's view of the aged as being unattractive and unacceptable sexual partners. Television holds the mirror to our view of sexual behavior among older persons; it is generally presented as humorous, ridiculous, repugnant, appropriate for patronizing response, or extraordinarily exceptional. On the other hand, some older persons do get together as sexual partners. Unlike health and other stubborn problems, the constraints of societal attitudes and norms can be defied; to do so, one simply does not conform to expectations.

Adult Children's Resistance

It is said that the humorist, Sam Levinson, related the following story. "When I first found out how babies were born, I couldn't believe it! To think that my mother and father would do such a thing." Then, after reflection, he added "My father—maybe, but my mother—never!" (Claman, 1966). Many adult children, even those who hold permissive standards regarding their own sexual behavior, cannot believe that their mothers and fathers would want to do such a thing, particularly with a partner other than the other parent. Resistance may stem from disbelief, from aversion, and from financial considerations of the parent's inheritance. Resistance ranges from informal but powerful negative sanctions, such as ridicule, to extreme legal action to gain control over a parent's actions. Some middle-aged children may be getting back at their parents.

> Often repression of parental sexuality stems from disillusionment and hidden resentment. Some adult children who inhibited their own sexuality many years in deference to their parents' restrictive sexual values simply cannot tolerate the feelings of betrayal and loss engendered by their parents' turned-about, sexually liberated values and behaviors [Sviland, 1978, p. 99].

There may develop an amusing corollary to the problem of the obstinate children. Now that population trends have developed in such a way that many older persons themselves have older parents (Treas, 1979), we can imagine the disapproving reactions of very old parents in their 80s to the young–old persons in their 60s, their "children," who are embarking on new sexual adventures of romance and marriage. This is a possible scenario that is to date unnoticed in the gerontological literature.

Institutional Barriers

In recent years there has been increasing recognition that most long-term care institutions do not—but should—respect the individual resident's need for various forms of sexual expression, whether they involve masturbation, hugging and petting activities, or overnight conjugal visits (Butler, 1975a; Lobsenz, 1981; Miller, 1978; Wasow and Loeb, 1978). Pfeiffer (1978) calls for the granting of privacy in nursing homes for residents, for both partnered and nonpartnered sexual expressions.

The implementation of such recommendations is not simple, however. Administrators have been criticized for yielding to the demands of adult children who are outraged by permissive institutional practices. Moreover, many residents are themselves shocked by the sexual expressions of other residents. Their privacy must be respected, and they need to be protected from being offended by other residents' intrusive sexual behavior. Although it is hazardous to generalize in this regard, the present generation of older people behave sexually more conservatively than younger generations. Many residents, especially the very old, do not appear to be aware of sexual needs. One researcher found that residents identified increased physical attractiveness, rather than direct sexual expression, as their sexual need (Kaas, 1978). Undoubtedly the administrator needs to find ways to meet the needs of the sexually interested and active as well as those of the sexually restrained and uninterested.

Disadvantages Women Face

Older men and women face quite different sets of circumstances that affect their sexual behavior, and it is appropriate to consider them separately.

Although there are some cultural restrictions on the elderly male, his sexuality is primarily limited by physical factors. In contrast, those elderly females who remain physically capable and responsive are primarily limited from sexual expression by cultural factors [Sviland, 1978, p. 102].

If the deck is stacked against the sexual expression of older persons, it is older women who face the greater disadvantages. Women are confronted by an unfavorable sex ratio, the related likelihood of widowhood, norms against marriage to younger men, reduced remarriage probabilities, a double standard of aging and desirability, and conventionally inhibiting sex roles.

The Sex Ratio

To continue Comfort's metaphor, if you do not have a bicycle, you cannot ride; and, if you do not have an acceptable partner, you cannot have a sexual relationship. Older women, because of their greater longevity, are faced with a distinct shortage of male partners, a demographic phenomenon that is so recent in our history that it is not often fully realized.

At the present time there are only 69 males for every 100 females 65 and over in the United States. Only forty years ago just as many males as females were reported at ages 65 and over, but there has been a steady decline in the proportion of men and an increasing excess of women since that time [Siegel, 1976, p. 12].

The older a woman is, the fewer men there are her age (Figure 4.1). The number of men per 100 women in 1975 was 77 for the 65 to 74 year-olds, 62 for the 75 to 84 year-olds, and 49 for those women 85 years and over (Siegel, 1976, p. 13).[1] [Older women in Alaska and Hawaii, it might be noted, are not disadvantaged by a preponderance of women over men, due to migration patterns in earlier periods.]

Marital Status

Whereas older men participate in sexual activity outside marriage, older women generally do not (Verwoerdt *et al.*, 1970). Lobsenz has observed that nonmarital sex is more available to men than it is to women.

The "double standard"... enables the older man to purchase sex without the guilt or social disapproval that it would create for the older woman. (And from a purely practical viewpoint, there are far more women who will sleep for money with an older man than there are men who will do the same for an older woman) [Lobsenz, 1981, p. 236].

A marriage partner is considered necessary for the sexual expression of most of today's older women, but most older women are not married (see Figure 4.2).

Most men 65 and over are married and live with their wives. In March, 1975 three out of four men in this age range were married and living with their wives. Only one out of seven men 65 and over was widowed .... In March, 1975 only one out of three women 65 and over was married and living with her husband. Over half of the women were widowed [Siegel, 1976, p. 45].

[1]In 1980, there were 131 women/100 men aged 65–74, 181 women/100 men over 75 and 229 women/100 men over 85 (Weg, 1981).

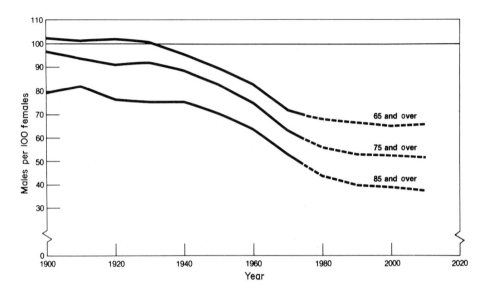

Fig. 4.1 Sex ratios in the older ages: 1900-2010. Estimates(—) and projections (--) as of July 1, except for 85 and over, 1900-1930, which relate to April 1. Points are plotted for years ending in zero, except for 1975. Source: Siegel, 1976, p. 12.

Differences between men and women in the likelihood of widowhood are greatest at the very oldest ages. Whereas 4% of men and 19% of women aged 55–59 are widowed, at age 75 and over 24% of men and 68% of women are widowed (U.S. Bureau of the Census, 1981). These differences in marital status between older men and women reflect the greater mortality of men and the pattern of men marrying women younger than themselves.

Relative Age of Husbands and Wives

Women outlive men (by about 8 years), and yet they marry men who are several years older than themselves, thus increasing their chances of eventually facing widowhood. Older women face fewer physiological limitations on sexual activity than older men. It would seem, then, to be reasonable for women to marry younger men. Nevertheless, because of standards of acceptability of marriage partners, there are powerful negative sanctions against women marrying men younger than themselves, and men usually select younger women as wives. Among older (65 and over) men who do marry, one out of five marries a partner under 55,

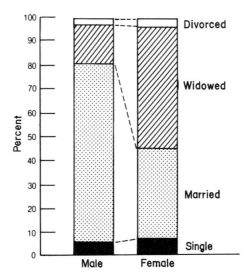

Fig. 4.2   Percentage distribution of the male and female population 65 years and over by marital status: 1975. Source: Siegel, 1976, p. 45.

compared to less than 3% of older women who marry (Treas and Van Hilst, 1976). Male mortality and social norms concerning the relative ages of sexual partners thus combine to limit the availability of sexual partners for older women.

The Chances of Remarriage

Treas and Van Hilst (1976) report the discouraging facts of low marriage–remarriage rates among older persons (65 and over), with no indication of increases in marriage rates. The likelihood of marriage in the later years is low for both men and women, but it is lower for women; as was noted earlier, marriage appears to be a necessary condition for sexual activity for older women, more so than for men of similar age.

> It is estimated that [in 1970] there were fewer than 3 brides out of 1,000 older single women; the marriage rate for males, while higher, was estimated to be only 17 grooms per 1,000 older single men [Treas and Van Hilst, 1976, p. 133].

According to the analysis by Treas and Van Hilst, marriage possibilities among the elderly are most reduced in the oldest age categories. In California, in 1971, a woman in the 65–69 age group was twice as likely to wed as one in the 70–74 age group. Older men and women who reside in the South or West are about twice as likely to marry as those who live in the Northeast and North Central states. Pressures against remarriage, beyond the availability of appropriate partners, include Social Security and pension eligibility rules that penalize widows who remarry.

Sex Roles

Although some exchange between men and women of conventional sex roles may occur in the later years, the male advantage in courtship persists, and the male is more likely to assume the prerogative of taking the sexual initiative (Lobsenz, 1981). Thus, older women who face a numerical disadvantage in the ratio of men to women, and who could be inclined to seek a male partner competitively, also face the likelihood of disapproval if they do so. The current generation of older men and women may be particularly sensitive to the niceties of traditional courtship. The rules of the game do work against the older woman who would actively seek a sexual partner.

The Double Standard of Aging

De Beauvoir has commented in regard to sexuality in the later years that "Biologically men are at the greater disadvantage: socially, it is the women who are worse off, because of their condition as erotic objects" (1972, p. 321). Because of their evaluation in terms of physical attractiveness, women are disadvantaged in aging.

> Women become sexually ineligible much earlier than men do.... Thus, for most women, aging means a humiliating process of gradual sexual disqualification.... Getting older tends (for several decades) to operate in men's favor, since their value as lovers and husbands is set more by what they do than how they look [Sontag, 1972, pp. 31–32].

The double standard of aging is reflected even in admonitions by the experts on sexuality and old age.

> Where the wife is the basic cause of the impotence, obviously she must be involved in measures to correct it. Sometimes the husband can be induced to accept a change that has occurred as inevitable and make the best of it. In other cases, the wife must take such necessary measures as dietary regulation, *plastic surgery*, or any step to correct the factor that is inhibiting her husband's potency [Rubin, 1965; p. 146, quoted in Botnowick, 1973, p. 44; italics added].

Butler (1975a) presents the opposite and exceptional view, admonishing both partners to take responsibility for their appearance.

Women are thus at a greater disadvantage than men in finding opportunities for sexual expression in the later years on several scores:

there are many fewer older men than women,

older men tend to be married, whereas older women tend to be widowed,

older men tend to marry younger women,

older women are not approved sexual partners for younger men,

older women are not expected to take the initiative in courtship, and

women become "old" in sexual terms at younger chronological ages than men do, because they are devalued as unattractive.

Disadvantages Men Face

The emphasis has been placed on the disadvantages women face. Physiologically, the deck is stacked against aging men; problems of impotence are discussed in the chapters by Felstein, Finkle, and Weg, and they have been analyzed by Masters and Johnson (1981). The ways in which social and psychological factors exacerbate these physiological problems are discussed in the chapter by Weg.

Although older men are advantaged by the sex ratio and are more likely than older women to be married and to remarry if divorced or widowed, they do face certain role disadvantages. Conventional role behavior assigned to men throughout the life cycle has emphasized the initiating, active, performing aspects of work and social relationships. Having relinquished the active work role in his retirement years, and facing changes in his sexual performance, the older male may suffer some loss of self-esteem. Gender roles, unless relaxed in old age, militate against the benefits of the woman's sharing of sexual initiative and the benefits of deemphasizing the performance aspects of sexuality. Today's older generation is more closely tied to traditional gender roles than tomorrow's elderly will be. Role changes and consequences are discussed at length elsewhere in this volume.

A BROADER LOOK AT SEXUALITY IN THE LATER YEARS

In counting the constraints against sexuality in the later years, we have been operating under several common assumptions: the need for heterosexual, marital relationships, with the emphasis on sexual intercourse as sexual expression. When these assumptions are relaxed, there is some evidence supporting an optimistic view of the potential for sexual expression.

Sexual Liberation

Butler has cautioned us to be wary of generalizations about the aged. "The present generation, now in their seventies, were among the early experimenters in the flapper age of the 1920's" (1975b, p. 394). Older persons today may share to some extent in "the eroticization of the backdrop" of everyday life:

> While there is a heightened sense of the sexual in today's daily life this backdrop only affects behavior indirectly, without supplying the social networks for acting out the behavior. And although it does not directly affect behavior, the shifting of the backdrop does create new sexual expectations in both older and younger generations [Gagnon and Simon, 1973, p. 291].

Liberation includes the appreciation of sexuality as a positive value, permission to explore alternative forms of sexual expression, a broader definition of the acceptable sexual partner, and a release of men and women from narrowly constructed male and female sex roles. Some of these factors, which contribute to a more optimistic picture of sexuality in the later years, are discussed below.

Older Married Women

There is more than one way to read statistics. We have stressed the fact that 52.1% of older women are widowed and thus have limited opportunities for sexual relationships. We might also emphasize that 38.5% of older women are married, and, although that proportion does not correspond favorably with the 77.1% of older men who are married (Weg, 1981), it nevertheless represents a great many women, as well as men, whose marital status affords optimism for their sexual lives.

Success of Remarriage

Although remarriage is not a readily available option for most older persons, and especially for older women, there is some indication that it is satisfying to those who do remarry. In a study conducted by Vinich (1976) of a small sample of 24 older couples married several years, three out of four of the older women were satisfied, or very satisfied, with their marriages.

Positive Aging Effects

Aging may bring some improvements in a sexual relationship. Some older persons report increases of interest and activity. There is the potential in retirement for relief from preoccupation with work roles and responsibilities that can be troublesome for sexual relationships (Botnowick, 1973). Although the passage of time itself is often acknowledged as having a negative effect on relationships, through the destructiveness of boredom with the partner and with the familiarity of routines of sexual behavior, time and experience can be beneficial:

> Couples can learn ways of utilizing the differences and changes to enhance their closeness and to increase the pleasure and gratification they can give to each other. Lovemaking techniques can accommodate each partner's changing needs for stimulation and gratification, and the marriage relationship can be enriched by a sensitive and mutually generous adaptation to each partner's age-related changes in sexual functioning [Kaplan, 1974, p. 114].

Lowenthal's research substantiated that optimistic perspective (Lowenthal et al., 1975):

> [Among] older people who did report increasing sexual satisfaction (about one-third)...men spoke of heightened "enjoyment" and "appreciation" deriving from growing emotional involvement and compatibility. Women spoke of "better understanding of one another," of becoming more "honest and comfortable," and made implicit references to early inhibitions [p. 34].

Timing Effects

It has been observed by those involved in sexual counseling that the older male is better able to, or needs to, engage in longer periods of love play leading up to climax, a phenomenon that can enhance the enjoyment of the female, for whom more drawn out lovemaking is beneficial at all ages (Kaplan, 1974; Sviland, 1978).

> Freed of the intense need for fast orgastic release and of the inhibitions of his youth, more satisfying and imaginative love play is often enjoyed by the older man and his partner [Kaplan, 1974, p. 109].

In the case of age-related physiological changes in the timing of sexual responses, the changes can be experienced to the advantage of increased mutual satisfaction.

Sex Roles

It has been speculated that, in the later years, men and women move toward each other's gender roles, although universal consensus on this belief is lacking (Puglisi and Jackson, 1981). Women, who have assumed submissive and passive roles generally, and in sexual behavior specifically, may become more assertive, instrumental, and initiating in their behavior. Men, in turn, may take on more nurturant and expressive role behavior. Such a merging of role behaviors is timely in that it corresponds to the older male's increased need for greater physical stimulation in order to achieve erection and ejaculation (Kaplan, 1974). Thus, certain specifically physiological aspects of sexual behavior in the later years are understood best in the context of learned role behavior. The merging of gender roles is a positive adaptation.

Sensuality

As we move away from the restrictive assumptions delineated earlier, including that of a narrow focus on sexual intercourse, other positive aspects of sexuality in the later years emerge. Romance is claimed as the province of youth, but, in fact, the more romantic, sentimental, and tender aspects of sexuality may become salient again, in the later years, when affectionate relationships include, but transcend, physical expressions of love through sexual intercourse (Broderick, 1978). Reedy (1978) reports some of the positive aspects of growing old together in a love relationship; although sexual intimacy may be less centrally important, it may be better—warmer and mellowed— with affectionate embraces becoming more important.

There seems to be a merging of male and female sexual styles, as well as roles, in the later years:

> As the biologic urge lessens with age, older males become more like women in their sexual behavior in that fantasy and ambience become more important in lovemaking, and there is relatively less preoccupation with orgasm. In older men, as the physical factors that motivate sexuality decline, psychic determinants become heavier contributors to the final sexual response [Kaplan, 1974, p. 112].

Sensuality as a broader experience than sexuality is not confined to heterosexual relationships. Women have always enjoyed greater license than men to express affection physically to friends and family members, through such gestures as walking arm in arm, hugging, and kissing. The male liberation that accompanies the current female liberation offers some optimism that the negative sanctions against expressions of affection among males with be relaxed. Sensual, but not strictly sexual, touching relationships may substitute for or complement heterosexual relationships for older men and women.

Alternative Forms of Sexual Expression

Once the definition of sexuality is broadened beyond marital, heterosexual relationships, the potential for fulfillment of sexuality in the later years appears to be less constrained. The older woman, faced with a distinct shortage of available men of her age, might expand the options that she defines as acceptable to include masturbation, a relationship with another woman, or a relationship with a younger man (Butler and Lewis, 1973; Genevay, 1978; Huyck, 1977; Solnick, 1978; Sviland, 1978).

A relationship with another woman might be sexual in a strict sense, or it might serve broader sensual needs by providing the hug and kiss, which seem to be important needs for all individuals at all ages. Some women choose a relationship with another woman as the *preferred* lifestyle and do not define it as an alternative to or substitute for a heterosexual relationship.

Variants of the marriage relationship that are open to older people have been described as polygyny, pair cohabitation, a group of women, group marriage, and comarital relationships, or swinging (Cavan, 1976). These arrangements are outside the range of options imagined by most older people, but older people reflect the changes that are occurring in other age sectors of society. "According to the 1977 Census tabulations, there were 106,000 households of unmarried members of the opposite sex, in which the head of the household was 65 and over" (Metropolitan Life, 1979).

Benefits of Sexuality

The best news of all must be that sex in the later years is even good for us. Two physicians offer the following advice:

There is some evidence, for example, that sex activity helps arthritis, probably because of adrenal gland production of cortisone. The sexual act is itself a form of physical activity, helping people stay in good physical condition. It helps to reduce tensions, which are both physical and psychological [Butler and Lewis, 1973, p. 102].

Sex offers the elderly the kind of relief from anxieties that others find, for example, in alcohol, eating, tranquilizers, marijuana and hard drugs, and violent behavior [Kassel, quoted in the Los Angeles Times, 1974].

Breakthroughs for Future Generations

We can be optimistic that future generations of older women will achieve greater sexual expression. Riley and Foner (1968) speak of the differences among generations in sexual responsiveness, citing Kinsey's finding that "women born before 1900 have been, on the whole, less likely than the more recently born cohorts to achieve orgasm during marital intercourse" (Kinsey *et al.*, 1953, p. 262). Calderone (1975) also projects the sexual fulfillment of the generation of older women of the 1990s, those who are experiencing today fuller and earlier "sexualization." Christenson and Gagnon (1965) found that earlier sexual experience predicted later orgasmic experience in a sample of older women.

Although there are some real impediments to the full realization of sexuality in the later years for some older persons, we have noted that, in some ways, sexual relationships become even better over the years. The love relationship may become stronger, and men's and women's roles and sexual styles may come into closer correspondence. A look beyond the traditional models of heterosexual and marital relationships may afford some older persons, especially women, the opportunity for sexual and sensual fulfillment that would otherwise be impossible. Future generations of women and men will probably find fuller sexual expression in their old age, but sexual liberation has not entirely bypassed today's older generation. Many of them are finding pleasure in sexuality in their later years.

IMPLICATIONS

Many of the problems of sexuality in old age have had a lifetime to develop and are not easily overcome. The corollary is that it is possible, on the basis of what we already understand about sexuality, to invest during the earlier years in sexual pleasure in old age.

Individuals and Couples

A young woman who is now choosing a mate could consider those factors that would help her to avoid widowhood in old age. It makes sense, from this perspective, to marry a man who is younger, or at least no older, than oneself. Although such marriages are uncommon in the United

States, there is evidence of an increasing trend in marriages between an older wife and a younger husband in recent years in West Germany, Britain, and Sweden (Butler, 1975a). Furthermore, because so much of male mortality is linked to smoking, a nonsmoking male could be a much better marriage risk. Also, it is possible to provide one's marriage partner with social supports that will reduce known mortality risks through lowered stress, proper diet, and exercise. Mortality is, to a great extent, beyond individual control, but we often do not exercise even that measure of control that is within our present knowledge.

Continuity has proven to be crucial to sexual potential in the later years. The individual who maintains an active sexual life in the middle years is contributing to his or her sexual potential in the later years (Masters and Johnson, 1966; Kaplan, 1974; Pfeiffer and Davis, 1972). 'A common expression of this fact is "Use it or lose it." Couples, therefore, have a mutual stake in maintaining an active sexual relationship. Two therapists have worked out a program of future sexual planning that is similar to financial investment planning; they are quoted as follows:

> A couple may believe that they are "too busy" for sex or spending intimate time together now, "but later, when we're retired," then there'll be time. . . . . . . The couple with no practice in intimacy will find it difficult to achieve it in later life . . . the couple who rely totally on sexual intercourse to communicate may have trouble adapting to the changes that occur as they grow older. . . . People can diversify their lovemaking to include touch for its own sake rather than touch merely as a way station to intercourse [Los Angeles Times, 1978].

Institutions

Institutions, as well as individuals, can engage in practices that make feasible the sexual fulfillment of both the current and the future older generations. An emphasis on the social origins of sexual behavior in old age leads to the realization that sexual attitudes and behavior that are socialized, or learned, can be learned differently by future generations and can be relearned by older persons. The physiological possibilities of sexual interest and behavior in old age, the attractiveness of the physically aging man or woman, and the propriety of sex between older persons are examples of learned ideas we share that are subject to redefinition. Educational programs in general, and preretirement programs in particular, might very well include attention to the sexual as well as the financial, health, and leisure aspects of old age.

The media are potent educational forces that shape our perceptions of what older people actually do in their sexual lives and of what they should and should not do. Sexual behavior among the aging is one of the few private areas that have not yet been opened up for scrutiny by television.

Legislation, through provisions regarding benefits, taxes, and inheritance, can either discourage or make feasible the combinations of older persons in couples, whether the couple is heterosexual or homosexual, married or unmarried.

Universities, government agencies, and private funding agencies can encourage research on the life-cycle aspects of sexuality. Research endeavors can become much more advanced. For instance, the first improvement should be to abandon attempts to generalize about old age per se, and instead to distinguish at least between the young–old (in their 50s or 60s) and the old–old (in their 70s or 80s) in discussing sexuality among older persons.

Many institutions in which older persons reside are following humanitarian trends to allow for (and even encourage) opportunities for older residents' sexual expression. Legislation is in effect or under consideration in some states to require the recognition by institutions of individual human rights to sexual expression.

CONCLUSION

The sexual behavior of older persons is now a politicized arena because of such forces as women's and men's liberation, raised levels of consciousness about aging issues, increased organized advocacy by older people, and the push for liberalized legislation affecting institutional residents and the financial benefits of older couples. Further liberalization of sexual behavior in the later years will be resisted by conservative forces that defend against modifications of the conventional family, and by the traditional control over sexual behavior by some religious organizations.

This chapter does not pretend to be "value neutral" in its sociological approach to sexuality in old age. The author obviously favors the encouragement of opportunities for sexual expression among the aged. On the other hand, we should not neglect the preferences and privileges of those older men and women who do not choose to define quality of life in terms of sexuality or in reference to a member of the opposite (or the same) sex, and who place sexuality low on their ranking of the important things in life. Permissiveness works both ways (Whitcomb, 1981).

This chapter has emphasized the contraints against the fulfillment of sexual interests among older men and women, stressing the effects of social roles, attitudes, and norms. We are experiencing a period of marked social change in sexual attitudes and behavior, however, and many of today's elderly will benefit from such change. The real breakthrough will occur in the future sexual experiences of those men and women who are now in their 40s and 50s. Many of them will carry into their old age broader experience and higher levels of expectation.

REFERENCES

Botnowick, J. (1973). "Aging and Behavior." Springer Publishing Co., New York.

Broderick, C. (1978). In "Sexuality and Aging" (R. L., Solnick, ed.), rev. ed., pp. 1-8. Andrus Gerontology Center, Univ. of Southern California Press, Los Angeles.

Butler, R. N. (1975a.). In "The Later Years" (L. E. Brown and E. O. Ellis, eds.), pp. 129-143. Am. Med. Assoc., Acton, Massachusetts.

Butler, R. N. (1975b). "Why Survive? Being Old in America." Harper & Row, New York.

Butler, R. N., and Lewis, M. I. (1973). "Aging and Mental Health: Positive Psychosocial Approaches." Mosby, St. Louis.

Calderone, M. S. (1975). In "No Longer Young," pp. 111-115. Institute of Gerontology, University of Michigan–Wayne State University, Ann Arbor.

Cameron, P., and Biber, H. (1973). Gerontologist **13**, 144-147.

Cavan, R. S. (1976). In "The Sociology of Aging: Selected Readings" (R. C. Atchley and M. M. Seltzer, eds.), pp. 141-144. Wadsworth, Belmont, California.

Christenson, C. V., and Gagnon, J. H. (1965). J. Gerontol. **20**, 351-356.

Claman, A. D. (1966). Can. Med. Assoc. J. **94**, 201.

Comfort, A. C. (1974). J. Am. Geriatr. Soc. **22**, 440-442.

De Beauvoir, S. (1972). "The Coming of Age." Putnam, New York.

Gagnon, J. H., and Simon, W. (1973). "Sexual Conduct." Aldine, Chicago.

Genevay, B. (1978). In "Sexuality and Aging" (R. L. Solnick, ed.), rev. ed., pp. 9-25. Univ. of Southern California Press, Los Angeles.

Huyck, M. H. (1977). In "Looking Ahead" (L. E. Troll, J. Israel, and K. Israel, eds.), pp. 43-58. Prentice-Hall, Englewood Cliffs, New Jersey.

Kaas, M. H. (1978). Gerontologist **18**, 372-378.

Kaplan, H. S. (1974). "The New Sex Therapy." Brunner/Mazel, New York.

Kinsey, A. C., Pomeroy, W. B., and Martin, C. E. (1948). "Sexual Behavior in the Human Male." Saunders, Philadelphia.

Kinsey, A. C., Pomeroy, W. B., and Martin, C. E. (1953). "Sexual Behavior in the Human Female." Saunders, Philadelphia.

Kleemeier, R. W., and Kantor, M. B. (1962). In "Determinants of Human Sexual Behavior" (G. Winokur, ed.), pp. 201-205. Thomas, Springfield, Illinois.

Kuypers, J. A., and Bengtson, V. L. (1973). Hum. Dev. **16**, 181-201.

Lobsenz, N. M. (1981). In "Aging in America" (C. S. Kart and B. B. Manard, eds.), pp. 233-243. Alfred Publ. Co., Port Washington, New York.

Los Angeles Times (1974). "Tolerance for Sex Among Elderly Urged." March 29.

Los Angeles Times (1978). "Reviewing One's Sexual Portfolio." October 4.

102   Pauline K. Robinson

Lowenthal, M. J., Thurner, M., Chiriboga, D., and associates (1975). "Four Stages of Life."
    Jossey-Bass, San Francisco.
Ludeman, K. (1981). *Gerontologist* **21** (2), 203–208.
Masters, W. H., and Johnson, V. E. (1966). "Human Sexual Response." Little, Brown, Boston.
Masters, W. H., and Johnson, V. E. (1981). *J. Am. Geriatr. Soc.* **29**, 385–390.
Metropolitan Life (1979). *Stat. Bull.* **59**, 7–11.
Miller, D. B. (1978). *In* "Sexuality and Aging" (R. L. Solnick, ed.), rev. ed., pp. 163–175.
    Andrus Gerontology Center, Univ. of Southern California Press, Los Angeles.
Palmore, E., ed. (1970). "Normal Aging." Duke Univ. Press, Durham, North Carolina.
Pfeiffer, E. (1975). *In* "Modern Perspectives in the Psychiatry of Old Age" (J. G. Howells, ed.),
    pp. 313–325. Brunner/Mazel, New York.
Pfeiffer, e. (1978). *In* "Sexuality and Aging" (R. L. Solnick, ed.), rev. ed., pp. 26–32. Andrus
    Gerontology Center, Univ. of Southern California Press, Los Angeles.
Pfeiffer, E., and Davis, G. C. (1972). *J. Am. Geriatr. Soc.* **20**, 4.
Pfeiffer, E., Verwoerdt, A., and Wang, H. (1970). *In* "Normal Aging" (E. Palmore, ed.), pp. 299–
    303. Duke Univ. Press, Durham, North Carolina.
Population Reference Bureau (1975). "The Elderly in America," Population Bulletin, vol. 30,
    no. 3. Population Reference Bureau, Washington, D.C.
Puglisi, J. T., and Jackson, D. W. (1981). *Inter. J. Aging and Human Dev.* **12**, 129–138.
Ragan, P. K., and Davis, W. J. (1978). *Society* **15**, 50–53.
Ragan, P. K., and Wales, J. B. (1980). *In* "Handbook on Mental Health and Aging" (J. E. Birren,
    ed.), pp. 377–399. Prentice-Hall, Englewood Cliffs, New Jersey.
Reedy, M. N. (1978). *In* "Sexuality and Aging" (R. L. Solnick, ed.), rev. ed., pp. 184–196.
    Andrus Gerontology Center, Univ. of Southern California Press, Los Angeles.
Riley, N. W., and Foner, A. (1968). "Aging and Society," Vol. I. Russell Sage Foundation, New
    York.
Rubin, I. (1965). "Sexual Life After Sixty." Basic Books, New York.
Siegel, J. S. (1976). "Demographic Aspects of Aging and the Older Population in the United
    States," U. S. Bureau of the Census Ser. P-23, No. 59. U. S. Gov. Printing Office,
    Washington, D. C.
Silverstone, B., and Hyman, H. K. (1976). "You and Your Aging Parent: The Modern Family's
    Guide to Emotional, Physical and Financial Problems." Pantheon, New York.
Solnick, R. L. (1978). *In* "Sexuality and Aging" (R. L. Solnick, ed.) rev. ed., pp. 33–47. Andrus
    Gerontology Center, Univ. of Southern California Press, Los Angeles.
Sontag, S. (1972). *Saturday Rev.* September 23.
Sviland, M. A. (1978). *In* "Sexuality and Aging" (R. L. Solnick, ed.), rev. ed., pp. 96–114.
    Andrus Gerontology Center, Univ. of Southern California Press, Los Angeles.
Treas, J. (1979). *In* "Aging Parents" (P. K. Ragan, ed.), pp. 58–65. Univ. of Southern California
    Press, Los Angeles.
Treas, J., and Van Hilst, A. (1976). *Gerontologist* **16**, 132–136.
U.S. Bureau of the Census (1981). "Marital Status and Living Arrangements: March 1980,"
    Current Population Reports, Series P-20, no. 365. U.S. Govt. Printing Office,
    Washington, D.C.
Verwoerdt, A., Pfeiffer, E., and Wang, H. (1970). *In* "Normal Aging" (E. Palmore, ed.), pp. 282–
    299. Duke Univ. Press, Durham, North Carolina.
Vinich, B. (1976). *Behav. Today* August 23.
Wales, J. B. (1974). *Case West. Res. J. Sociol.* **6**, 82–105.
Wasow, M., and Loeb, M. B. (1978). *In* "Sexuality and Aging" (R. L. Solnick, ed.), rev. ed., pp.
    154–162. Andrus Gerontology Center, Univ. of Southern California Press, Los Angeles.

Weg, R. B. (1978). *In* "Sexuality and Aging" (R. L. Solnick, ed.), rev. ed., pp. 48–64. Andrus Gerontology Center, Univ. of Southern California Press, Los Angeles.
Weg, R. B. (1981). "The Aged: Who, Where, How Well." Leonard Davis School of Gerontology, University of Southern California, Los Angeles.
Whitcomb, M. (1981). *50 Plus*, January, pp. 30–31.

5

Gender Identity: A Life-Span View of Sex-Role Development

INTRODUCTION

According to a Moroccan parable, each boy is born surrounded by 100 devils and each girl by 100 angels. With each passing year, a devil is exchanged for an angel. When they reach 100 years of age, the man is surrounded by angels, and the woman is surrounded by devils (Gutmann, 1977). An American Indian parable tells of a warrior chief to whom, in middle age, the Great Spirit appeared in a dream. The spirit announced to

SEXUALITY IN THE
LATER YEARS

him that from then on he must sit among the women and children, wear women's clothes, and eat the food of women. He obeyed the dream without suffering a loss of prestige.

Like most artistic creations, folktales can be interpreted as metaphor. They reflect the unconscious concerns and hidden agenda of a culture. These two parables have in common an implicit model of human development—specifically, of sex-role development. They imply a reversal of sex roles in the second half of life. The male relinquishes his aggressiveness and war-like capability for gentler, more feminine ways. The female takes on the man's fighting spirit (if I may so interpret Moroccan devils). Equally important, each culture regards this transformation as a normal, expectable life event. Each culture sanctions, and in this sense socializes, its members to some reversal of sex-role norms in the second half of life.

According to Jung (1933 p. 108), folktales such as these are true expressions of a psychic revolution in the middle years of life. "[The man] discovers his tender feelings and [the woman] her sharpness of mind." Jung regards this shift as generated from within, as a genuine developmental phase in the human life cycle that transcends cultures and historic periods. He suggests that the roles we fulfill in the first half of life—being useful, achieving and nurturing of the young—require that we develop selected parts of ourselves at the expense of other parts, which we suppress. But, in the second half of life, the individual turns inward to greater awareness of the parts of the self that were suppressed earlier. Jung asserts that the person can achieve true individuation only when she or he integrates latent sides of the personality, and that it is most important for the man to integrate his feminine side and for the woman to integrate her masculine side.

Bakan (1966) proposes a similar view. Bakan views agency and communion as the basic modalities of all living organisms. Agency is concerned with the assertion of individuality and self-interest, and communion is concerned with integration with other organisms. He proposes that the basic developmental task for survival, for the individual or the society, is to integrate these two modalities so that neither overrides the other. Thus, the fundamental developmental tasks for men and women differ: the man must develop qualities of communion to modify his agentic orientation; the woman must adopt agentic qualities for greater self-actualization.

Changes in the quality of maleness and femaleness over the life span have been topics of increasing interest to social scientists as well as philosophers in recent years. A growing body of empirical research suggests that sex typing does indeed become less rigid in the second half of life. In this chapter, I will review evidence that casts light on the evolution of gender identity in men and women over the life span. My focus will be on sex-role development in our own culture, primarily in the white urban middle class, but data from other groups and societies will be cited when relevant. My approach will be neither exclusively developmental, in the sense of an inner unfolding, nor exclusively social. I assume that social, psychological, and biological determinants all interact with one another to shape the development of human beings. However, I will not focus on biological determinants here. I assume, too, that the course of development differs from one historical period to another, along with changes in the definitions of age and sex roles (Baltes *et al.*, 1977; Riegel, 1976; Neugarten, 1978). Chiriboga and Thurnher (1980) point out that in our own age of rapid social change, even the rhythm of the life cycle is changing: puberty comes earlier, and the climacterium comes later. People live longer, become parents and grandparents earlier, and spend most of their lives in the postparental stage of life. Women outlive men by an increasing margin. Neugarten refers also to the emergence of a "fluid" life cycle that is marked by the disappearance of traditional timetables. People of all ages marry and remarry, enter and reenter the labor force, change careers or return to school, and rear first and second families. Our society, she points out, has become age-irrelevant. And, I would add, it is on the way to becoming, if not gender-irrelevant, at least more fluid with respect to sex roles. Thus, the trajectory of change in the quality of maleness and femaleness over the life cycle can be traced only against a moving background of shifting roles for men and women at different ages and in different times and places.

There are, however, certain regularities in the experiences of most women and men in our own as well as other societies that justify a developmental approach to the study of gender identity. Certain issues that arise in the course of the life cycle—for example, a sense of time running out in the middle years—impel a reworking of what it means to be male or female.

With these assumptions in mind, I will propose a life-span model of sex-role development and will review, as far as possible, empirical evidence to document the model. One additional caveat: the returns are just beginning to come in. The evidence is sketchy. Most studies of sex differences and sex-role development end with adolescence. There is relatively little systematic research on gender identity in the older adult years. That which exists is often peripheral to, or must be inferred from, studies addressing other issues in adulthood. Thus, the model is tentative and the data are suggestive.

A MODEL OF SEX-ROLE DEVELOPMENT

The model of sex-role development to be described in this chapter is an adaptation of those models proposed by Block (1973), Pleck (1975), and Hefner *et al.*, (1975). These theorists suggest that sex-role development has much in common with more general processes of cognitive, moral, and ego development (Kohlberg, 1966, 1973; Loevinger, 1966, 1976; Piaget, 1965). Their models propose that the individual moves through a hierarchy of stages that are increasingly complex and that occur in a fixed order. The number of stages varies with each theorist. Block's model, the most elaborate and differentiated of the three, corresponds to Loevinger's theory of ego development and proposes six stages of gender development. Following Pleck, I will outline three broad phases common to all of the models: (a) a global or undifferentiated stage, in the first years of life, in which gender is unorganized and amorphous; (b) a highly differentiated, conforming stage, beginning in middle childhood, in which sex roles are rigidly polarized; and (c) an integrated stage, in which sex-role norms are transcended, leading to psychological androgyny. This final stage corresponds to Loevinger's highest stage of ego development, in which conflicting forces in the self are integrated and resolved internally. It is also analogous to Kohlberg's higher and more complex stages of moral reasoning.

Block's Model

Block (1973) points out that the conforming stage is a critical period in the acquisition of gender identity. It is at this stage that boys internalize masculine role norms: they learn to stress agentic skills (achievement and mastery) and to disown dependency and emotionality. Girls internalize feminine norms: they develop their communal or affiliative side and disown aggression. Both sexes at this stage are intolerant of deviance in self or others. This phase reaches a peak in adolescence with its emphasis on courting and confirming same-sex identity. Terman and Miles (1936) found, for example, that sex-typed interests are highest during the eighth grade for girls and during the eleventh grade for boys, and that they decline later.

With the exception of Hefner *et al.*, these authors do not explicitly focus on continuing sex-role development in the adult years. Evidence is accumulating, however, that sex-role integration is fully established only in mature adulthood, some time during the middle of life. [For a similar point of view, see Sedney (1977)]. I suggest that individuals who do reach the androgynous stage of development by the end of adolescence may do so only partially or tentatively. In response to early adult role demands, they may regress to an earlier, more polarized stage of gender development.

Livson's Model

The model I am proposing deviates from a structural model in that it allows the possibility of reversal in the individual's progression through successive stages, at least in the postadolescent years.

Traditional roles in early adulthood—career building, marriage, parenting—tend to maintain or recreate the polarization of sex roles that is apparent in adolescence. To perform these roles efficiently—to nurture children, achieve occupational success, and be a traditional wife or husband—individuals may need to disown cross-sex characteristics developed only tentatively, if at all, by the end of adolescence. They may regress to an earlier, more conventional level of sex-role development. Indeed, individuals may regress and progress more than once before fully transcending sex-role norms with the approach of middle age; however, children leave home, occupational goals change, and retirement becomes imminent, so that the nurturant role for women and the achieving role for men become less demanding. Individuals may now allow themselves to reclaim unused parts of their personalities. Beginning with this period of life, they may more solidly integrate or transcend sex-role norms. Kohlberg (1973) proposes that the highest and most complex levels of moral development occur in response to life experience rather than to developmental changes in cognitive functioning. Similarly, I propose that life experience stimulates the individual to move toward a more complex level of sex-role development. But, insofar as shifts in life tasks and roles expand consciousness and increase the freedom to accept conflicting parts of the self, sex-role integration is linked to a more complex level of cognitive functioning. There is evidence to support the view that women and men do indeed integrate cross-sex characteristics in the second half of life.

Androgyny of Later Life

Drawing on cross-cultural observations in folk and traditional societies in all parts of the world, Gutmann (1977) documents what he calls the "normal unisex of later life." Men become less power oriented than they were when they were younger, and women become more power oriented, at least in domestic settings. Young men are instrumental and productive. As warriors, hunters, and farmers, they deal with the world by active mastery. But in later life, communal concerns take priority over agency. A receptive attitude, particularly in regard to women, tends to replace independence, and affiliation with a supernatural power takes the place of individual strength. According to Gutmann, adult men move from active to passive mastery. He finds that women, however, reverse this process, moving from passive to active mastery. In early adulthood, women are dependent on, and deferent to their husbands (and, in some cultures, to older women). But, in later adulthood, they take on increasingly active and powerful roles, at least within the family. "Across cultures and with age they seem to become more domineering, more agentic, and less willing to trade submission for security" (Gutmann, 1977, p. 309).

Gutmann concludes that sex roles are distributed not only by sex but also by age. The explanation he proposes is that the demands of parenthood account for this shift. Each sex suppresses opposite-sex characteristics in order to provide the optimum conditions for the care of the young: nurturance and physical security. When parenting is completed in the second half of life, each sex is able to live out potentials that were relinquished earlier.

Studies in our own society suggest that men and women integrate opposite-sex characteristics as they age. Neugarten and Gutmann (1968), analyzing Thematic Apperception Test (TAT) stories of men and women beteween ages 40 and 70, found that women, as they age, become more tolerant of their aggressive and egocentric impulses. Men, as they age, become more tolerant of their nurturant and affiliative impulses. Lowenthal et al. (1975), in their study of men and women at four life transitions, report a similar shift. Among young newlyweds, men saw themselves as active and energetic, whereas women's self-images lacked energy. But, at the preretirement stage (about age 60), women's assertiveness contrasted with the expressive orientation of men. At the same time, the self-concepts of preretirement women were less feminine than those of younger women. Both men and women in this study agreed that men are less likely and women are more likely to be "boss" in the family in the later life stages than in the earlier ones. Chiriboga and Thurnher (1980) report similar age-related changes in the balance of domestic power in another sample.

Several studies find that older men are more affiliative and more sensitive to human relations than are older women (Kelly, 1955; Kerchoff, 1966; Kuhlen, 1964). Terman and Miles (1936) and Strong (1936) observed increasing "femininity" with age among men from ages 18 or 19 on, although their data on changes in women are less clear.

Fantasy productions and dreams, along with projective tests, tap a different level of consciousness. Lehner and Gunderson (1953) compared men's and women's self-images at successive ages as expressed on the Draw-A-Person Test. They found that women's self-images expand during the 30s, reaching a peak around age 40. Men's self-images begin to contract after age 30. Brenneis (1975) used dreams to explore women's self-images at different ages. Women over 40 depict themselves as more robust and energetic and less concerned with the effects of aggression than adolescent girls or young adults. Conversely, men's daydreams regarding heroic action or personal advancement decline steadily with age (Giambra, 1973).

All of these studies are limited by the fact that age changes are inferred from cross-sectional comparisons of persons in different age groups. Thus, all are subject to the possibility that apparent differences actually reflect cohort differences. Also, it is hazardous to generalize from studies of varying quality using different measures on different populations. The cross-cultural observations, however, lend support to the findings of more systematic studies. Together they strongly suggest that there is a tendency, if not to reverse roles in later life, for each sex to develop qualities conventionally defined as appropriate to the opposite sex.

This proposition finds support in a longitudinal study of my own in which I compared personality changes in the same women and men from adolescence to age 50 (Livson, 1976b).[1] Individuals who were psychologically healthiest at age 50 showed increasing androgyny over time.

---

[1]These women and men are part of an ongoing longitudinal study at the Institute of Human Development, University of California, Berkeley.

Women became more assertive and analytic while remaining nurturant
and open to feelings. Men became more giving and expressive while they
continued to be ambitious and assertive. Also, psychologically less healthy
men became more androgynous by age 50; they became more accepting of
dependent needs and less power oriented. The only group who failed to
become more androgynous were psychologically less healthy women, a
finding to which I will return later. The point to be made here is that the
other three groups developed cross-sex characteristics by age 50 *without*
relinquishing same-sex characteristics. The sexes did not reverse roles;
they became more androgynous.

Altogether, these studies lend support to the view that the most
complex level of gender development is generally not achieved before
middle life (and is probably not achieved by everyone). The fact that this
level is more evident in older adults than in younger adults suggests that
maturational factors are involved: for example, increased capacity to
resolve conflict. I am in agreement, however, with Gutmann (1977), that
changes in life tasks play a key part in the androgyny of later life. Gender
roles become less rigid when mates have been chosen, children reared,
careers won, and dragons conquered. There is, in short, less conflict
between masculine and feminine role norms in later life. With less actual
role conflict, the individual may be able to tolerate more complexity in
role behavior and to define the self more flexibly. This pattern may be
changing, however; with more fluid age norms and sex-role definitions,
we can expect increasing variation in sex-role conformity across the life
span.

Paths to Androgyny: His and Hers

How do men and women differ as they progress through the earlier
stages of gender development? Sex-role norms define what is appropriate
and inappropriate in one's behavior and self-image at each stage of
development. They influence one's style of coping and sense of self. Thus,
sex roles shape the course of ego development.

In this section, I review evidence that suggests that women in our
society move more slowly and gradually than do men into full adulthood.
Many of the polarities confronting the individual over the life span are
subsumed in our culture by gender. I refer to polarities such as those
between dependence and independence, attachment and separation, submission and dominance, and emotionality and self-control. In each
dimension, the more self-oriented, assertive pole belongs to the masculine
stereotype, and the more person-oriented or expressive pole belongs to the

feminine. Men are socialized to individuate—to develop a separate and autonomous sense of self—early in life. Women are socialized to affiliate. Thus, individuation develops more slowly in women than it does in men. This leads to advantages and disadvantages for both sexes at different stages of the life cycle.

L. W. Hoffman (1977) argues that girls and boys are socialized to develop qualities that are congruent with their major adult roles as mother and economic provider and to disown qualities that do not fit these roles. The socialization of girls reinforces communal qualities such as affiliation, nurturance, and dependence, and discourages agentic qualities. As a result, a woman learns early in life to express herself for and through others and to suppress aspects of herself that are necessary for self-actualization. Boys are socialized to develop skills that are useful in instrumental roles—independence, self-assertion, and mastery. In turn, they learn to suppress their emotionality and vulnerability and to tone down affiliative needs.

Sex Differences: Socialization to Different Life Scripts

I will not attempt to review here the vast literature on psychological sex differences. Nor will I consider the influence of biology on sex differences (Rossi, 1977). Rather, I will focus on the ways in which socialization creates different life scripts for women and for men. I will draw mainly on comprehensive reviews by Block (1979, 1981) and L. W. Hoffman (1975, 1977).

In almost all societies there are similar sex differences in temperament and in division of labor. Men are more aggressive than are women, and women are seen as more nurturant, cooperative, tender, and expressive of emotions (D'Andrade, 1974; Whiting and Edwards, 1974). Women perform tasks, such as gardening, crafts, and cottage industries, that are in or near the home and that do not require constant commitment to work. Men are big-game hunters and warriors. This universal division of labor is based on the fact that, until recently, women devoted most of their lives to the care and feeding of children (L. W. Hoffman, 1977).

Studies of sex differences in temperament and other psychological traits in our contemporary culture yield conflicting results. In their thorough review of this literature, Maccoby and Jacklin (1974) conclude that very few differences are empirically established. Boys are more aggressive physically and are superior in visual–spatial ability and mathematical skills. Girls are superior in verbal skills. Other differences are questionable or nonexistent. But these conclusions have been seriously challenged by Block (1979), and recent data point to many differences between the sexes, although with considerable overlap between them (L. W. Hoffman, 1977).

Girls and boys are born with different constitutions, and they stimulate different responses in mothers. At birth, girls are more mature physiologically and more resistant to disease. They are more sensitive to touch, and they verbalize more. Boys fuss more and sleep less than do girls. Though girls are more sturdy, parents play more vigorously with infant boys. The assumption that girls are more fragile begins in infancy.

Girls are more affiliative than boys, and more dependent. They are more concerned with approval, have less confidence in their ability, and are more likely to cope by seeking help and assurance from others. They are more likely to change their opinions when challenged and are more compliant with adults, at least at younger age levels (Block, 1979). Girls are also more empathic (M. L. Hoffman, 1977). Although girls are no less achievement oriented than boys are, their motivations differ. Male achievement is motivated by mastery. Female achievement is motivated more by a desire for social approval (V. C. Crandall, 1964; V. J. Crandall, 1963). When achievement and affiliative goals conflict—for example, in adolescence when competition conflicts with popularity—girls evidence "fear of success" (Horner, 1975). They either underachieve or achieve with anxiety. In sum, girls are less independent in their coping styles, more conforming, less confident of their own abilities, and more dependent on the opinions of others.

Hoffman (1975) outlines three major differences in the socialization experiences of girls and boys. First, girls are given inadequate encouragement by parents in early strivings for independence. They are more protected than boys, who are encouraged to move about and explore the environment more freely (Block, 1981). Boys' toys allow more potential for manipulation and inventive use. Assignment of household tasks more often takes boys out of the home. Parents put more pressure on sons to achieve and to control feelings. Moreover, children's literature continues to portray males as more instrumental and active, and less expressive than females. Hoffman concludes that girls do not seem to be trained in dependency as much as they are deprived of the training in independence that boys get.

Second, girls have more difficulty establishing a separate sense of self, because they are the same sex as their mothers, with the same role expectations. Their identification and their bond are with the same person. But boys must learn to identify with their fathers or with other male figures. To do this, they need to separate themselves from their mothers earlier and more fully than do girls.

Third, boys find it easier to establish a separate sense of self, because they have more conflict with parents than girls have. More active, and generally more aggressive in the use of large muscles from infancy on, boys are disciplined more than are girls and the discipline is more likely to be the power-assertive kind. These kinds of conflict, if not carried to extremes, facilitate separation of self from parents.

Given these and other socialization experiences, a girl is less likely than a boy to develop confidence in her ability to cope independently with her environment and she is not likely to develop the skills needed to do so—at least not to the same degree. She is more likely to retain infantile fears of abandonment and to feel that safety and effectiveness lie in her emotional ties with adults. Boys learn to be effective through mastery, but girls learn to be effective through the help and protection of others. Girls, in this sense, are more dependent than boys, and this often continues into maturity (Hoffman, 1975).

I would add that wife and mother roles in early adulthood perpetuate the woman's affiliative orientation and her bond with her own mother— either her actual mother or the "mother" in her husband. Pressures to regress in marriage, to retreat into dependency or to inhibit individuality, are often greater for women than they are more men. Wives make more of the adjustments in marriage and conform more to husbands' expectations than husbands do to wives' expectations (Bernard, 1972). Wives are encouraged to assume a complementary role to their husbands' assertiveness by supressing their own competitiveness and power drives. Many women respond by projecting power and competence onto men. They define themselves through their husbands and their children; for example, through *his* career or *their* performance. As a result, they depend on others for their satisfaction and sense of worth. Though the man may also regress in marriage in the sense of depending on maternal qualities in his wife, he retains his instrumental roles in the occupational world and is less likely to borrow his wife's identity as his own. A national survey found that women demand more of their husbands than men demand of their wives, and that they are more likely to blame their spouses for marital unhappiness (Gurin et al., 1960). There is considerable evidence to indicate that wives are more unhappy in marriage than husbands, as is described in the following section.

To generalize: I suggest that women are "late maturers." Traditional gender roles, socialization experiences, and incomplete separation from mother all converge to delay the formation of a separate sense of identity in women well into the adult years. Only in middle life, when parenting is no longer salient, do women fully actualize their autonomy. Men, by contrast, are "early maturers." Traditional male roles and socialization encourage them to actualize their selfhood much earlier in life. It would not be suprising to find that there are advantages and disadvantages to both positions at different stages of the life cycle, as has been found with respect to physical maturation in adolescence. Early maturing boys, for example, have more social skills than late maturers, but they are more rigid emotionally. Late maturing boys are more open to new experiences, but they are less likely to commit themselves to occupational choices or marriage, even by the age of 30 (Peskin, 1967). Similarly, the delayed identity formation of traditional women may be compensated by greater flexibility later in life. The early (and possibly premature) independence of men may result in rigidity and more stress later in life. Do men and women differ in overall mental health and in the ways in which they cope with stress at different stages of the life cycle?

GENDER IDENTITY AND MENTAL HEALTH

Masculine Traits: Positive Image

Studies of sex-role stereotypes reveal that traits ascribed to men are positively valued more often than are traits ascribed to women (Broverman et al., 1975). Desirable masculine traits reflect competency. Relative to men, women are seen as dependent, passive, and illogical. Desirable feminine traits reflect warmth and expressiveness. Both men and women internalize these stereotyped traits. Since more feminine traits are seen as undesirable, women can be assumed to have more negative self-images than have men. This conclusion is confirmed by a national mental health survey; women are indeed more self-critical than are men (Gurin et al., 1960).

Epidemiological studies of depression, and of mental illness in general, reveal consistently higher rates for women (Gove and Tudor, 1973; Weissman and Klerman, 1977). More women than men in every population group and age group suffer from depression. This trend holds up in community surveys as well as psychiatric treatment centers. It is neither an artifact of help-seeking patterns, nor a reflection of greater willingness on the part of women to admit symptoms. This pattern has been found not only in the United States, but also in a wide variety of countries, both industrialized and developing.

Men, on the other hand, use (and abuse) alcohol and commit crimes more frequently than do women. They also commit suicide more often (Breed and Huffine, 1979). The suicide rate for males increases steadily after age 35 into the decade of the 80s. The suicide rate for females, consistently lower than that for males, peaks before age 50 and then declines steadily. However, more women than men *attempt* suicide. Most attempts are made by women under 30 years of age.

These patterns are consistent with more general sex-role norms. Men cope with distress by taking action (suicide or crime) or by exhibiting sanctioned masculine behavior (drinking). Women cope with distress by seeking help directly [women use medical and psychiatric treatment more often than do men (Gurin *et al.*, 1960)] or indirectly (by attempting suicide). In general, it is more consistent with feminine sex-role norms to admit vulnerability openly, and it is more consistent with masculine norms to deny (or mask) vulnerability and take action.

With all other forms of mental illness, however, women have higher rates. This difference is largely accounted for by higher rates of mental illness among married women (Gove and Tudor, 1973; Radloff, 1975). But among single persons, men are more likely to be mentally ill. Apparently, being married has a protective effect for males but a detrimental effect for females (Bernard, 1972).

It is generally agreed that domestic roles for women have lost status in this country with increasing industrialization and urbanization. The disadvantages of the housewife role—particularly for mothers of young children—in contemporary society have been well documented (Campbell, 1975; Pearlin, 1975). The only community in which married women do not have higher rates of mental illness is in close-knit, traditionally family-oriented and culturally isolated areas where housewives have more central functions and greater prestige (Gove and Tudor, 1973).

An economic study of women in underdeveloped nations concludes that the position of women declines as industrialization rises (Boserup, 1970). Blake (1974) traces the evolution of women's secondary economic status in industrialized nations.

> The migration of industrializing peoples out of rural settings into urban factories and bureaucracies ... progressively removed work from the family milieu and put men in jobs away from home ... gradually, both wives and children became economic liabilities to men .... Industrializing societies [developed] all kinds of rationalizations and legitimations for the wrenching change in the position of women that was accompanying the Industrial Revolution and the demographic transition. In particular they asserted that women's personalities and behavior actually conformed by nature to the restrictions of their new way of life [p. 92].

Thus, our society socializes women to adopt a self-image that fits their secondary economic status. As a result, conflicts and anxieties over assuming adult roles in the larger society can be postponed, sometimes indefinitely. A woman may resent her dependency while gaining security from it, and she may feel helpless to modify either. A woman who later divorces or is widowed may suddenly be confronted with issues that are typical of adolescence: developing independence and an identity apart from her family. Many women, as I have suggested, actualize a separate identity only in middle life, when they disengage from mothering.

For men, the converse is true. With their earlier training in independence and earlier separation from mother, men move more quickly into adult roles in the larger society. This transition, of course, can be stressful for a man, and it may evoke self-doubt, but more often than not the transition is negotiated successfully (Levinson *et al.*, 1978; Vaillant, 1977). As economic providers, men continue to develop competence and to actualize their sense of self. Lowenthal *et al.* (1975) found that men's self-concepts become increasingly clear-cut over the life course, whereas women's self-concepts remain more diffuse. A longitudinal study of college students found that men make greater gains than do women in resolving their identity crises during their four college years (Constantinople, 1969).

Masculine characteristics have been found to be a necessary condition for high self-esteem in both men and women (Bem *et al.*, 1976; Spence *et al.*, 1975). For males, however, high levels of masculinity are sufficient; for females, both *masculinity* and *femininity* are required for high esteem. [See Kelly and Worell (1977) and Kaplan (1978) for reviews of this research literature.] As noted, men generally have more positive self-concepts than women. Androgyny seems to be more important for psychological health in women than in men; and women may have more to gain from less polarized sex roles in later life.

My longitudinal study of personality change in women and men mentioned earlier supports this proposition (Livson, 1976b). All of the men, but only the more independent women, improved in psychological health by age 50. The one group who failed to improve were the highly feminine, submissive, dependent women. This group, significantly, was most anxious at age 50 and was the only group to decline in tested IQ since adolescence. In men, oversocialization to the masculine roles does not seem to inhibit later life development. But, in women, oversocialization to the feminine role (i.e., to the dependent aspects of the feminine role) does inhibit later development. Male sex roles allow more options for growth throughout the adult years.

Gender Identity and Mental Health in Later Life

Highly feminine women may be at an even greater disadvantage at older ages than they are at younger ages. A longitudinal study of elderly women and men suggests that traditional, family-oriented women are more vulnerable in widowhood than are more autonomous women; they are more dependent on the proximity of family members for successful adaptation (Maas and Kuypers, 1974). The life-transitions study found an increase with age in the degree to which a feminine self-concept in women is correlated with self-criticism (Lowenthal *et al.*, 1975). A study of adjustment to divorce reveals a similar age difference. Women and men over 40 who have more androgynous life-styles in their marriages have better morale after separation, but marital life-style is irrelevant to adjustment among younger divorcees (Chiriboga and Thurnher, 1980). Several studies suggest that androgynous personalities of both sexes age more successfully and even live longer (Sinnott, 1977). As we have seen, however, both men and women become more androgynous in later life, on the whole. There is evidence that sex differences in self-esteem diminish accordingly.

Although women are more depressed and have poorer self-concepts than men at all ages, the difference is diminished among older persons, in part because women improve. National survey data reveal that women over 55 are less critical of themselves, relative to men of the same ages, than women under 55 (Gurin *et al.*, 1960); however, they are still more self-critical than their male age-mates. Another national survey finds, similarly, that sex differences in psychic distress decline after age 60, mainly because women improve. The proportion of men reporting high distress declines slightly to age 60, when there is a small rise. But the proportion of women reporting high distress remains consistently high (and higher than the proportion of men) to age 60, when it declines sharply (Mellinger *et al.*, 1978).

Smaller, more intensive studies also find that psychological health improves among women in later middle age. This improvement seems to reflect changing role expectations in middle life rather than chronological age per se. Life satisfaction improves, for example, after children have left home (Neugarten, 1970). The study of life transition found that 50-year-old women with children still at home are relatively pessimistic and dissatisfied with themselves, whereas 60-year-old women are more expansive and confident, but only after their children are launched (Lowenthal *et al.*, 1975). Correspondingly, 50-year-old men, still at the peak of their careers, reveal a sense of competence and control over self and environment. But 60-year-old men anticipating retirement are more mellow; that is, less ambitious and restless, more nurturant and self-accepting. The critical factor for both sexes seems to be life stage rather than chronological age. But the cricial transition for the two sexes differs: for women, it is disengaging from mothering; for men, it is disengaging from work (Lowenthal *et al.*, 1975).

Turning Points: The Mid-life Transition

Career and parenting are not, of course, the only roles that change or are shed in middle life. A number of events, within and outside the individual, converge to propel middle-aged women and men into a new life stage. Perhaps the most universal is a growing awareness of death as a personal reality. The sense of timelessness and infinite possibility, common in youth, gives way to the reality that one's life span is finite and one's options are limited. There is a shift in the way in which one counts the years, from time since birth to time left to live (see Neugarten, 1970). Along with this shift in the sense of time, there is often a heightened consciousness of self that is comparable to that of adolescence. Issues of identity—of who one is, where one is going, and whether one is satisfied with one's life-style—become prominent. Awareness of aging shakes one's sense of control over destiny and undermines youthful fantasies of omnipotence. The individual may have to discover new roles in order to shape a new self that is more suited to her or his changing life perspective. The press to redefine oneself at mid-life is accentuated in contemporary society. Women and men disengage earlier today from life tasks that polarize sex roles. Technological and medical advances have extended life expectancy; at the same time, they have removed many of the social roles that once occupied a major part of the life span. The older man and woman today are likely to be in better health than their grandparents at the same ages; they are also likely to be more affluent and freer of family responsibilities. At the same time, the man is likely to retire earlier and the woman to be widowed longer. And both are likely to be more isolated from their families.

With increased longevity, fewer children, and the earlier departure of children, a woman can now expect a longer period in the postparental phase of family life. The youngest child today leaves home when the woman, on the average, is 48 and has approximately 2 decades left to live (Neugarten and Moore, 1968). As noted, the departure of children is comparable in many ways to occupational retirement in men. In both, a major role that contributes to the individual's identity is lost. But even before retirement, often in the 40s, many men begin to question their commitment to occupational goals, either because they have not realized their "dream" or because they have done so and found it wanting (Levinson *et al.*, 1978). At this point a man may begin to reshape his image of what it means to be male.

Widowhood is becoming an increasingly common status for older American women. Women, on the average, outlive men in this country by about 8 years. With the probability that husbands are older than wives, and the smaller likelihood of remarriage for women, it is not suprising that there are five widows for every widower in this country (Kimmel, 1974). The average widow has lost her spouse at age 61, leaving her with approximately 16 years to live in this status. Loneliness and withdrawal are the most serious difficulties reported by widowed women (Lopata, 1973). As noted, however, more autonomous women, and those with multiple roles, cope best with widowhood (Maas and Kuypers, 1974).

It is beyond the scope of this chapter to review in depth the many psychological and social changes that affect the development of men and women in later life. I will, however, briefly consider two biological changes that pertain directly to gender identity.

From about age 30, there is a gradual decline in the secretion of androgens in the male. The production of estrogen in the female is drastically reduced after menopause. To what extent do these hormonal changes contribute to more androgynous personality styles in men and women in the second half of life? Or to the vulnerability to stress? Little is known about the effects of hormonal changes on personality in later life; conversely, little is known about the effects of personality and life-style on hormone production. We do know, for example, that sexual potency in older men is maintained by sexual activity (Masters and Johnson, 1966). We also know that in societies in which women's status rises in later life, menopause is not seen as stressful (Bart, 1971). Studies in our own society also suggest that menopause is less stressful than is commonly believed (Neugarten, 1970). Relationships between emotions and biology are complex and clearly not one-way.

Both sexes in our youth-oriented society tend to be concerned about physiological decline in middle life. Men, particularly, are concerned about loss of health and sexual adequacy during this period of life (Neugarten and Datan, 1974). But physiological aging poses special problems for women. Growing old strikes at the core of a woman's pride.

Sontag (1972), in a strong polemic against the "double standard of aging" for men and women in our culture, calls attention to the damaging effects of aging on a woman's desirability and sense of worth. A man's attractiveness is enhanced by signs of aging, such as lines on the face and graying hair. Moreover, his attractiveness is enhanced by what he does, and by his power, achievement, and wealth, which increase with age. Insofar as women are valued for beauty, and female beauty is equated with youth, aging robs a woman of her main source of value and self-esteem. The loss of youthful attractiveness, like the loss of the mothering role, may be a major force requiring a woman to redefine what it means to be female.

Concern over the loss of youth and beauty has been found to peak for women in their late 40s, declining later (Nowak, 1977). To the extent that a woman develops a more agentic orientation in later life, she is more likely to value herself for what she does rather than whom she attracts. The double standard of aging is most damaging to older women who fail to develop more androgynous values.

CONCLUSIONS

The evidence is fairly clear that women and men follow different paths over the life cycle, but somewhere in the middle years of life each becomes a little more like the other. Men begin to soften and develop a more expressive orientation. Women become more assertive and achieving; they assume more power within and outside the family. Men and women do not reverse roles, however; men do not give up their masculinity nor women their femininity. Nor, of course, do men and women become really alike. What the evidence does suggest is that they develop some new ways of dealing with the world and with themselves—ways that traditionally are defined as appropriate to the opposite sex. Thus, each moves toward a more androgynous, or integrated, stage of sex-role development.

In reviewing the evidence, I have assumed that the dialectic between masculinity and femininity, and its corollaries—between agency and communion, and separateness and attachment—are continuing polarities in the inner lives of men and women. I have assumed further that in each sex, one pole or the other has more expression at different stages of the life cycle as a function of social and biological role expectations.

Women are socialized to be less autonomous and more attached than men. From early childhood on, they place affiliative concerns before independence. Their roles in early adulthood—mother, wife, and caretaker—further delay or interrupt the process of individuation. The evidence suggests that the traditional woman comes fully into her own only in middle adulthood, when disengaging from mothering and other age-related events allows her to actualize the other side of the polarity: the assertive, agentić, independent side of herself. For a woman, identity formation is a lengthy and complex task that is often not fully accomplished until well into middle life, sometime in the 50s or 60s. It is in this sense that I have suggested that women are late maturers. (The process of individuation, however, may get underway much earlier, often when children enter school; and, of course, it has its roots in childhood and adolescence.)

Men are socialized to individuate at much younger ages. Their childhood experiences and their adult roles stress separateness, independence, and competence in the outside world. As a result, men form their identity earlier in life. Men, in this sense, are early maturers. [In my opinion, Erikson's (1950) model proposing identity formation as the central task of adolescence fits men more than women.]

There are advantages as well as disadvantages to both of these developmental paths. Women suffer more than men from depression and mental illness, particularly during the first half of life, and they devalue themselves more. On the other hand, women may acquire more role flexibility. Women follow a less clear-cut, linear path through life. They experience more discontinuities in roles (marital, parental, and occupational) and life-styles than do men over the life span (Kline, 1975; Maas and Kuypers, 1974). They adapt to more complex or conflicting role demands (for example, work and family) and experiment with more role options (jobs, volunteer work, continuing education, and organizational activity). Women, in brief, are more likely than men to learn to cope with change; as a result, they may be better equipped to cope with change in later life. There is some evidence to suggest that women do adapt better than men to aging (Kuhlen, 1964). (Also, the disengagement process is more gradual for women than it is for men.)

Not all women and men, of course, develop androgynous personality styles in later life. Integrating cross-sex characteristics is one route to psychological health in the older years, but it is not the only route. A key factor seems to be the "fit" between an individual's personality and her or his life-style. In a longitudinal study of successfully functioning middle-aged women and men, I found that androgynous personalities improve in psychological health by age 50, when changing role expectations allow them to develop more flexible life-styles. But traditional women and men continue to function successfully by maintaining a life-style that supports their personality needs (Livson, 1976a, 1978). Similarly, Maas and Kuypers (1974) found that work-centered and organization-centered older women adjust best to aging, and that family-centered women also are content, as long as they continue to have the support of family life. A study of patterns of adjustment in older men found that both andro-gynous and traditionally masculine men adjust well to aging, depending on the degree to which they are able to support their preferred personality style (Reichard *et al.*, 1962). All of these studies suggest that androgynous personalities are more poorly adjusted in early adulthood, when they are locked into traditional sex roles, but they improve when aging and role changes permit a more flexible expression of self. More traditional personalities adjust well to aging insofar as they continue to maintain a life-style that supports their sex-role preferences.

Sex-role norms are changing. We are living in a society that is becoming more fluid with respect to gender, as it is with respect to age. Future generations will undoubtedly have greater flexibility in their gender roles prior to their middle years. Even in the current generation, many individuals live androgynous life-styles in early as well as late adulthood. In this review, I have not focused on single women, career women, or men who do not follow conventional career lines. Nor have I addressed issues of sex-role development in the black community or in other ethnic groups. My focus has been on traditional patterns of sex-role development. Most of the research evidence is drawn from the current older generation of white, middle-class members of contemporary society. In this generation (and apparently in more traditional cultures), women and men develop along different paths with different timing—in some ways to the disadvantage of both, but the later years bring fresh options to diversify gender roles and expand the boundaries of the self.

REFERENCES

Bakan, D. (1966). "The Quality of Human Existence." Rand McNally, Chicago.
Baltes, P. B., Cornelius, S. W., and Nesselroade, J. R. (1977). *In* "Minnesota Symposium on Child Psychology" (W. A. Collins, ed.), Vol. II, pp. 1–63. Univ. of Minnesota Press, Minneapolis.
Bart, P. (1971). *In* "Women in Sexist Society" (V. Gornick and B. K. Moran, eds.), pp. 163–186. Basic Books, New York.
Bem, S. L., Martyn, A. W., and Watson, C. (1976). *J. Personality Social Psychol.* **34**, 1016–1023.
Bernard, J. (1972). "The Future of Marriage." Bantam Books, New York.
Blake, J. (1974). *In* "The Human Population" (D. Flanagan, ed), (A Scientific-American Book), pp. 91–101. Freeman, San Francisco.
Block, J. H. (1973). *Am. Psychol.* **28**, 512–526.

Block, J. H. (1979). In "Psychology of Women: Future Directions of Research" (F. Denmark and J. Sherman, eds.), pp. 29–87. Psychological Dimensions, New York.

Block, J. H. (1981). In "Cognitive and Affective Processes in Development: A Developmental–Interaction Point of View (E. Shapiro and E. Weber, eds.), pp. 147–169. Lawrence Erlbaum Associates, New York.

Boserup, E. (1970). "Woman's Role in Economic Development." St. Martin's Press, New York.

Breed, W., and Huffine, C. L. (1979). In "Psychopathology of Aging" (O. J. Kaplan, ed.), pp. 289–309 Academic Press, New York.

Brenneis, C. B. (1975). Arch. Gen. Psychiatry 32, 429–435.

Broverman, I. K., Vogel, S. R., Broverman, D. M., Clarkson, F., and Rosenkrantz, P. S. (1975). In "Women and Achievement" (M. T. S. Mednick, S. S. Tangri, and L. W. Hoffman, eds.), pp. 32–47. Wiley, New York.

Campbell, A. (1975). Psychol. Today 8, 37–41.

Chiriboga, D. A., and Thurnher, M. (1980). J. Divorce 3, 379–390.

Constantinople, A. (1969). Dev. Psychol. 1, 357–372.

Crandall, V. C. (1964). Young Children 20, 77–90.

Crandall, V. J. (1963). In "Child Psychology: The 62nd Yearbook of the National Society for the Study of Education," Part I (H. W. Stevenson, ed.), pp. 416–459. Univ. of Chicago Press, Chicago.

D'Andrade, R. G. (1974). In "Culture and Personality: Contemporary Readings" (R. A. Levine, ed.), pp. 16–39. Aldine, Chicago.

Erikson, E. H. (1950). "Childhood and Society." Norton, New York.

Giambra, L. (1973). Pap., 81st Ann. Meet. Am. Psychol. Assoc., 1973.

Gove, W. R., and Tudor, J. F. (1973). Am. J. Sociol. 78, 812–835.

Gurin, G., Veroff, J., and Feld, S. (1960). "Americans View their Mental Health." Basic Books, New York.

Gutmann, D. (1977). In "Handbook of the Psychology of Aging" (J. F. Birren and K. W. Schaie, eds.), pp. 302–321. Van Nostrand-Reinhold, New York.

Hefner, R., Rebecca, M., and Oleshansky, B. (1975). Hum. Dev. 18, 143–158.

Hoffman, L. W. (1975). In "Women and Achievement" (M. T. S. Mednick, S. S. Tangri, and L. W. Hoffman, eds.), pp. 129–150. Wiley, New York.

Hoffman, L. W. (1977). Am. Psychol. 32, 644–657.

Hoffman, M. L. (1977). Annu. Rev. Pscyhol. 28, 295–321.

Horner, M. S. (1975). In "Women and Achievement" (M. T. S. Mednick, S. S. Tangri, and L. W. Hoffman, eds.), pp. 206–220. Wiley, New York.

Jung, C. (1933). "Modern Man in Search of a Soul." Harcourt, Brace, New York.

Kaplan, A. G. (1978). Pap., 55th Ann. Meet. Am Orthopsychiatr. Assoc., 1978.

Kelly, E. L. (1955). Am. Psychol. 10, 659–681.

Kelly, J. A., and Worell, J. (1977). J. Consult. Clin. Psychol. 45, 1101–1115.

Kerchoff, A. (1966). In "Social Aspects of Aging" (I. Simpson and J. McKinney, eds.), pp. 133–192. Duke Univ. Press, Durham, North Carolina.

Kimmel, D. C. (1974). "Adulthood and Aging: An Interdisciplinary, Developmental View." Wiley, New York.

Kline, C. (1975). Gerontologist 15, 486–492.

Kohlberg, L. (1966). In "The Development of Sex Differences" (E. Mccoby, ed.), pp. 82–173. Stanford Univ. Press, Stanford, California.

Kohlberg, L. (1973). Gerontologist 13, 497–502.

Kuhlen, R. G. (1964). *In* "Relations of Development and Aging" (J. E. Birren, ed.), pp. 209–246. Thomas, Springfield, Illinois.

Lehner, G. F. J., and Gunderson, E. K. (1953). *J. Personality* **21**, 392–398.

Levinson, D. J., Darrow, C. N., Klein, E. B., Levinson, M. H., and McKee, B. (1978). "The Seasons of a Man's Life." Knopf, New York.

Livson, F. B. (1976a). *Int. J. Aging Hum. Dev.* **7**, 107–115.

Livson, F. B. (1976b). *Pap., Meet. Gerontol. Soc.*

Livson, F. B. (1978). *In* "The Life Cycle: Development in the Middle Years" (D. Levinson, chairman). Am. Assoc. Adv. Sci., Washington, D.C.

Loevinger, J. (1966). *Am. Psychol.* **21**, 195–206.

Loevinger, J. (1976). "Ego Development." Jossey-Bass, San Francisco.

Lopata, H. Z. (1973). "Widowhood in an American City." Schenkman, Cambridge, Massachusetts.

Lowenthal, M., Chiriboga, D., and Thurnher, M. (1975). "Four Stages of Life." Jossey-Bass, San Francisco.

Maas, H. S., and Kuypers, J. A. (1974). "From Thirty to Seventy." Jossey-Bass, San Francisco.

Maccoby, E. E., and Jacklin, C. N. (1974). "Psychology of Sex Differences." Stanford Univ. Press, Stanford, California.

Masters, W. H., and Johnson, V. (1966). "Human Sexual Response." Little, Brown, Boston.

Mellinger, G. D., Balter, M. B., Manheimer, D. I., Cisin, I. H., and Parry, H. J. (1978). *Arch. Gen. Psychiatry* **35**, 1045–1052.

Neugarten, B. L. (1970). *J. Geriatr. Psychiatry* **4**, 71–87.

Neugarten, B. L. (1978). "Time, Age, and the Life Cycle." Am. Psychiat. Assoc., Atlanta, Georgia.

Neugarten, B. L., and Datan, N. (1974). *In* "American Handbook of Psychiatry" (S. Arieti, ed.), 2nd ed., pp. 592–608. Basic Books, New York.

Neugarten, B. L., and Gutmann, D. L. (1968). *In* "Middle Age and Aging: A Reader in Social Psychology" (B. L. Neugarten, ed.), pp. 58–71. Univ. of Chicago Press, Chicago.

Neugarten, B. L., and Moore, J. W. (1968). *In* "Middle Age and Aging: A Reader in Social Psychology" (B. L. Neugarten, ed.), pp. 5–21. Univ. of Chicago Press, Chicago.

Nowak, C. A. (1977). *In* "Looking Ahead" (L. E. Troll, J. I. Israel, and K. Israel, eds.), pp. 59–64. Prentice-Hall, Englewood Cliffs, New Jersey.

Pearlin, L. I. (1975). *In* "Life-Span Developmental Psychology: Normative Life Crises" (N. Datan and L. H. Ginsberg, eds.), pp. 191–207. Academic Press, New York.

Peskin, H. (1967). *J. Abnorm. Psychol.* **72**, 1–15.

Piaget, J. (1965). "The Moral Judgment of the Child." Free Press, New York.

Pleck, J. H. (1975). *Sex Roles* **1**, 161–178.

Radloff, L. (1975). *Sex Roles* **1**, 249–269.

Reichard, S., Livson, F., and Petersen, P. G. (1962). "Aging and Personality: A Study of Eighty-seven Older Men." Wiley, New York.

Riegel, K. F. (1976). "Psychology of Development and History." Plenum, New York.

Rossi, A. S. (1977). *Daedalus* **106**, 1–31.

Sedney, M. A. (1977). *In* "Sex-role Development in Adulthood: Growing Beyond Polarities." (M. A. Sedney, chairman), *Pap., 85th Ann. Meet. Am. Psychol. Assoc.*, San Francisco.

Sinnott, J. A. (1977). *Gerontologist* **17**, Part I, 459–463.

Sontag, S. (1972). *Saturday Rev. Soc.* October, pp. 29–38.

Spence, J. T., Helmreich, R., and Stapp, J. 1975). *J. Personality Soc. Psychol.* **32**, 29–39.

Strong, E. K. (1936). *J. Soc. Psychol.* **7**, 49–67.

Terman, L., and Miles, C. (1936). "Sex and Personality." McGraw-Hill, New York.
Vaillant, G. E. (1977). "Adaptation to Life." Little, Brown, Boston.
Weissman, M. M., and Klerman, G. L. (1977). *Arch. Gen. Psychiatry* **34**, 98–110.
Whiting, B., and Edwards, C. P. (1974). *In* "Culture and Personality: Contemporary Readings" (R. A. Levine, ed.), pp. 188–207. Aldine, Chicago.

PART **II**

LIFE-STYLES: CHANGING ROLES AND BEHAVIOR

6

Old and Alone:
The Unmarried in Later Life

Nan Corby
Judy Maes Zarit

INTRODUCTION

In most areas of sex research, including sex and aging research, women have been somewhat neglected as subjects, compared to men; however, in the area of sexuality and sensuality of unmarried older people, men have been given short shrift. It is not that the data on single older women are so extensive; rather, it appears that single older men are simply fewer in number, and so they are seldom reported as a separate category. In addition, marital status appears to have little effect on the sexual activity of older men.

Among older adults, gender appears to be the best overall predictor of sexual expression in later life (Pfeiffer and Davis, 1972). Thus, a greater number of men are more likely to engage in sexual activity with a higher frequency than is the case for women. Among women, those who remain most sexually active in later life have socially acceptable, active, and health partners (i.e., husbands) (Pfeiffer and Davis, 1972). In a recent Swedish study it was found that in a sample of 166 men and 266 women over 70 years of age, 46% of the men and 16% of the women were still having sexual intercourse (Persson, 1980). Among those in the sample who were married, 52% of the men and 36% of the women were still having intercourse. Both men and women who continued to be sexually active gave themselves a better mental health rating than those who were not married, and they had a more positive attitude toward sexual activity among the aged (Persson, 1980).

Data: Confounding Categories

According to census data, in the United States there are only 69 men for every 100 women over 65 years of age. Almost 80% of these men are married, compared to only 38% of the women (U.S. Bureau of the Census, 1977). This reduces the ratio to 24 unmarried men for every 100 unmarried women over age 65. For these women, whose culturally acquired attitudes often require marriage as a condition of sexual activity, opportunities to engage in heterosexual activities continue to diminish with age.

Typically, women have selected partners who are older than they are, and men have chosen younger women. Whereas 20% of males over 65 marry women who are younger than 55 years of age, only 3% of women over 65 marry men who are younger than 55. The average difference in ages between older marriage partners is 4 years (Newman and Nichols, 1960). Moreover, females live approximately 7 or 8 years longer than males, which implies at least 11 years of widowhood should a woman not remarry after her husband's death (Brotman, 1981; Pfeiffer and Davis, 1972). Furthermore, women get caught in the double standard of aging, which defines a woman as sexually unattractive at an earlier age than a man (Treas and VanHilst, 1976). A small sample of formerly married women over 60 was interviewed on the subject of their sexuality; most of them continued to be interested in sex, but none saw themselves as sexually appealing (Ludeman, 1981).

The probability of a woman finding a suitable sexual partner continues to decrease with age. Approximately 84% of the men between the ages of 65 and 74 are married, as opposed to 49% of the women in that age group. Of those 75 and older, only 37% of the population is male, and 70% of them are still married. Conversely, of the women 75 and older, 70% are widowed, and only 22.5% are still married (U.S. Bureau of the Census, 1977).

The incidence of sexual activity is higher among older married women than it is among older unmarried women (Christenson and Gagnon, 1965; Kinsey *et al.*, 1953; Pfeiffer and Davis, 1972). Among women who are currently unmarried, the divorced have a higher incidence of sexual activity than do the widowed (Gebhard, 1971). However, marital status does not appear to have a measurable influence on sexual behavior among men, whose late-life sexuality seems to be more dependent on the importance they attached to sex early in life (Pfeiffer and Davis, 1972).

Complicating attempts to use marital status categories in evaluating the sexuality of human beings is the problem of which marital status categories to use. Previous researchers have categorized people according to whether or not they have ever been married, are presently married, presently married and living with a spouse, formerly married, widowed, divorced, divorced and separated, single, never-married, and not presently married. Some data are not presented by marital status at all. Therefore, the comparison of sexuality by marital status is exceedingly difficult.

The complexity of this evaluation is compounded by the problem of varying measures of sexuality. Indices of sexuality used include sexual interest, activity, frequency, fantasy, masturbation, thought, attitudes, coitus, dreams, dreams to orgasm, homosexual contact, etc. However, evaluations based solely on these indices lack information about sensuality and sensual contacts and interests. Perhaps the difficulties of defining sensuality for research purposes, explaining it to subjects, and collecting and interpreting data have precluded its incorporation into most studies. Then again, perhaps sensuality has not been recognized until recently as a valid and important part of sexual expressiveness. Whatever the reasons, there are few data to report on, other than genital-oriented sexual behavior.

Sexual Behavior: Potential Barriers and Constraints

As is suggested by the Duke University studies (Pfeiffer and Davis, 1972), there is some evidence that a continuity of life-style is at work in the sexual lives of older people. This suggests that the influences of a low-level interest in sex and negative sexual experiences during early life continue into old age. Individual differences must be taken into consideration when viewing data that indicate an overall decline in sexual activity with age. For instance, never-married women who have not achieved orgasm and who remain virgins into maturity contribute data that significantly depress incidence and frequency reports.

There are also certain very real physiological impediments to sexual expression that develop after menopause. Although medical literature now suggests that females can maintain their ability to enjoy sexual expression almost indefinitely, postmenopausal estrogen starvation can reduce vaginal lubrication sufficiently to cause pain during intercourse. Simple medical treatment can alleviate this condition in most women who experience it, but, for many older women, there are cultural and psychological impediments to seeking such help. A woman's attitude toward menopause can have a damaging effect on her sexuality if she considers intercourse to be properly related only to childbearing. (The physiological characteristics of late-life sexual–sensual expression are examined in more detail elsewhere in this volume.)

Physical restraints are even more evident in men as they age. In order to function coitally, the male must achieve an erection of sufficient strength and duration to complete the act of intercourse. Provided that a man is in good health, he can usually retain this capacity indefinitely. However, the excitement phase of arousal may be somewhat slowed, and full erection may not be achieved until immediately preceding orgasm (Verwoerdt et al., 1969). Ignorance of this fact can compound what may already be a sensitive situation. A man (or his partner) who does not realize that it will take more time and perhaps more stimulation to achieve erection may panic and refrain from further attempts at intercourse. Moreover, many older males are capable of achieving orgasm without ejaculation, an experience that may be disturbing to those who are not prepared for it (Long, 1976).

The amount of knowledge that both partners have about the physical aspects of sexuality and the changes concomitant with age will have a decided influence on the frequency and enjoyment of intercourse. However, many older persons have attitudes about sexuality that make it difficult to provide this education (Brower and Tanner, 1979). An important point, and one that is generally overlooked, is that sexuality does not begin and end with the act of sexual intercourse. Human sexual expressiveness includes masturbation, fantasy, homosexual contact, and all of those varying indices mentioned earlier, in addition to more subtle sensual expressions such as caressing, touching, feelings of warmth and closeness, and sexual interest in general. By focusing too much on the achievement of orgasm, we may interfere with these other equally valid expressions of sexuality and closeness in a special type of intimate relationship.

WIDOWED AND DIVORCED

Marriage Behavior of Widowers

The widowed describe themselves as lonely more than twice as often as either married or never-married people, according to a British study (Willmott and Young, 1960). For men, losing a spouse results not only in loss of love, but often in loss of family and social relationships as well, since women tend to be the facilitators in social situations (Blau, 1961; Cummings and Henry, 1961). Widowers tend to become very isolated and are more likely to commit suicide than are widows following the death of a spouse (Bernardo, 1968, 1970; Bock and Webber, 1972). When they survive the initial crisis, however, men are more likely than women to remarry, and they do so sooner. On the average, men remarry within approximately 3 years of a spouse's death, whereas those women who remarry do so after some 7 years of widowhood. About 20% of widowers remarry, compared to only 2% of widows (Treas and Van Hilst, 1976).

Characteristics and Sexual Behavior of Widows

Women who are widowed tend to mourn the loss of a spouse somewhat longer than men do (Goodman, 1978). The death of a husband causes a disruption of the widow's social system, particularly in the case of a woman whose marital relationship can be described as traditional. At other crisis points in her life, such a woman has relied on her relationship with her husband for support. The psychological and physical health of the surviving spouse is significantly related to the amount of emotional support he or she receives. Without the support of family members and friends, there is a greater probability of mental and physical pathology (Henderson, 1977; Maddison and Viola, 1968; Maddison and Walker, 1967; Miller and Ingham, 1976).

Many widows do not remarry. There are many reasons for this; primary among them is the shortage, with advancing age, of available males. Moreover, the older widow has a strong cultural role to step into—which may be more comfortable and less threatening than attempting to seek out a new marital partner. Divorced women, in fact, are three times more likely to remarry than are widows (Treas and Van Hilst, 1976). There are certain social expectations in our predominantly "couples" society that operate to keep single women out of the social mainstream. Married women tend to exclude single women from social activities, unless they have an escort. Unattached women are viewed as a threat to marriage (Adams, 1974), whereas, true to the double standard, men are not. Because unattached women are not invited to social functions, the possibility of meeting men is severely limited. The result is a vicious cycle that serves to segregate single women from the rest of the social world. When a woman is both single and old, the chances of reentry diminish still further. Alternatives occasionally develop as a result of extreme need. An example of this is a group of older, mainly widowed, women living in a working-class housing project in the San Francisco Bay Area. They attempted to create their own viable community, compelled by the ostracism and loneliness that ultimately gave them the impetus to form an alternative community.

In general, the strongest determining factor in whether a woman desires to continue coitus after the end of marriage (whether its end was caused by death or divorce) is her capacity to experience orgasm. Another important influence is the strength of her religious faith. Women who have strong religious beliefs show a somewhat greater decline in sexual activity than women whose religiosity is not strong (Christenson and Gagnon, 1965). This has its greatest impact postmaritally, when religious sanctions are most likely to come to bear. A question can be raised about these data: Would the more devout women be less likely to *report* actual postmarital sexual activity because of a greater concern about its impropriety? Possibly not, but the question is worth asking.

Although formerly married women over 65 have intercourse less often than do married women, they show a higher incidence of masturbation. The Duke University studies (Newman and Nichols, 1960) showed the incidence of coitus among postmarital women over 65 to be 0, whereas it was 50% for married women. About one-third of these formerly married women reported masturbating, compared to one-quarter of the married women. Similar levels of incidence of sexual dreams leading to orgasm were reported by both groups of women.

NEVER-MARRIED

Roles and Behavior

The group of people who do not marry at all are unique in several ways: they tend to be lifelong isolates, and they are not especially lonely in old age. Their life satisfaction is more comparable to married individuals than it is to the widowed and divorced. And they have the added advantage of not having experienced the bereavement that goes with the loss of a spouse (Gubrium, 1975).

These people may be self-selected or socially selected never-marrieds. Among the self-selected are those who chose a career over marriage (often seen as an either/or situation for women in the 65-and-over cohort), those who value personal independence and continuity in their life-styles, and those who prefer minimal social involvements. Some may have been unable to attract a spouse due to real or imagined handicaps.

Historically, there has been a limited number of culturally acceptable roles for those women who chose to remain single. It was accepted that a woman who became a schoolteacher would remain single and presumably celibate. Some employers made it clear to women they hired in secretarial or bookkeeping jobs that they were required to remain unmarried in order to keep their positions. Consequently, in the cohort of women who are currently over 65, there may be some individuals who were forced into a single role for survival.

There were also powerful social forces that influenced whether a woman chose a certain role, whether married or single, and much of that decision making depended upon which roles were perceived as possible alternatives. For those women who are over 65, few single roles were available: spinster, which carried the stigma of being unchosen; the family caretaker, often a younger daughter who cared for her parents as they became elderly, and then cared for her own siblings; the religious person, who chose celibacy; or the committed careerwoman.

There have been tremendous changes in the variety and number of social roles and rolé models for single life-styles in recent years. Women in their 30s who choose to remain single now may be more committed to intellectual and creative endeavors than to childrearing. Adams (1976) interviewed a sample of 26 women and 10 men and found that sex was lower on their list of priorities than independence and career goals. This does not imply a lower sex drive, per se, but rather a decreasing need for marriage as the most convenient relationship within which to engage in sexual activity. When this cohort reaches age 65, it may be quite different from those preceding it along many of the dimensions discussed in this chapter.

Potential Sexuality: Selection Process

Another interesting possibility for consideration is the fact that there may have been a selection process related to potential sexuality (Gubrium, 1975). In a study of never-married women based on Kinsey's data (Kinsey *et al.*, 1948, 1953), 71 women were found in the 50 to 69 age range. At that time (around 1950), never-married women represented 9% of the total population of white women in that age group. Of this sample, one-third (23 cases) revealed that they had never experienced overt sexual activity beyond petting. All of these women reported themselves to be virgins, and none were ever orgasmic. As a group, they showed a higher degree of religious devoutness than did the rest of the sample. Of the remaining two-thirds, 79% had masturbated to orgasm, 62% had experienced sexual intercourse, and 52% had orgasmic sexual dreams. Extensive homosexual contacts had been made by 17% of the women, but those contacts had ended by age 50, and none of the women reported being exclusively lesbian.

When the sample was divided into groups based on levels of sexual activity, it was found that such levels were consistent over the life span, with one important exception: those who reported low incidence and frequency of sexual activity before age 30 were not necessarily in the low level group later on. Some women appeared to be "late developers," reporting low levels of activity in young adulthood that increased dramatically between ages 30 and 40. A low level of sexual activity during that decade was a good predictor of the level of sexual activity in later years.

Never-married women who were currently sexually active showed a frequency of sexual activity comparable to formerly married women of the same ages, with masturbation being the most frequent sexual outlet. The small group of women with homosexual backgrounds showed an aging pattern not unlike sexually active married women (Christenson and Johnson, 1973). Clearly, there is a wide range of individual variation that must be considered when dealing with frequency and incidence data. Data on never-married men in this age group were not found.

ATTITUDES TOWARD SEXUALITY: A FUNCTION OF SOCIAL
AND PSYCHOLOGICAL FACTORS

Research

Social and psychological factors play an important part in an individual's continued interest in sexual activity as old age approaches. One's interest in sexual expression is molded and directed by the culture (Long, 1976). One measure of attitudes in the United States toward the sexual life of older people is the low level of substantial research literature on this topic. Although some research has been done on aging males, its focus has been on problems associated with impotence (Christenson and Gagnon, 1965) rather than on normal psychosexual functioning in later life. Other recent important studies on male sexual functioning have concentrated on physiological responsiveness. Some studies have even combined data on aging males and females (Newman and Nichols, 1960; Busse et al., 1955).

A study examining the attitudes of the aged toward nontraditional sexual behavior was conducted by Snyder and Spreitzer (1976). They surveyed attitudes of both men and women, married and unmarried, over 65 and under 65, toward premarital, extramarital, and homosexual activities. They observed more intolerance for nontraditional sexual behavior among women, married people, and older people.

Emphasis on Youth: Consequences for Self-Image

The American culture's focus on youth is reflected in the disinclination to think about the inevitable process of aging. Even though male sexual activity, at any age, is less disapproved of than female sexual activity, what may have been considered virility at age 25 is often labeled lechery at age 65 (Taylor, 1973), in spite of the few well-publicized examples of famous men who father children or marry very young women in later life. A 65-year-old man who shows sexual interest in a younger woman is still called a "dirty old man" by his acquaintances or, worse, his friends and family. On the other hand, no one would understand why he would show any interest in a woman his own age. This perspective can be a good reason for some men to give up sex (Roen, 1974) or, at least, become very discouraged. Teasing, conversational nuances, and overt flirting also may drop from the older man's repertoire of behavior. This is especially true if he has been married during the major portion of his life and, therefore, presumably has not been "courting." (This same is true of women, too, of course.)

The problem for the single woman is somewhat different in certain ways. For her, to be old is to be undesirable. Our culture finds it hard to believe that the aged could desire each other sexually (Felstein, 1970) or find each other attractive. Along with this internalized feeling of undesirability is a fear of rejection. A good example of social constraint that has turned into a psychological defense is the rationalization or sublimation of sexual desire. Convincing themselves that older people do not want or need sexual involvement may be adaptive to the extent that it forestalls depression (Long, 1976). It may also, however, prematurely end sexual activity for people who could still derive pleasure from it. Pfeiffer and Davis (1972) have postulated that the relatively low rates of sexual interest among older women may be a defense mechanism. Because of the relative scarcity of older men and, hence, the unlikelihood of finding an acceptable partner, women may inhibit all sexual feelings.

Older people consider themselves to be relatively uninterested in sexual activities and less capable of them, and they see themselves as having fewer opportunities to engage in sexual activities. They also expect a lower frequency of such activities. Middle aged people are judged and judge themselves to be the most sexually knowledgeable and skillful of any age group. Young people, however, believe that they are the most interested and the most physically capable, and they believe that they have the greatest access to sexual activities (Cameron, 1970). More people consider masturbation "credible" among the aged than consider intercourse "credible" (LaTorre and Kear, 1977). Brower and Tanner (1979) attempted to teach a workshop on sexuality at a senior center and found that many people objected to the language on the Sex Knowledge and Attitude Test, a standard measure of sexual knowledge, and that many people either refused to attend or walked out during the sessions.

These attitudes lead to practical problems for the elderly, primarily with regard to the issue of sufficient privacy for being intimate with one another. Married couples who live with their adult children or other adult relatives may experience this problem. Sometimes staff in nursing homes actively separate married couples who continue to engage in sexual activity (Falk and Falk, 1980). Older single people have an equally serious problem, since they are not believed to have a legitimate right to or need for sexual privacy.

Institutionalized Elders

The institutionalized elderly suffer especially from society's misconceptions, because they are subject to the direct control of the administrators of institutions. Among 124 nursing home residents, almost one-half agreed with the statement "Sex over 65 is ridiculous" (Kahana, 1976). Nursing home staffs may give positive responses to statements advocating freedom of sexual expression among their elderly residents, but their behavior does not support that expression in their own institutions. (Wasow and Loeb, 1977, 1979). Nursing homes and other institutions do not provide environments that are natural and socially (or sexually or sensually) attractive, where married (or unmarried) residents can engage in sexual activities (Burnside, 1975; Schlessinger and Miller, 1973).

Single elders are effectively discouraged from the expression of sexual behavior when the sexes are physically segregated in institutions. The introduction of a "heterosexual living space" in one institution resulted in better social adjustments for both male and female residents. The men groomed themselves more carefully, limited their profanity somewhat, and made more use of the privacy they had (e.g., shutting doors to their rooms while dressing). Overt sexual contacts were observed, and one sexual relationship developed (Silverstone and Wynter, 1975).

Inappropriate sexual behavior can be a problem in nursing homes. Institutions that allow the expression of heterosexual behavior are reported to have less of a problem with inappropriate behavior. Moreover, opportunities for such sexual expression add pleasure to the lives of residents (Wasow, 1977). However, families of some older people may find their relatives' sexuality to be anxiety-provoking (Dean, 1972). Older residents, their children, and institutional staffs can benefit from increased information about the function and role of sexuality in old age. The need for education on geriatric sexuality as part of the curriculum for physicians and nurses was acknowledged only recently (McCarthy, 1979; Renshaw, 1979; Turnbull, 1979; Zimring, 1979).

CONCLUSIONS

There is a continuing need for research on the effects of aging on human sexuality (and vice versa), especially among the not presently married. The literature is scarce, and much of it dates back to Kinsey's data from the late 1940s and early 1950s. Separated married couples have never been studied as a group; they usually are combined with the divorced. But the separation they experienced could have occurred as a result of spouse institutionalization rather than a deteriorating marriage, and that is likely to be an important difference. Alternatives to hetero- sexual marriages should be explored and studied, not merely suggested, as a solution to the disproportionate number of single women over 65. These alternatives might include polygamous marriage, cohabitiation without marriage to younger men, and homosexual relationships.

Sex education for the elderly could serve a very positive function, provided that it could be presented in a way that would not offend those who are sensitive to sexual language. Attitude surveys show that older people expect their sexual drives to diminish and finally cease. Educating people to the extent and variety of sexual expression could have a liberating effect for some (Felstein, 1970; Green, 1975). It could be threatening to others, and this must be considered. The various myths about masturbation also could be dealt with, releasing some individuals to experience their own sexuality anew and allowing self-determination in this sphere. Pfeiffer and Davis (1972) suggest increasing efforts to extend a vigorous life span for men, since they are the usual initiators of sexual activities among older persons. Men, it is said, set the lower limits on frequency of sexual intercourse, whereas women set the upper limits (Long, 1976).

Single men benefit from society's double standard. Marriage is not an important factor in their sexual expressiveness, and single men receive less censure for casual affairs than do women. A relaxation of personal and social attitudes might benefit single older women and help them to accept their sexuality—or at least to experience it—as fully as some men seem to to accept and experience theirs.

One of the clearest needs for change is in the design and admini- stration of institutions for the elderly. The gap between staff and family approval of sexual activity and the actual allowance of or empathy with intimate behavior represents emotional rejection of sexuality in the elderly by those operating the institutions. This could be circumvented by administrative education followed by decisions that would allow mingling of the sexes and provide sufficient privacy for physical and emotional intimacy.

Our society offers little impetus to marry in later life; instead, it throws up numerous impediments. Older people are encouraged to protect their estates for their children. The children may then exercise a strong negative influence over a parent who considers remarriage (Treas and Van Hilst, 1976). Social Security benefits decrease on the marriage of two individuals who had been collecting singly. There have been some widely publicized instances in which elderly couples have attempted to fight the Social Security regulations. At present, the most feasible solution for those who can accept it emotionally is cohabitation without marriage. For those whose beliefs will not allow that, the economic penalties can be great—even prohibitive, in some cases.

SUMMARY

A socially acceptable and sexually active partner—meaning a healthy husband—is the factor on which rests much of the older woman's sexual expressiveness. However, the opportunities for her to marry decreases with age due to the declining number of single men, for whom marital status is not as significant a factor in sexuality. Knolwedge of physical changes in sexual functioning with age can be helpful for both men and women in maintaining the ability to function sexually. By shifting the emphasis from genital intercourse per se to more general sexual activities, many individuals might prolong the enjoyment of sexual feelings.

Elderly widows and widowers have greater feelings of isolation and loneliness than have the divorced or never-married. Widowers remarry more often and sooner than do widows. Religious devoutness correlates with a lower rate of sexual activity among formerly married women. Capacity for orgasm and past sexual enjoyment levels correlate with continuing sexual interest and activity among these women.

The never-married differ from widows and divorced individuals in some ways. Although they may have been either self-selected or socially selected, they tend to express more satisfaction with their singleness, and they are aware of the advantages of not having to endure the loss of a spouse. Never-married women show the lowest rates of sexual activity of all currently single women over 65. Although lifetime patterns of sexual activity are usually fairly stable, some women are late developers, coming into their sexual prime after age 30.

Because of the smaller numbers of elderly single men than women, there is little information on their late-life sexual activities. According to the Duke University studies, marital status appears to have little effect on the sexual activities of older men; therefore, it appears reasonable to attribute to single older men a sexual life that is similar to that of their married counterparts, who are discussed elsewhere in this volume.

Cultural attitudes have had a negative influence on continuing sexual activity into old age. Sexual relationships between elderly singles are sometimes supported in theory but often discouraged in fact. The denial of sexual needs with advancing age may be an adaptive way of coping with the many barriers to sexual expression that the older person encounters, particularly in institutions. Feelings of undesirability, combined with lack of privacy, make an asexual old age the easiest choice.

There are no simple solutions to the sexual problems and the need for intimacy of the single older adult. Changes in Social Security regulations could make it possible for older individuals to marry without suffering a financial penalty. We need to examine the issue of sexuality in institutions in order to ensure privacy and protect the sexual rights of individual residents. More research is necessary; however, the implications of the current literature are that sensual and sexual activity can and should be of lifelong duration. To this end, there is a need for dissemination of information that would lead to a change in cultural attitudes toward sexual and sensual activity among the elderly. With the growth of societal knowledge and positive attitudes regarding human sexuality across the lifespan, older persons could look forward to more natural expressions of their desire and needs.

REFERENCES

Adams, M. (1974). In "Intimacy, Family and Society" (A. Skolnick and J. Skolnick, eds.), pp. 6–44. Little, Brown, Boston.
Adams, M. (1976). "Single Blessedness: Observations on the Single Status in Married Society." Basic Books, New York.
Bernardo, F. M. (1968). Fam. Coord. 17, 191–203.
Bernardo, F. M. (1970). Fam. Coord. 19, 11–25.
Blau, Z. S. (1961). Am. Sociol. Rev. 26, 429–439.
Bock, E. W., and Webber, I. L. (1972). J. Marriage Fam. 34, 24–31.
Brotman, H. (1981). "Every Ninth American," prepared for "Developments in Aging." Special Committee on Aging, U.S. Senate, Washington, D.C.
Brower, H. T., and Tanner, L. A. (1979). Nurs. Res. 28, 36–39.
Burnside, I. M. (1975). In "Sexuality and Aging" (I. M. Burnside, ed.), pp. 26–34. Andrus Gerontology Center, Univ. of Southern California Press, Los Angeles.
Busse, E. W., Barnes, R. H., Silverman, A. J., Thaler, K., and Frost, I. L. (1955). Am. J. Psychiatry 111, 896–901.
Cameron, P. (1970). Dev. Psychol. 3, 272–273.
Christenson, C. V., and Gagnon, J. H. (1965). J. Gerontol. 20, 351–356.
Christenson, C. V., and Johnson, A. B. (1973). J. Geriatr. Psychiatry 6, 80–96.
Cumming, E., and Henry, W. H. (1961). "Growing Old: The Process of Disengagement." Basic Books, New York.
Dean, S. R. (1972). Am. J. Psychiatry 128, 1267.

Falk, G., and Falk, U. A. (1980). *Nurs. Outlook* **28**, 51-55.

Felstein, I. (1970). "Sex and the Longer Life." Penguin, Baltimore.

Gebhard, P. (1971). *In* "Divorce and After" (P. Bohannan, ed.), pp. 125-151. Doubleday, New York.

Goodman, E. (1978). *Miami Herald* Feb. 12.

Green, R. (1975). *In* "American Handbook of Psychiatry," vol. 6 (S. Arieri, ed.), pp. 665-691. Basic Books, New York.

Gubrium, J. F. (1975). *Int. J. Aging Hum. Dev.* **6**, 29-41.

Henderson, S. (1977). *Br. J. Psychiatr.* **131**, 185-191.

Kahana, B. (1976). *Perspect. Hum. Reprod.* **2**, 89-95.

Kinsey, A. C., Pomeroy, W. B., and Martin, C. R. (1948). "Sexual Behavior in the Human Male." Saunders, Philadelphia.

Kinsey, A. C., Pomeroy, W. B., Martin, C. R., and Gebhard, P. H. (1953). "Sexual Behavior in the Human Female." Saunders, Philadelphia.

LaTorre, R. A., and Kear, K. (1977). *Arch. Sex. Behav.* **6**, 203-213.

Long, I. (1976) *Soc. Casework* **57**, 237-244.

Ludeman, K. (1981). *Gerontologist* **21**, 203-208.

McCarthy, P. (1979). *J. Gerontol. Nurs.* **5**, 20-24.

Maddison, D. C., and Viola, A. (1968). *J. Psychosom. Res.* **12**, 279-306.

Maddison, D. C., and Walker, W. L. (1967). *Br. J. Psychiatry* **113**, 1057-1067.

Miller, P. M., and Ingham, J. G. (1976). *Soc. Psychiatry* **11**, 51-58.

Newman, G., and Nichols, C. R. (1960). *J. Am. Med. Assoc.* **173**, 33-35.

Persson, G. (1980). *J. Psychosom. Res.* **24**, 335-342.

Pfeiffer, E., Davis, G. C. (1972). *J. Am. Geriatr. Soc.* **20**, 151-158.

Renshaw, D. (1979). *Med. Times* **24**, 595-596.

Roen, P. R. (1974). "Male Sexual Health." Morrow, New York.

Schlessinger, B., and Miller, G. A. (1973). *Med. Aspects Hum. Sex.* **3**, 46-52.

Silverstone, B., and Wynter, L. (1975). *Gerontologist* **15**, 83-87.

Snyder, E. E., and Spreitzer, E. (1976). *Arch. Sex. Behav.* **5**, 249-254.

Taylor, R. B. (1973). "Feeling Alive After 65." Arlington House, New York.

Treas, J., and Van Hilst, A. (1976). *Gerontologist* **16**, 132-136.

Turnbull, J. M. (1979). *Tex. Med.* **75**, 46-48.

U. S. Bureau of the Census (1977). "Statistical Abstract of the United States: 1977." U. S. Gov. Printing Office, Washington, D. C.

Verwoerdt, A., Pfeiffer, E., and Wang, H. S. (1969). *J. Geriatr. Psychiatry* **2**, 163-180.

Wasow, M. (1977). *Concern Care Aging* **3**, 20-21.

Wasow, M., and Loeb, M. B. (1977). *In* "Sexuality and Aging" (R. L. Solnick, ed.), rev. ed., pp. 48-65. Andrus Gerontology Center, Univ. of Southern California Press, Los Angeles.

Wasow, M., and Loeb, M. B. (1979). *J. Am. Geriatr. Soc.* **27**, 73-79.

Willmott, P., and Young, M. (1960). "Family and Class in a London Suburb." Routledge & Kegan Paul, London.

Zimring, J. G. (1979). *N. Y. State J. Med.* **79**, 752-753.

7

Intimacy and Adaptation[1]

Lawrence J. Weiss

[1]This research was supported in part by the Administration on Aging, Grant No. 90-A-455/01 and the National Institute on Aging, Grant No. AG00002-005. Some of the findings were initially presented at the 30th Annual Scientific Meeting of the Gerontological Society of America, San Francisco, California, November 1977.

INTRODUCTION

This chapter explores the relationship between interpersonal intimacy and adaptation to stress throughout adult life, especially in late life. Intimacy, an emotional closeness between two human beings, has been defined as a human need with basic, or instinctual, characteristics (Bowlby, 1958; Freud, 1922; Harlow and Zimmerman, 1959; Maslow, 1970). It has been argued that a lack of fulfillment of interpersonal intimacy can inhibit psychological health, growth, and development (Erikson, 1963; Maslow, 1970; Sullivan, 1953) and can result in various forms of maladaptation (Jourard, 1964; Montagu, 1966; Otto and Mann, 1968). Jourard (1964, pp. 46–48) argues that "when we are not truly known by other people in our lives, we are misunderstood . . . worse, when we succeed too well in hiding our being from others, we tend to lose touch with ourselves, and this loss of self contributes to illness in its myriad forms." The inability to disclose oneself to another, an important dimension of intimacy according to Taylor (1968), is potentially lethal. Modern men, being the "instrumental experts" and not as "socioemotionally" expressive as women (Parsons, 1964), are perhaps more susceptible to the lethal aspects of the lack of disclosure. This may contribute to the shorter life expectancy among men. The main objectives of this chapter are to define intimacy more distinctly (including the factors that constitute greater depth or higher levels of intimacy), to explore the changes with the advent of later life, and, most importantly, to assess the degree of association between intimacy and adaptation to life stress.

Whereas the link between interpersonal intimacy and one's state of well-being or adaptation may seem evident, there is very little documentation of the qualitative nature of intimacy or its role as a resource for adaptation in the face of stress. Nevertheless, some indirect documentation of the need for intimacy with others can be observed in a variety of ways. For example, extreme forms of isolation, as portrayed in various literary works (e.g., Conrad, 1910) or symbolically displayed in the form of a catatonic state, demonstrate the devastating qualities associated with the lack of intimate contact with others. Harlow and Zimmerman (1959), in their work with animals, demonstrated empirically that a lack of physical contact or intimacy between an infant and its mother (or surrogate mother) produced maladaptation later in life. In another example, Spitz and Wolf (1946) found that isolated institutionalized infants had higher illness and mortality rates than those infants who had human contact. Therefore, it is quite reasonable to suggest that there is a close association between the lack of physical and emotional contact in early life among higher animals and humans and a variety of forms of maladaptation or illness, including death, later in life.

Research has established that in normal aging, with the loss of various social roles, the aged become isolated and alone (Townsend, 1963). This reduction in social interactions has a deleterious effect on feelings of well-being (Lowenthal and Boler, 1965). Whether such reductions in social interaction of later adulthood are accompanied by definitive changes in the qualitative nature of intimacy carried over from earlier adulthood is not known. Perhaps developmental changes in intimacy contribute to a decrease in the sense of well-being in the older person (e.g., Pineo, 1961). It is known, however, that the process of loss, rather than the state of isolation, has a much more serious consequence with regard to adaptation. Lowenthal (1964) and Gubrium (1976) make the additional point that lifelong isolation may be adaptive in old age. If there is no one to lose, then there is no need to experience a loss and the accompanying trauma. However, for those people who experience the stressful impacts of loss, especially the loss of significant others that inevitably results with increasing age, a variety of adaptations must occur (Morris, 1956; Parkes, 1971). It is posited here that a remaining intimate relationship with a close friend or spouse will act as a positive psychological resource in meeting these losses, and other life stresses, as one ages.

DEVELOPMENTAL PERSPECTIVE

Developmental theorists, such as Erikson (1963) and Sullivan (1953), locate the origin and major emphasis of the development of intimacy either in adolescence or in the beginning stages of adulthood. Given this emphasis on the development of same-sex "chums" or heterosexual partnerships during young adulthood, the question arises of how intimacy varies in later adult life stages.

Unfortunately, very little scientific investigation has occurred that would shed light on the developmental life-course perspective of intimacy. Other developmental theorists maintain that interpersonal style and behavior change qualitatively with age. Consequently, the depth or level of intimacy and intimate relationships also should change with age or life stage. For example, Loevinger's (1966) theory of ego development maintains that as one increases in age or maturity and, in essence, increases in competence, a corresponding change in interpersonal style occurs. In other words, one moves from a dependent, manipulative, and superficial style of interaction to a more conscientious, responsible, and considerate mode. This change in interpersonal style reflects a greater probability that older persons will have knowledgeable, respectful, concerned, and responsible relationships with significant others. According to Fromm (1956), the four elements of knowledge, respect, concern, and responsibility determine the success of all relationships. Therefore, older persons potentially have closer, more successful intimate relationships than younger persons. These relationships are not necessarily closer or more intimate per se; they are simply more valuable resources for the considerate and responsible older person. In other words, older, mature individuals may not experience a greater degree of intimacy in their relationships than younger, less mature persons, but older persons' relationships may be perceived as more important, meaningful, mutually satisfying, or supportive due to their increase in considerate and responsible sensitivity. Even though this sensitivity may be achieved only by a select few, perhaps only by the self-actualized (Maslow, 1970), the potential, or capacity, is greater for those older persons to accomplish closer, more intimate relationships.

Confounding the assumption of this greater potentiality are the rather rapid social changes that have occurred in the moral attitudes and values associated with the establishment and maintenance of intimate relationships. One cannot ignore the increase in divorce rates, cohabitation, and promiscuous sexual and emotional expression, especially among younger people. With the proliferation of such trends, one wonders what impact these attitudes and experiences have on the level of intimacy achieved. Perhaps the movement toward increased emotional expressivity and openness among the young generation contributes to greater levels of intimacy. On the other hand, maybe this increase in expressivity and openness acts as a substitute for intimacy. Whether in fact these changes have occurred among the young, or whether they affect the level of intimacy in relationships, is beyond the scope of this chapter. What is important in the context of this chapter is the degree of association between intimacy and one's age or developmental stage. This investigator proposes that changes occur in intimacy from its original inception during either adolescence or young adulthood to the older adult life stages. These changes occur in the qualitative nature of perceived intimacy, in the degree or level of intimacy in relationships, and in the impact of intimacy on adaptation.

In contrast to the notion that intimacy increases from late adolescence or early adulthood to the older adult life stages, many researchers (especially those dealing with the marital relationship) suggest the opposite—a decrease in intimacy with age or life stage. Investigators such as Blood and Wolfe (1960), Pineo (1961), Burr (1970), and Thurnher (1975) have documented a significant decrease in marital satisfaction or favorable perceptions of the marital relationship with age or life stage. Such marital dissatisfactions peak during the period preceding the loss of the parental role and are followed by increased satisfaction in the post-parental stages (Thurnher, 1975). There seems to be an antithesis between parent and spouse roles; parenting "interferes with the capacity of a spouse either to give or receive attention and love from the other spouse" (Bohannan, 1971, p. 58). If perceived dissatisfaction and conflicting parent and spouse roles reflect the degree or level of intimacy in a relationship, then a decrease in intimacy (or at least a waxing and waning) would seem to occur through middle and older adult life stages. Therefore, in contrast to the potential for increasing levels of intimacy to occur with age or life stage, many researchers have found a tendency toward declining levels of intimacy with age. The present study will shed some light on these contrasting views by assessing the level of intimacy throughout adult life.

LEVEL OF INTIMACY: ITS MEDIATING IMPACT ON ADAPTATION TO STRESS

Intimacy is not a static state that, once achieved, remains constant. Instead, it is a dynamic process that changes over time in specific relationships. In order to conceptualize and define intimacy, we need to delineate the various parameters involved and accept the assumption that intimacy is the central dynamic to all voluntary interpersonal relationships. Given this assumption, the depths of exchange (or levels of relatedness) proceed from approach, to affiliation, to attachment. Newcomb's (1961) analysis of the acquaintance process provides some support for a level approach in which a progression occurs from superficial, objective characteristics at the outer, or peripheral, layers of personality to the closer, more centralized, or core, layers of personality in an intimate acquaintance.

Kerckhoff and Davis's (1962) filtering theory of pair formation is based on data collected from dating couples at various points in the courtship process. They propose that a series of successive filters operates in the development of intimacy. Initially, filters involving similarity in background and other social status factors operate. Then, similarity in attitudes and values (value consensus) and, finally, complementarity of deeper social or personality needs become important filtering factors in intimate relationships. Levinger *et al.* (1970) were unable to replicate

Kerckhoff and Davis's (1962) findings, but they also support a "levels" model.

The present framework adopts a levels-of-relatedness approach and proposes to define the qualities associated with higher levels of intimacy. In addition, the framework for conceptualizing stress and adaptation utilized in this research is a modification of Selye's (1955) paradigm of the stress response, translated into social and psychological terms by Dohrenwend (1961), Rahe and Holmes (1966), and Rahe (1974) and adjusted to accommodate social-interaction variables as intervening or mediating factors (Lowenthal et al., 1967; Lazarus et al., 1974). This stress-adaptive framework displays a variety of stressors as antecedent events or agents in one's life that produce a condition of stress or emotional discomfort. An assumption is made that the greater the amount of negative events, the greater the stress. The mediating factors consist of external social interaction variables that potentially provide social support and, consequently, influence the level of adaptation. In short, the present framework not only adopts a levels approach to the concept-ualization of intimacy, but it also postulates intimacy as a mediating factor in adaptations to stress.

AN EXAMINATION OF THE "BUFFERING EFFECT" OF INTIMACY

The mediating, inhibiting, or buffering effects that varying depths or levels of intimacy have on the experience of stress may occur on both a psychological and a physiological level. In a pioneering social-psychological study, Lowenthal and Haven (1968) concluded that the presence of a confidant (or intimate other) served as a buffer both against gradual social losses in roles and interaction and against more traumatic losses accompanying widowhood and retirement. Some earlier supporting physiological evidence of this mediating effect was presented by Back and Bogdonoff (1964). They found that a group of friends experiencing the physical stress of blood withdrawal had lower levels of fatty acids in their blood than did a group of strangers; therefore the full impact of the stressor was inhibited. On a more encompassing level, Bruhn and asso-ciates (1966) found that a cohesive and mutually supportive community with strong family and neighborly ties had a lower mortality rate due to heart disease than either a noncohesive or nonsupportive matched community or the United States as a whole. Therefore, it seems evident that the mere presence of others during stressful situations has an impact on both physiological and psychological adaptation. In addition, it is apparent that the more qualitative aspects of the relationship (i.e., the level of intimacy) or the social environment seem to have a greater effect on the outcome. This buffering effect appears to extend beyond the particular time and place of stress; it influences one's general state of physical and mental well-being.

DEFINITION AND OPERATIONALIZATION

In order to explore the association between intimacy and adaptation to stress during adult life, a series of studies were undertaken to define and operationalize the concept of intimacy. In short, the results produced the following 16 items that defined the parameters of intimacy and provided the content for the measurement instrument, Weiss's Intimacy Rankings (WIR):

1. Has a similar or complementary personality
2. Has similar interests
3. Has similar attitudes (ideas, values, beliefs, morals, ethics)
4. Shares activities with me
5. Likes me
6. Is comfortable and easy to be with
7. Is enjoyable, entertaining company
8. Knows me well
9. I respect him or her
10. Is supportive and accepting
11. Is dependable and trustworthy
12. Would help me out in a crisis
13. Is someone I can confide in
14. Is physically attractive
15. Provides sexual satisfaction
16. We feel a strong emotional attraction for each other

These 16 intimacy dimensions were then rank ordered by an independent sample of 35 professional judges for the degree of importance in an ideal opposite-sex and same-sex relationship. The results indicated that different configurations of important dimensions for inclusion in deeper or higher levels of intimacy existed for men and women and for the sex of the intimate other. Consequently, four profiles were established in order to determine greater depth in intimacy and to establish the operational definition for same-sex friendship intimacy and opposite-sex spouse intimacy. The dimensions comprising higher levels of intimacy

TABLE 7.1
Dimensions Comprising Higher Levels of Intimacy

Males		Females	
Same sex	Opposite sex	Same sex	Opposite sex
Confidant	Emotional attraction	Supportive	Emotional attraction
Comfortable	Confidant	Dependable	Likes me
Dependable	Comfortable	Likes me	Confidant
Respect	Provides sexual	Confidant	Supportive
Supportive	satisfaction		Respect
Knows me well	Likes me		
Likes me	Supportive		

are shown in Table 7.1.[2] The summation of inverted ranks of each appropriate dimension for the four criteria groups in Table 7.1 was used in determining a level-of-intimacy score.[3]

The intimacy instrument WIR, which assesses levels of friendship and spouse intimacy, was administered to a sample of 171 women and men drawn from an existing study population.[4] The majority were white, middle- and lower-middle class people residing in a large urban city. The people in the sample ranged in age from 21 to 72. Primarily, they were chosen because they were experiencing one of the following major life transitional stages: high school graduation, recent marriage and pregnancy (newlywed), the departure of the youngest child from home (empty nest), and retirement.

The methodological tools for data collection consisted of the intimacy instrument, WIR; a stress index; and two adaptation measures (Morale and Symptoms Checklist). A level-of-intimacy score was determined by combining the inverted ranks of each appropriate dimension for the four profiles previously mentioned. The four intimacy profiles provided the appropriate items, or sex-relation norms, that serve as a basis of the intimacy score. The ranks of each item in the profile were inverted so that a higher score would indicate higher levels of intimacy. The instrument utilized for measuring presumptive stress was the Life Event

[2]The interested reader is encouraged to write the author for more methodological details.

[3]Level-of-intimacy scores were standardized $(\bar{X} = 50)$ and ranged from 22 to 77. Higher scores indicated more intimacy. Test–retest reliability (R) ranged from .67 to .77.

[4]The larger study is the Longitudinal Study of Transitions, Human Development Research Program, University of California, San Francisco.

Questionnaire. This instrument, as adopted by Lowenthal *et al.* (1975), is a modification of the Holmes and Rahe (1967) social stress scale. The Life Event Questionnaire lists 125 events containing common episodes that evoke changes, whether pleasurable or painful. A life-stress score was determined by the summation of the number of unhappy, painful, or negative adult life events checked (a high score indicated a high level of stress).

Adaptation was measured by two instruments: The General Morale Index and the Symptoms Checklist. The General Morale Index was a self-evaluation of well-being formulated by Lowenthal *et al.* (1975) and originally adopted from the Bradburn Morale Scales (Bradburn and Caplovitz, 1965). A high score indicated high morale and increased psychological well-being and adaptation. A second measure of adaptation was the 42-item Symptoms Checklist. The items on this self-administered checklist of psychosomatic impairment were determined by a team of psychiatrists and reported by Lowenthal *et al.* (1975). The higher the score or total number of positive responses, the lower the respondent's degree of adaptation. In short, the data generated by these methodological tools were tested by a correlational research design, and they provided the operational model for assessing the degree of impact that friendship and spousal intimacy have on adaptation to stress in various adult life transitional stages.

RESULTS

Association of Gender with Intimacy

The amount of influence that gender has on intimacy was treated in the discussion of the operationalization of the concept of "levels of intimacy" (see "Definition and Operationalization"). In short, there were enough differences between men and women and same-sex and opposite-sex relationships in the way in which the qualitative dimensions of intimacy were ranked (see Table 7.1) to warrant the development of four separate profiles defining the criteria for deeper levels of intimacy.

Life Stage and Sex Similarities and Differences in the Level of Friendship and Spouse Intimacy

Not only did the results indicate that men and women perceive friendship and spouse intimacy differently, but they also indicate that the level of intimacy differs from one adult life-stage cohort to another. The cross-sectional data revealed highly significant differences in the level of *spouse* intimacy from one life stage to another ($F = 7.29$, $p \le .001$) and interaction between life stage and sex ($F = 3.69$, $p \le .001$). Clearly, the level of spouse intimacy differs from one life stage to another, with a dramatic shift toward lower levels of intimacy among the older sample (see Figure 7.1). In addition, an interaction between life stage and sex occurred, indicating different trajectories for men and women across the life span. The men successively decreased in intimacy from high school to retirement. The women, on the other hand, initially displayed an increase in spouse intimacy during the newlywed stage, but the level of intimacy decreased drastically among the empty nest (middle-aged) cohort, and then increased among those women who were retired.

The level of friendship intimacy, however, remained constant across the life span, with a slight, nonsignificant tendency to decrease with each stage of cohorts (see Figure 7.1). This constant level of intimacy may imply that the important functions of close friends remain fairly stable throughout life. Moreover, it may suggest that the situational factors that affect each life stage have little or no relationship to the level of friendship intimacy attained.

Therefore, given this stability and situational independence, the potential resource of close friends in times of stress should be greater than that of marriage partners. This should be especially true when the stress and strains of a particular stage focus on family or marital affairs (as in the empty nest stage). Therefore, these data generate the following question: "What kind of relationship exists between the level of intimacy and adaptation to stress?"

Relationship between Life Stress and Adaptation for Varying Levels of Intimacy for Younger and Older Adults

The results for the total sample generally do not support the role of intimacy as an intervening or mediating factor in adaptation to stress. However, when life stage, sex, and type of relationship are taken into consideration, significant differences result. Some differences in the strength of the correlation between stress and adaptation existed for the friendship intimacy level. The major differences occurred for the spouse intimacy level, indicating its greater potential as an intervening factor.

Looking first at the levels of friendship intimacy and dichotomizing the intimacy scores at the mean into high and low levels, the difference between correlations for stress and morale was significant only for the

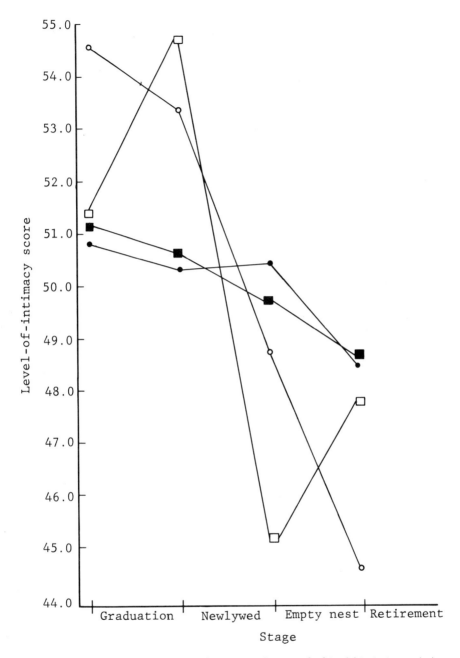

Fig. 7.1 Level-of-intimacy scores by stage and sex; male friendship intimacy (●), female friendship intimacy (■), male spouse intimacy (○), and female spouse intimacy (□).

oldest group—those in the retirement stage. Among the people in this stage, a low level of intimacy significantly increased the negative correlation between stress and morale. The men in the retirement stage contributed the most to the association between stress and morale. On the other hand, the correlations between stress and psychosomatic symptoms were significantly higher and positive for the young (primarily young women), who had a high level of intimacy. The men reversed this pattern: those who were low on friendship intimacy displayed a stronger positive link between stress and symptomatology (the higher the stress, the more reported symptoms).

The level of spouse intimacy influenced many more correlations between stress and adaptation than did friendship intimacy. The correlations between stress and morale were significantly higher and negative among those young people (graduating high school students and newly-weds) who had a high level of intimacy. These differences occurred primarily for the young newlywed women. However, for the older people (in the empty nest and retirement stages), the negative correlations between stress and morale were greater for those who had a low level of intimacy. The older men and women, predominately in the retirement stage, contributed the most to this direction. In addition, older people manifested higher negative correlations between stress and symptoms when they had a low level of intimacy with their spouse. This relationship occurred primarily among the older women rather than the men.

In summary, the results indicate that older people manifest a higher negative correlation between stress and adaptation when they have a low level of intimacy, whereas the reverse is true for younger people. The implication of this finding is that intimacy (primarily with a spouse) can be conceived as having a mediating or intervening effect on adaptation for older adults, but not for younger adults.

DISCUSSION AND CONCLUSION

Levels of Intimacy: Qualitative Differences

The results of the qualitative differences indicate that intimacy is not a universal phenomenon that crosscuts different types of relationships. Instead, different qualitative dimensions contribute to higher levels of intimacy, depending on the sex of the respondent and the significant others in the relationship; this results in four intimacy profiles (see Table 7.1). Looking first at friendships, men emphasized respect in close friendships more than women did. This finding appears to be consistent with Rubin's (1973) contention that respect is a fundamental dimension of liking, but not of loving, and Reiss's (1960) finding that respect is more important to men than to women in loving relationships. One implication is that sex-role differences have a tremendous impact on the importance or value of respect in intimate relationships as well as in work-role functions.

Similarly, the inclusion of comfort and ease as an important dimension of intimacy in male friendships, but not in female friendships, tends to support the social stereotype or caricature of male companionship as a respite from more intense or demanding interactions with females. Apparently, intimacy with male friends or companions centers on a more relaxed, open compatibility that is relatively free from anxiety and fear. This comfortable interaction is complemented not only by respect for the other, but also by the perception that the other knows one well. Therefore, the important dimensions in male friendships, above and beyond those that are common to female friendships, imply a greater degree of compatibility based on respect, comfort, and knowledge of the other. In addition, even though the inclusion of more dimensions in male friendship intimacy implies a greater degree of complexity, these relationships seem to be locked into or at least conform to stereotypical sex-role patterns.

The qualities of an ideal female friendship tend to emphasize emotional support, acceptance, dependability, and reciprocal affection. Male friendships emphasize the same qualities, but to different degrees and with additional factors included. Female's conception of same sex friends do not emphasize respect as much as the males' conception. Instead, women desire the support and trust that friends provide. Dependability and emotional validation seem to be valued more in a close friend than the knowledge of the other or comfort and ease in the relationship that men seek. The ideal female companion provides a trusting ear for sharing confidences and accepting behaviors that denote reciprocal affection. The importance of these dimensions in female friendship seem to support the role of women as being the socioemotional experts.

Qualitative differences also exist between those dimensions that are considered important in friendship intimacy and those that are considered important in spouse intimacy. For example, both men and women unquestionably value a strong emotional attraction for their spouses. This emphasis on reciprocal, passionate feelings reflects elements of tenderness, caring, and eroticism that seem appropriate to opposite-sex intimacy. Perhaps this emphasis on passionate feelings with regard to spouse intimacy reflects the importance of a sexual component. Interpretation of this sexual component extends beyond mere egocentric gratification; instead, it includes reciprocal passionate feelings. The importance of this dimension in spouse intimacy supports Walster and Bersheid's (1971) theory of passionate love, which claims the necessity in a heterosexual love relationship of an aroused state of passion, and the labeling of such a state accordingly.

Friendship intimacy, on the other hand, does not emphasize a strong emotional attraction, but rather the dependable and trustworthy nature of a friend. The ability to have confidence in another person, and the ability to rely on that person for aid and security, appear to be essential elements of intimacy among friends. A dependable friend fits the social image of what friendship is all about. However, an emphasis on the dependability of a spouse appears to be antagonistic or contradictory to the image of independence that our society so vehemently promotes, especially with regard to the male role. Ideal marriages do not appear to focus on dependability, as friendships do, but rather on more romantic, loving qualities of strong emotional attraction, passionate feelings, and shared confidences.

The influence of stereotypical images on the intimacy profiles is reflected in the gender differences found for spouse intimacy. Males stressed the importance of having their spouses provide sexual satisfaction, whereas females placed more importance on respect for their spouses. This finding is consistent with the cultural emphasis on the males' demand for sexual prowess (with the marital relationship being no exception) and the females' expressed need or desire for status and respect for their partners. These differences between the sexes appear to reinforce the mythology of sex bias and to structure the relationships between men and women in a way that perpetuates the subservient position of women. Women in this sample do not define sexual satisfaction as a dimension of higher level intimacy. However, these women acknowledge that they must provide sexual satisfaction if they want to please their spouses. Consequently, a woman may come to perceive herself as a sex object. If a woman wants to please herself in the development of a close relationship, she needs to respect her partner. However, by looking up to her spouse, she puts herself in a position that reinforces her subservient role. Although there are additional less sexually biased factors that contribute to higher levels of intimacy, culturally determined sex roles do seem to influence our ideal intimacy profiles.

One final gender difference requires explication. One dimension exists for the male friendship and spouse intimacy profiles that does not exist for either of the female profiles. Namely, males perceive comfort and ease in being with another as an important and perhaps a necessary dimension in intimacy, whereas the females do not. Since this degree of comfort, quiet presence, or compatibility is reflected in both friendship and spouse intimacy profiles for men it refutes the earlier mentioned stereotype of male friends seeking each other's company as a relief from their more intense, demanding, or anxiety-producing relationships with the opposite sex. Instead, men also desire comfort and ease in their relationships with the opposite sex; this reflects a general desire for respite from demanding relationships, regardless of the sex of the significant other.

In summary, the qualitative differences in intimacy that contribute to the conceptualization of four profiles indicate the influence that our cultural stereotypes have on intimate relationships. The commonalities among the intimacy profiles reflect a configuration of reciprocal affection, support, and self-disclosure that lend credence to the potential role intimacy has in adaptation to stress.

Intimacy across the Adult Life Span

In contrast with the finding that friendship intimacy remained stable across the adult life span, the level of spouse intimacy significantly changed from one adult life stage to another. These results support a deterioration or disenchantment theory of marital relations (e.g., Pineo, 1961). The changing pattern involved in women's intimacy levels among the four cohorts (the empty nest cohort having the lowest levels) appears to coincide with the developmental processes of the formation and culmination of the parental role. The woman's roles as parent and spouse are so intricately connected that each reflects the stresses and strains of the other. More realistically, however, the marriage relationship may well be subordinate to the demands of children and motherhood, resulting in a greater distance and a lower level of intimacy between spouses.

The men's lowest level of intimacy for the four adult life stages occurred at the retirement stage. This finding suggests that a developmental link exists between the change or loss of occupational status and a man's lack of intimacy with his spouse. Rollins and Feldman (1970) provide some support for these findings, showing that not only does a steady decline exist in marital satisfaction from the beginnings of marriage to the point at which the children leave home, but that marital crises exist for men who are anticipating retirement. In addition, Lowenthal *et al.* (1975) report marital crises among women who are facing the empty nest stage. Consequently, since marital intimacy is the lowest for those older adults experiencing major life transitions (namely, the empty nest women and the retired men), the implication is that the lack of intimacy during these later stages contributes to the crises or, at least, is influenced by the stressful situation. Each of these traditional crises seem to be associated with the sex-role behavior and identity of men and women.

In summary, the overriding explanation for the fluctuation of spouse intimacy with each adult life stage for women and the smoothly declining intimacy for men suggests that an anticipated or actual loss in one network or area of life may threaten or change other networks or areas. A loss or change in the parental role for women or the occupational role for men is generalized to, and similarly affects, other roles and relationships, specifically with regard to a spouse.

Figuratively, one can image a mobile balanced with various relationships and social roles. When a change occurs and one role becomes weightier or is cut loose, the whole mobile or network is affected, resulting in a generalized loss. The overall affect of a decrease in the actual level of spouse intimacy (and, to some extent, friendship intimacy) from the younger to the older cohorts lends uncertainty to the notion that older adults have the potential for greater levels of intimacy which is related to an increase in sensitivity and competence through considerate and responsible interaction. Perhaps higher levels of intimacy are reserved for a select few who are actualized. In any case, these results do not disprove the notion that older adults have a greater potential for intimacy, nor do they state that older people are inconsiderate or irresponsible. Given the existence of a lower level of intimacy among older adults, the question arises concerning the relationship between intimacy and adaptation, especially with regard to those identified as at-risk groups; that is, cohorts experiencing major life transitions.

The Relationship between Intimacy and Adaptation to Adult Life Stress

The findings concerning the relationship between intimacy and adaptation to stress revealed that those older people who had a low level of intimacy (especially with their spouses) became more maladapted with increasing stress. On the other hand, older people who had a high level of spouse intimacy did not display a significant relationship between stress and adaptation. Therefore, one can speculate that intimacy serves as a critical intervening, mediating, or buffering factor in adaptation to stress. There are certain conditions that seem essential for intimacy to act as a mediator: (a) the relationship applies only to older people, (b) spouse intimacy appears to be more important than friendship intimacy, and (c) an apparent ceiling effect, or point of satiation, exists in the level of intimacy.

The value of intimacy as a resource for older people lies in its mediating power to intervene in or buffer the effects of stress or adaptation. For younger adults (who have graduated from high school and/or newlywed), the reverse function of intimacy in adapting to stress occurs suggesting that what is a resource for an older person in adaptation may be an impediment for a younger person. The results discussed here indicate that even though younger people appear to have a multitude of resources (including their working and parental roles, health, large social networks, etc.), the additional weight of a highly intimate relationship seems to contribute to stress, rather than alleviate it. Many older people are losing or do not have work or work associates for support. Their parents are either ill or dead, and their children have moved away from home. Therefore, the availability of accessible resources is diminished. This diminished availability of resources, coupled with the greater potential for the older person to be more considerate and responsible in social interactions, provides some basis for understanding the increase in importance of the level of intimacy as a mediator in adaptation to stress among older adults.

An additional modifier of the mediating effect of intimacy on adaptation to stress is the fact that the level of intimacy among older married couples is a more effective mediator than the level of intimacy among friends. This finding supports Erikson's (1963) emphasis on a heterosexual relationship. Clearly, as Erikson's theory would suggest, a marriage partner has a greater effect on adaptation to stress later in life than a same-sex friend. This association seems to remain effective, even though friendship intimacy among the older sample is comparatively higher than their spouse intimacy. Furthermore, this mediating effect of spouse intimacy occurred with regard to morale and degree of satisfaction among older men and for both morale and psychosomatic symptoms among older women. The obvious implication is that women suffer more than men do, both emotionally and physiologically, as a result of the lack of intimacy with a spouse. However, a minimum level or threshold of intimacy, once established, appears to have the power to buffer older married partners from the stresses accompanying the aging process.

The above findings cited in this chapter do not directly reflect the homosexual relationship or the single adult. In the research design of this study, there was no attempt by the investigator to include gays or to compare the same-sex friendship with a homosexual relationship. However, an investigation of the role of intimacy in a homosexual relationship, incorporating the present research methodology, would be a fascinating area of future study. It would be this author's contention that intimacy serves a similar mediating function for both older homosexual and heterosexual couples.

The role of intimacy in adaptation to stress among single persons would appear to depend more on the recency of their status and on the levels of intimacy in their other relationships than on their status per se (i.e., recently widowed, or a lifelong single). Lowenthal (1964) found that lifelong isolates were more adaptive than those people who tried and failed in relationships. This finding implies that singlehood itself is not maladaptive. A more important factor would seem to be the role and level of intimacy in relationships, not whether a person is married or single. The study of intimacy among single persons (i.e., widowed, divorced, or never-married), especially in late life, would significantly contribute to the stress–adaptation equation.

One final modifying factor that seems important to the function of intimacy as a mediator between stress and adaptation is an apparent ceiling effect, or satiation point, which limits the buffering capacity of higher levels of intimacy. Since lower levels of intimacy increased the chance for maladaptation, and higher levels decreased or had no effect on the relationship between stress and adaptation for the older adult, the power of close relationships to increase the buffering effect seems to diminish. In other words, the attainment of a minimum critical level of intimacy among older spouses is an essential factor in mediating adaptation to stress. Below this critical minimum level, the buffering effect of intimacy becomes nonexistent. When a point of satisfaction is achieved, however, and one's apparent need for intimacy is gratified, the buffering effect loses its strength and fails in its effectiveness, thereby producing a ceiling effect. One implication of this is that if the returns do not increase proportionately or significantly with increases in the level of intimacy with one's spouse, then the time, effort, and energy involved in establishing and maintaining such interpersonal intimacy should be devoted to other more rewarding relationships. In other words, for an older couple, once a minimum level of intimacy that results in a buffering effect on adaptation is attained, it would seem expedient to invest in other more advantageous or resourceful relationships, such as a relationship with a friend or a child. This suggestion implies a somewhat egocentric or pragmatic approach embodying an exchange-theory perspective—an approach that is, nonetheless, potentially important for survival. This implication, along with the issue of palled intimacy, is not clearly substantiated in the present data and, therefore, requires further research, including an investigation of the point at which a minimum critical level of intimacy is achieved.

In summary, intimacy can be conceived as an intervening or mediating factor in adaptation to stress when certain modifying factors are taken into consideration. When an older person attains a minimum critical level of intimacy with a spouse, the functional capacity of intimacy acts as a mediator, or perhaps even as a buffer, in adaptation to stress. This mediating function of intimacy may be a requirement for survival as one ages.

REFERENCES

Back, K. W., and Bogdonoff, M. D. (1964). *In* "Psychobiological Approaches to Social Behavior" (P. H. Leiderman and D. Shapiro, eds.), pp. 36–39. Stanford Univ. Press, Stanford, California.

Blood, R. O., and Wolfe, D. M. (1960). "Husbands and Wives: The Dynamics of Married Living." Free Press, New York.

Bohannan, P. (1971). *In* "Kinship and Culture" (F. L. K. Hsu, ed.), p. 58. Aldine, Chicago.

Bowlby, J. (1958). *Int. J. Psychoanal.* **39**, 350–373.

Bradburn, N. M., and Caplovitz, D. (1965). "Reports on Happiness: A Pilot Study of Behavior Related to Mental Health." Aldine, Chicago.

Bruhn, J. G., Chandler, B. C., Miller, M., Wolf, S., and Lynn, T. (1966). *Am. J. Public Health* **56**, 1493–1506.

Burr, W. R. (1970). *J. Marriage Fam.* **32**, 29–37.

Conrad, J. (1910). "Heart of Darkness." Harper, New York.

Dohrenwend, B. P. (1961). *J. Abnorm. Psychol. Soc. Psychol.* **62**, 294–302.

Erikson, E. H. (1963). "Childhood and Society," 2nd ed. Norton, New York.

Freud, S. (1922). "Group Psychology and the Analysis of the Ego." Hogarth, London.

Fromm, E. (1956). "The Art of Loving." Harper & Row, Bantam ed., New York.

Gubrium, J. F. (1976). "Time, Roles and Self in Old Age." Human Sciences Press, New York.

Harlow, H., and Zimmerman, R. (1959). *Science* **130**, 412–432.

Holmes, T. H., and Rahe, R. H. (1967). *J. Psychosom. Res.* **11**, 213–218.

Jourard, S. M. (1964). "The Transparent Self," pp. 46–48. Van Nostrand, Princeton, New Jersey.

Kerckhoff, A. C., and Davis, K. E. (1962). *Am. Sociol. Rev.* **27**, 295–303.

Lazarus, R. S., Averill, J. R., and Opton, E. M., Jr. (1974). *In* "Coping and Adaptation" (G. V. Coelho, D. A. Hamburg, and J. E. Adams, eds.), pp. 249–315. Basic Books, New York.

Levinger, G., Senn, D. J., and Jorgensen, B. W. (1970). *Sociometry* **33**, 427–443.

Loevinger, J. (1966). *Am. Psychol.* **21**, 195–206.

Lowenthal, M. F. (1964). *Am. Sociol. Rev.* **29**, 54–70.

Lowenthal, M. F., and Boler, D. (1965). *J. Gerontol.* **20**, 363–371.

Lowenthal, M. F., and Haven, C. (1968). *Am. Sociol. Rev.* **33**, 20–30.

Lowenthal, M. F., Berkman, P. L., and associates (1967). "Aging and Mental Disorder in San Francisco: A Social Psychiatric Study." Jossey-Bass, San Francisco.

Lowenthal, M. F., Thurnher, M., Chiriboga, D., and associates (1975). "Four Stages of Life: A Comparative Study of Women and Men Facing Transitions." Jossey-Bass, San Francisco.

Maslow, A. H. (1970). "Motivation and Personality," 2nd ed. Harper, New York.

Montagu, A. (1966). "The Human Dialogue." Bantam Books, New York.

Morris, C. (1956). "Varieties of Human Value." Univ. of Chicago Press, Chicago.

Newcomb, T. M. (1961). "The Acquaintance Process." Holt, Rinehart, & Winston, New York.

Otto, H., and Mann, J. (1968). "Ways of Growth." Growsman, New York.

Parkes, C. M. (1971). *Soc. Sci. Med.* **5**, 101–115.

Parsons, T. (1964). "Social Structure and Personality." Free Press, New York.

Pineo, P. C. (1961). *Marriage Fam. Liv.* **23**, 3–11.

Rahe, R. H. (1974). *In* "Life and Stress and Illness" (E. K. E. Gunderson and R. H. Holmes, eds.), pp. 58–78. Thomas, Springfield, Illinois.

Rahe, R. H., and Holmes, T. H. (1966). "Life Crisis and Disease Onset: Qualitative and Quantitative Definition of Life Crisis and its Association with Health Change." Reprint from the Dept. of Psychiatry, University of Washington School of Medicine, Seattle.

Reiss, I. L. (1960). *Marriage Fam. Liv.* **22**, 139–145.

Rollins, B. C., and Feldman, H. (1970). *J. Marriage Fam.* **32**, 20–28.

Rubin, Z. (1973). "Liking and Loving: An Invitation to Social Psychology." Holt, Rinehart, & Winston, New York.

Selye, H. (1955). *Science* **122**, 625–631.

Spitz, R. A., and Wolf, K. M. (1946). "Anarlitic Depression. Psychoanalytic Study of the Child," Vol. 2, pp. 313–342. International Universities Press, New York.

Sullivan, H. S. (1953). "The Interpersonal Theory of Psychiatry." Norton, New York.

Taylor, D. A. (1968). *J. Soc. Psychol.* **75**, 79–90.

Thurnher, M. (1975). *In* "Four Stages of Life" (M. F. Lowenthal, M. Thurnher, D. Chiriboga, and associates), pp. 24–47. Jossey-Bass, San Francisco.

Townsend, P. (1963). "The Family Life of Old People." Penguin, Baltimore.

Walster, E., and Berscheid, E. (1971). *Psychol. Today* **5**, 47–62.

8

Long-Term Care Institutions

Victor Kassel

All would live long, but none would be old.
Anonymous

INTRODUCTION

Discussions dealing with the lives of those aged who are confined to long-term care institutions must differ from those dealing with others of the same age who have the freedom of living outside these institutions.[1] One cannot equate these two groups of aged people, anymore than one can equate the life of an incarcerated felon with that of the average unjailed citizen. This relates particularly to studies of the sexual behavior found in the noninstitutionalized aged as contrasted with the institutionalized aged.

The institutionalized aged are wholly dependent upon the moods, largess, whims, prejudices, attitudes, and enlightenment of the personnel working in the institution. The nursing home resident is a controlled person without the freedom of decision. The literature written during the early days of this century to describe social interactions in long-term chronic care tuberculosis hospitals approximately describes the relationships. The single major difference is the age of the patient; the chronic tubercular was much younger. For the aged in the long-term care institution, the internal and external milieu has a serious destructive effect upon sexuality. One cannot interpret sexuality studies about the aged that have been made outside of long-term care institutions as indicative of life in such institutions.

Many of the aged who find themselves banished to long-term care institutions (approximately 10% of the elderly population), growing old is a miserable experience. They now live with two kinds of adversity: old age in America and serious, limiting incapacities. These aged, relegated to spending their final days in the typical nursing home, carry stigmata and are stigmatized.

EVOLUTION OF THE NURSING HOME

There are a number of causes of insensitivity to the sexuality of the aged, long-term institutionalized person. The first cause stems from the origin of the American nursing home (Kassel, 1973). Our tradition of the American nursing home began in England. Its history goes back to the Elizabethan Poor Laws enacted during the sixteenth century. The society had encountered a population increase, closure of the commons (the common pasture of a village community), the beginnings of manufacturing, improved agriculture, and colonization. There was social and economic upheaval. What was to be done with the orphans, the helpless

---

[1]The terms *long-term care institution* and *nursing home* are used interchangeably throughout this chapter. They indicate facilities that render nursing care to the chronically impaired aged.

chronically sick, the widowed, the old, and the blind? Their care and welfare became the responsibility of the state. No longer was private charity able to deal adequately with these problems, and local government divisions assumed responsibility for these needy people. The poor farm was developed. The orphans, the blind, the infirm, and the sick became the wards of the state. The needy were moved to the local poor farm, where they resided, worked if they were able, and were provided for if they were not.

This tradition was transferred to America at the time of the original thirteen colonies. In our country, poor houses, county farms, and asylums were established to cater to the needs of helpless infancy, decrepit old age, abandoned widows, and orphans. For the affluent, private institutions were built to serve the expensive tastes of the infirm.

On the governmental level, separate state institutions for the needy gradually evolved: sanitariums for chronic tuberculosis care, insane asylums for the mentally ill, orphan asylums for orphaned children, prisons for law breakers, and chronic disease hospitals for the old and the infirm.

At the same time, the private sector of society began to recognize the lack of facilities for people who were neither poverty-stricken nor very wealthy. In many instances, a daughter began to give home nursing care to an elderly, infirm parent. As long as her time was taken up totally with the care of one elderly person, it seemed reasonable to include more people. This was done, and the neighborhood elderly infirm were added to the nursing load. It was in this way that many private nursing home operators began their establishments.

In a general way, this was the status of things until Title 18 and Title 19 of the Social Security law (Medicare and Medicaid) were passed in 1966. There were (a) government-sponsored nursing homes, like certain Veterans Administration (VA) domiciliaries, state hospitals, county hospitals, and city hospitals; (b) nursing homes sponsored by religious groups, fraternal organizations, and labor unions (e.g., the Elks, the Good Samaritan Group, and the Jewish Home for the Aged in New York); and (c) small private nursing homes, usually converted residences, established by concerned women who were unhappy with government institutions.

Following the White House Conference on Aging in 1961, the needs of the aged became more widely recognized. Discussions of the nursing home needs of the aged produced a concern for adequate facilities. Medicare focused on the lack of high quality institutions for the aged chronically ill. From this, there developed a fourth group, the incorporated nursing home chains, which, in many instances, used the marketing techniques of the large hotel and motel chains. The fourth group has now become the nursing home industry. Long-term custodial care of the aged in nursing homes, rest homes, convalescent homes, chronic disease hospitals, skilled nursing facilities, extended care facilities, self-care units, or personal care units has become big business, and in many institutions the major emphasis is on profit. In many cases, greater investment is made in brick and mortar for the public image of the institution; the lesser investment is in enlightened quality care.

Senator Frank E. Moss's study of America's nursing homes included 23,000 homes with 1.3 million beds and 1 million patients (Moss and Halamandaris, 1977). He profiled the patients as old. The average age of the patients was 82, and 70% were over 70. The women outnumbered the men 3 to 1. Only 10% had a living spouse. More than 50% had no close relatives. Less than 50% were ambulatory. At least 55% were mentally impaired, and 33% were incontinent. In any discussion of the sexuality of nursing home patients, one must give serious consideration to the last three figures cited here (Downey, 1974).

This accounts for the negative stereotype of average nursing home residents. They are considered neutered by menopause or eunuchoid by testicular atrophy and looked upon as demented and confused, with brain failure. They are physically frail as a result of accumulated chronic degenerative disease; both the men and the women are bewiskered because shaving is too much trouble. Women wear unfashionable dresses for the convenience of the nursing personnel, and men wear unzippered and drooping pants hanging by overstretched suspenders with walked-upon cuffs. Egg stains trailing down the front, fingernails dirty and uncut, toenails grotesque with onychogryposis, all bottomed with perianal "dangleberries"; these are all-too-common images. The thought of sexuality and the long-term institutionalized aged is repulsive. Perhaps not in *all* nursing homes, but far too many live this way in the twentieth century of American geriatric unenlightenment.

STEREOTYPE OF THE SEXLESS ELDER

The second cause of the insensitivity to the sexuality of the aged, long-term institutionalized person results from unenlightened attitudes manifested by the people who work in and administer nursing homes. It reflects Cato the Elder's *"De Senectute"* (quoted by Cicero).

> Next we come to the third allegation against old age. This was its deficiency in sensual pleasures. But if age really frees us from youth's most dangerous failing, then we are receiving a most blessed gift.

"The most fatal curse given by nature to mankind," said Archytas, "is sensual greed; this incites men to gratify their lusts heedlessly and uncontrollably."

Nature, or a god, has given human beings a mind as their outstanding possession, and this divine gift and endowment has no worse foe than sensuality [p. 228].

For such feelings cloud a man's judgment, obstruct his reasoning capacity, and blind his intelligence: let sensuality be present, and a good life becomes impossible [p. 229].

Because the weakening of temptation to indulge in them, far from supplying a pretext to reproach old age, is a reason for offering it the most cordial compliments [p. 230].

When its campaigns of sex, ambition, rivalry, quarrelling, and all the other passions are ended, the human spirit returns to live within itself—and is well off. There is supreme satisfaction to be derived from an old age which has knowledge and learning to feed upon [p. 232. Copyright © 1967. Reprinted by permission of Penguin Books Ltd.].

Sexual Revolution—For the Young

The American sexual revolution of the 1960s was responsible for communicating more liberal concepts of male–female relationships than was understood by the general population during earlier years. An appreciation of Freud's all-inclusive concept of sex had not filtered down through all of society. Many of the educated understood; most of the uneducated did not understand. All seemed to be involved in or involved with sex without a hint of understanding of sexuality. The major sufferer was the resident of the nursing home, who, being older, was obviously asexual and believed physiologically desexed. Although the sexual revolution and communication about it was nationwide during the 1960s, I still recall the local nursing homes' reaction to a proposed lecture that I had been invited to give at a community college. I had planned to present a workshop on the "Sexual Needs of the Elderly" in 1974. However, the nursing home administrators were up in arms, and they refused to listen to "dirty talk" about their residents. Their refusal appeared to be based particularly on a report in their local newspaper of a quotation from a previous talk: "that a special room might even be set aside in nursing homes in which patients might engage in sex" (Kassel, 1974).

There still is a pervasive ignorance, an antireaction throughout America as a major response, when one conjures up maleness and femaleness in older people in nursing homes. Sexuality, the state and reaction of an individual based on gender and the relationships included in the male–female psychological, social, and physical being of the person, is an all-encompassing phenomenon. In contrast, sex, as it relates to physical contact between persons, has a more limited connotation. Yet, unfortunately, the differentiation between sexuality and sex is frequently ignored.

The *Salt Lake Tribune* (1971) reported a senior citizen "shotgun wedding." According to the newspaper two elderly residents of a nursing home, both confined to wheelchairs, were forced to get married. The imposition made upon them by the nursing home administrator resulted from an in-house regulation that did not allow couples to enjoy each other's company after 9:00 P.M. The ignorance concerning sexuality on the part of the nursing home operator forced the two residents to get married in order to enjoy each other's company, sitting together in separate wheelchairs, after hours.

Nursing Home Personnel

Nursing home personnel generally come from social classes in which attitudes toward sex are far from enlightened. "With regard to sex behavior this class is probably the most puritanical of all. For them, sex is an ugly aspect of the human situation and they do their best to ignore it" (Ferdinand, 1969; p. 42).

Thus, elderly residents in nursing homes can often expect very little understanding from their nurses or, in far too many instances, from their physicians and attendants. Instead, some unfortunate elderly people have forced upon them religious values, moral judgments, archaic mythologies, and projected anxieties belonging to the so-called trained and enlightened professionals.

Attitudes in nursing homes still are basically Victorian, despite academic studies that try to show otherwise. Wasow and Loeb (1975, 1978) accurately put the position with their statement: "The staff of nursing homes are generally quite permissive in their attitude about sexuality of older people, but we have not any good information on what they actually do in specific situations" (p. 41). I still recall the disgust expressed by a daughter-in-law when she described the giggling and tittering of the personnel in a nursing home while they spied upon her mother-in-law and a male companion petting in a secluded garden spot (Kassel, 1976).

Many elderly people have instinctively discovered the relief obtained through masturbation. It affords solitary sexual solace, and it is practiced by a number of nursing home residents. Unfortunately, some personnel react with shock and horror when they come upon a masturbating patient. When an elderly man is found masturbating, the reaction is not as explosive as it is when an elderly woman is discovered masturbating. In the Salt Lake area, the most common reason for a request that I transfer a woman out of a nursing home is that she masturbates. Furthermore, most nursing home operators refuse to discuss the "problem" with the patient's family. The prevailing attitude is that an elderly women who masturbates is a vile, filthy, reprehensible undesirable who contaminates the wholesome living of nice, respectable old ladies.

In some cases, elderly men are admonished with such threats as "I'll cut that thing off!" when they are "caught " masturbating. It was not too long ago that I received a request for an order to put an old man in a straitjacket because of his incorrigible masturbating. Jacobson was correct when she wrote "When it comes to human sexuality, nursing is still in the Dark Ages—ignorant and prudish about this important aspect of patient care" (1974; p. 50). Estrogen still is used to control sexual urges of male patients. How many patients are tranquilized with phenothiazines into a state of zombiism in order to control "aggressive sexual behavior"? It would be instructive to experiment with genital fondling as a therapeutic control of "disturbed behavior" in a nursing home. What is the agitated, demented lady agitated about? Why does she keep tearing off her clothes? What is she searching for with her incessant pacing? What is the underlying meaning of her "senseless babbling"?

SOCIETAL ATTITUDES AND LAWS

Unenlightenment pervades the surrounding society. Legislation dealing with sex has evolved to protect the family. Adultery, divorce, homosexuality, rape, incest, abortion, and pregnancy out of wedlock are all threats to the stability of the family, which has been the basic unit of society. Anything that might destroy the family by interference with the support of the dependent mother and her immature offspring works against the strengths of the social group.

Impact on Older Persons

Are these same laws relevant in situations in which the potential for pregnancy does not exist; where no family exists, just lonely old widows and widowers? Where does the possibility for social destruction lurk under these circumstances? Antifornication and antisodomy laws have no meaning for this age group. Restrictions against free agency through legalisms established by the attitudes of the "lower-middle-class mentality" described by Ranulf (1964) inflict severe limitations upon the behavior of nursing home residents. More details of the evolution of these mores can be learned from Calverton (1932).

In these circumstances, crimes without victims are punished not only when the perpetrators are caught; rather, the fear of these laws on the part of nursing home administrators leads to stricter policing due to fear of a reacting moral indignation arising from the cultural psychology of one segment of society (Fox, 1977).

Often, organized religions display the same degree of unenlightenment as do regulating governmental agencies. What meaningful insight can a senior citizen expect from celibates? Mainline religious organizations do administer nursing homes, but is treatment any better from fundamentalist, religious sects or cults who are in the nursing home business? Judaism and Christianity have made a self-serving interpretation of the Onan incident (Genesis 38:9). Given the acceptance of polygamy and concubinage in the Old Testament, the seventh commandment against adultery (Exodus 20:14) was a legalism against the female. There are many Bible scholars who insist that immorality, as defined in the Bible, is worship of idols, and that the proscription of certain sexual behavior was intended to prevent pagan temple-worship practices, not sexual behavior as we know it today (Edwardes, 1967; Epstein, 1967).

Should a senior citizen be forced to abide by a defined custom, governmental or religious, that has no pertinence to his/her life? Most nursing homes in the United States follow a restricting morality defined by the Judeo-Christian tradition. All nursing homes in the United States follow a restricting genital sexual morality defined by governmental agencies. Neither government nor religion sees the individual aged person and his or her needs as the object of prime importance.

When a nursing home resident has a natural drive, an appetite for a sexual experience, and has an opportunity for its expression, should it be forbidden because of another person's moral system, religious values, or concept of proper behavior? Too many overseers, whether they are nurses, physicians, or clergy, obtrude upon the inclinations of nursing home residents. Whether one interprets this intrusion as a power play (Waitzkin and Waterman, 1974) or simply as a manifestation of ignorance regarding the normal sexuality of the aged (Rubin, 1967) the fact is that the nursing home resident is the lowest person on the social totem pole, the end of the pecking order.

Signs of Change: For People's Sake

Puritanical antisexual attitudes have begun to wane a bit in recent years. Initially precipitated by the sexual revolution brought about by young people, this change seems to have been further stimulated by social needs. A reason for change is illustrated by contemporary cost problems. Some years ago, it was necessary for me to hospitalize a confused elderly man for a medical evaluation. The only person who could control his erratic behavior was his wife. My plan was to hospitalize the patient and to have his wife share the double room with him. The hospital administration was aghast at the thought of a man and a woman in the same room, despite the fact that the two were legally maried and had been so for 30 years. The major consideration by the administration was "What would people think?" And now we have intensive care units that mix unmarried people of different sexes in the same room. What happened to the sexual prohibitions? They have been erased by the cost factor.

Mores change at different rates, under different circumstances, in different places. It seems that new perceptions are gained through liberal education, particularly education attained in schools with enlightened graduate studies in the behavioral sciences. People with such educations are moving into programs that serve the aged.. At the twenty-first annual meeting of the American Nursing Home Association in 1970, I spoke on "Sex in the Seventies." The *Miami News* was comfortable with my statement, which they headlined "Put life in nursing homes with dose of prostitution." The audience was terribly upset. To most of them, the image still was "dirty old men"; to many of us, it was "sexy senior citizen."

Today, some of the more informed nursing homes are hiring ancillary staff who have had gerontological training. Despite the fact that all nursing home patients are impaired by a variety of medical–surgical, psychiatric–psychological, and social problems, these residents are people who are alive. Their needs are not limited to basic vegetable functions. Limitations may exist for comprehensive interpersonal relations and social interactions, but still these needs are present. The staffs of modern nursing homes now include medical social workers (MSWs), who have learned about sex and sexuality; recreationists, who instigate activities in which the sexes mix; empathetic volunteers, who participate in residents' outside activities; and nurses and nurses' aides, who have received advanced training and who comfortably comprehend the erotic. (Schools of nursing during my medical school days omitted nursing instruction about male patients that dealt with any problem betwen the umbilicus and the knees.)

Social attitudes concerning nursing homes are changing. In spite of the majority for-profit, private nursing homes that have developed in America, most of the heavy costs are carried by the taxpayers. The taxpayers support these institutions through governmental programs; therefore, more private citizens are looking into the care policies developed by nursing homes. Also, nursing home advisory groups are forming throughout the country to advocate for justice and quality care for the nursing home resident. Many of the citizens are disturbed by what they have come to learn about the level of care offered in the nursing home. They are not satisfied. They demand that nursing home administrators be trained to appreciate quality care (Kassel, 1972). No longer will these groups settle for room, board, and minimal nursing service. These advocate groups, in order to understand more completely the various problems the aged encounter in nursing homes, are demanding classes from the universities' gerontological departments. These people demand answers to their penetrating and incisive questions. Many of them are young and in the full bloom of their own sexuality. They are curious. No longer will they accept the old myths. And they demand that the concepts they learn be instituted in long-term care institutions. Nursing homes can no longer lock their doors and keep the outside world away. The taxpayers support the institutions, and, increasingly, the taxpayers are demanding competent service for their money (D'Erasmo and Burger, 1978; Horn and Griesel, 1977; National Citizens' Coalition for Nursing Home Reform, 1978).

INSTITUTIONALIZED ELDERS: A CHANGING POPULATION OF THE 1960s AND 1970s

What about the sex act and the aged resident in a nursing home? One can turn to various studies: Finkle et al. (1959), Freeman (1961), Kinsey et al. (1948, 1953), Newman and Nichols (1960), Newsweek (1959), Pearlman (1972), Pfeiffer (1969), Pfeiffer et al. (1968), Weinberg (1971), and more. Men overstate; women understate! The present generation of aged, most of whom continue to be misled by the prevailing antisex myths, generally manifest a diminished interest in sexual intercourse. It was the style 10 years ago for declaiming social gerontologists to wax indignant about the decline of available sex in nursing homes. Now, we must consider what sort of elderly people reside in nursing homes.

Decreased Libido and Potency

It becomes obvious to anyone rendering care to the institutionalized aged that the majority of these people have accumulated a number of serious disabling illnesses (Shanas and Maddox, 1976). Stricter governmental regulations resulting from the ever-increasing expense of long-term care have established rules dealing with the criteria for admission to all levels of care. Originally, one might have assumed that patients in nursing homes, like inmates in prisons, "couldn't come to grips with sexual tensions, doubts, fantasies, anxieties and hunger" (Campbell, 1974, p. 385). It was thought to be this way in nursing homes—a major seething of sexual frustration precipitated by the insensitivity of administrators. But it is not so. From whatever causes—and there are many—there exists a major lack of sexual hunger, libido, and sexual potency among nursing home residents (Ford and Orfirer, 1967). This does not deny the existence of sexual proclivities in these elderly men and women; rather, it points out that there are valid reasons for the extinguishing of these desires and competencies among the elderly who are sick. This is an intuitive determination gained from friendly conversations with may elderly patients who reside in long-term care institutions. Most of these patients find themselves far more concerned with their day-to-day well-being and their ability to enjoy a tasty meal than with their ability to attain the privacy required to indulge in sexual intercourse. Would they indulge if this privacy were readily available? It seems unlikely, considering the widower's syndrome and the necessary therapeutic manipulations required to convert a hormone-starved vagina (with vaginitis) to a premenopausal state (Kassel, 1975). Furthermore, many of these patients receive medications that interfere with sexual competencies (Glover, 1977). Many of them have had their "sex center" destroyed by a stroke (Ford and Orfirer, 1967). Most of them remember youthful sexual activities with their spouses as having occurred in a different lifetime. Their "sexual functioning . . . is dependent on adaptation between physical capacities, societal mores, and individual desires" (Kaas, 1978, p. 372).

These facts should not be misinterpreted: an undetermined number of aged have lingering sexual desires and definite sexual wishes for their fulfillment. The number of these persons is not the same as that published by the gerontological sexologists studying the aged who are active and well. Lust among the aged is the province of burlesque-house jokes, not the nursing home. We are considering the institutionalized aged who require long-term care.

Many residents of institutions who, in former years, were fairly well, but were confined to nursing homes because of social need, have been able to return to independent home living due to recent home health-care services. As a result, the residual group of nursing home residents are elderly people with far more serious disabilities and less likelihood of a continued interest in sex and sexuality. Yet, a description of the functions of sex is pertinent to their lives. Morris (1974) listed four separate functions of sexual intercourse, the "four Rs of sex," which are reproduction, relational, recreational, and relief. Morris simply extended Alex Comfort's "three Rs" with the addition of relief. The reproduction function is of no consideration. The modern sex manuals have come to stress the relational and recreational aspects of sex. Nonwestern cultural attitudes find that sex has a therapeutic effect. Crying babies are quieted by their parents through genital fondling, a technique used by some of the Southwest Indians.

In the past in Salt Lake City, there was a "depraved" nursing home attendant who found that she could quiet her patients at night, without sedatives, by means of soporific masturbation (Goldberg, 1972). "How contented they seemed," she said. "Didn't have to give any of them sleepers." The horrifed state examiners took her license away after learning of this "disgusting behavior." Her error was that she tormented authority with concepts that were beyond their grasp. She was right at the wrong time: in her day, taking a stand against sedatives was considered deviant nursing.

Wolpe (1958) wrote about techniques used to extinguish anxiety. Anxiety, a manifestation of the sympathetic nervous system, could be extinguished by activating the parasympathetic nervous system. In clinical studies, it has been shown that sexual orgasm can relieve anxiety. Thus, Morris's inclusion of relief as a function of sexual intercourse is a reasonable consideration for the inclusion of sex as acceptable behavior in a nursing home.

The Institutionalized Environment: The Nature of the Barrier

For the long-term resident of a nursing home, how conducive is the environment to the sex act? In the average nursing home, doors cannot be locked, most rooms are occupied by two people of the same sex, and nursing home personnel have ready access to all areas; as a result, privacy becomes impossible. Interruptions are guaranteed. Most nursing homes have pervasive repugnant odors caused by the intermixed stench of stale food, decomposing urine, incontinent diarrheal stools, and penetrating disinfectants.

Illustrative of the problems encountered by nursing home couples is the story told of two elderly residents of a local nursing home. They visited an understanding physician and requested that he oversee, from his professional viewpoint, their lovemaking. He was to determine whether they were indulging in sexual intercourse properly. He agreed. After they completed the act, he told them that it was perfect, and then charged them $10 for the office visit. They returned weekly for 8 weeks, and each time they paid $10 for the office visit. Finally, the doctor told them the continuation of their visits was senseless because he repeatedly confirmed that their sex life was perfect. The couple then confided that they were residents of the Shady Nook Nursing Home, and that they could find no privacy for themselves. They could not go to their children's homes, and they could not afford $20 for a motel room. On the other hand, the doctor visits cost $10, and they received $8 refunds from Medicare.

An incident in the same vein is headlined in *National Enquirer* (1972) "100-Year-Old Man and Bride, 77, Elope from Old Folk's Home." They had to run away, because "the staff discouraged their romance. 'They did everything in their power to stop our secret meeting and our hand holding,' said Robert Koch, the groom." And, according to Gordon *et al.,* "A constant theme in the relevant literature is that sexual enjoyment is a capacity that is developed early in life and can be maintained throughout the entire life span, but only *with continual reactivation in a meaningful and unthreatening environment*" (1976, p. 325; italics added).

Homosexual Relationships

Studies describing sexual behavior in nursing homes are restricted to heterosexual encounters. Homosexual relationships have remained closeted. My initial introduction to homosexual activities in a long-term care institution occurred in the early 1950s at Fort Douglas Veteran's Administration Hospital in Salt Lake City. I had developed a geriatric service there. One morning, an aide sneaked into my office, embarrassed and upset, to whisper to me that he had "caught" two of the patients performing fellatio. Frankly, I was taken aback, not by the act of fellatio, but by the consideration that old men needed sex, too.

Following my presentation before the New England Hospital Assembly (Kassel, 1974), I received from England, from the Campaign for Homosexual Equality (CHE), a 20-page document presenting information about the emotional needs of retired and elderly homosexuals (1974). In the document, there was no description of the situation of homosexuals in nursing homes.

The ability to obtain a valid sexual history from the present generation of aged is difficult at best. It is even more difficult to get nursing home residents to admit to homosexual tastes. In my professional experience with homosexuals in nursing homes, of a single proven case, the difficulties did not make for a simple solution. The history was given to me by the former lover of an elderly female nursing home resident. The patient had become severely upset, agitated, and destructive. She was an unmarried schoolteacher who, until retirement at age 68, had lived with an unmarried female librarian who was 10 years her junior. Following retirement, she began to manifest evidence of brain failure with associated impaired memory and suspiciousness about her roommate. It became impossible for the two women to live together, and it was decided that the elderly schoolteacher would live alone in a separate apartment. In the meantime, the librarian found a younger, more attractive partner. The patient became disturbed over her replacement, and she finally had to be placed in a nursing home in order to control her agitated behavior. Phenothiazines were prescribed to prevent her from grabbing nearby woman; in doing so, she continued to seek her former lover to relive her past homosexual intimacies.

"The male homosexual over 45, regardless of his wishes, is faced with the fact that the homosexual world places a premium on youth" (Weinberg, 1969; p. 71). How the situation stands for the female homosexual over 45 is essentially unknown, although there appears to be an increase of interest in suggested and ongoing studies. One may infer that if overall sexual enlightenment and tolerance in the average nursing home is at a low level with regard to heterosexual behavior, homosexual residents are in for explosive reactions when they make their sexual preference manifest. Miller (1978) included a consideration of homosexual behavior and associated rules for the nursing home in one of her works.

Physicians and Sexual Expression in Institutions

The general tone of papers dealing with sexuality among the aged in nursing homes is derogatory with regard to nursing home personnel. My geriatric private practice experience confirms that this is deserved. What about the physicians? As a general statement, the physicians of America continue to abandon their patients after admitting them to nursing homes. In addition, they abandon concerns about sexuality to behavioral scientists with the insistence that sexuality and the aged bear no relevance to medical care. Perhaps recent medical school graduates have been exposed to the latest sexual concepts, sexual counseling, and information about sexuality in the family, but their ignorance is abysmal when it comes to sexuality and the aged. It is still an image of "dirty old men." At present, it is the rare medical student who has any exposure to geriatric medicine (Kassel, 1979). Furthermore, his/her exposure to geriatric sexuality is extremely limited. One can expect little enlightenment on this subject, as yet, from the medical profession. Frequently, members of this profession continue to be too preoccupied with their own aging and sexual anxieties. In the hospital coffee klatch, many continue to advertise their own inner concerns by casting aspersions at the aged and sexuality.

SUMMARY

How might one summarize sexuality in long-term care institutions? Certainly, the residents of these institutions are individuals. Statistical studies of sexuality in the aged vary countrywide and are dependent upon the locale and the customs of a particular area. The active, alert, healthy senior citizen who is participating in the life of the community maintains a sexual competency that differs from that of the nursing home resident. The latter, confined to a nursing home, is there because of serious, limiting competencies. Whatever degree of sexual interest or activity is pursued by the aged, the health limitations forcing institutionalization produce a real constraint on the sexual competency of the incapacitated aged. It is the factor of old age complicated by disability that hinders further sexual participation. Old age without disability does not appear to be the barrier.

Many nursing home residents are chronically ill with physical disabilities. An overwhelming number of them have a superimposed reactive depression precipitated by the circumstances of their living conditions. Long-term institutional care is too expensive to enable the resident to afford the luxury of privacy. The great majority of residents have no available sexual partners. Many of these people continue to believe that they have aged beyond an active sex life—that is, an active sex life for themselves. For "the others," it is all right.

Compounding the difficulties are the bureaucratic, restricting, governmental regulations imposed upon the nursing home resident. In addition, the level of society from which the majority of nursing home personnel are recruited dictates certain prejudices and beliefs; although these workers try to reflect an air of modern gerontological sophistication, when push comes to shove, they retreat into their antisexual biases.

Families continue to react adversely to the thought that a mother or grandmother still have a sexual appetite. Intellectually, children can discuss the right of sexual intercourse among the aged: "But don't let that dirty old man get near my sweet mother!" The younger adult generation finds liberal sexual behavior acceptable. Even their parents may find a number of these liberal ideas acceptable for themselves; yet, both generations continue to place emotional restrictions on this behavior among the oldest generation. Swinging is not for the aged!

It can be expected that the state of impotency that may be imposed upon the aged male, because of small blood vessel disease, pelvic nerve degeneration, and/or adverse effects of medication, will gradually be eradicated through newer medical and surgical techniques. The impotent, aged male can expect to develop a competency to perform the sex act. The loss of libido—that is, the sexual appetite—cannot be expected to be relieved too early in the near future. The devastating effect of multiple chronic degenerative diseases accumulated in the later years will continue to adversely react against the feeling of well-being. Many long-term chronically ill people just do not feel well, and their enthusiasm for the sex act has waned. Yet, it is important to keep in mind that, despite the physical and mental deviations produced by accumulated disease, in many elderly sick, there continues to be a strong sex drive.

A positive change in the attitude of the people dealing with nursing homes, as the result of their advocacy concern, their employment contingent on competent training, or their realization of the humanness of the aged, is forthcoming. The aged in nursing homes have minimal opportunity for many satisfying experiences and enjoyable pursuits. Within all of the limitations, sex is an opportunity for good, clean entertainment that provides laughter and joy in the heart and the intimate giving of one person to the other. Unfortunately, it is in the long-term care institution that the American aged remain most deprived of human intimacy.

REFERENCES

Calverton, V. F. (1932). "The Liberation of American Literature." Scribner's, New York.
Campaign for Homosexual Equality (CHE) (1974). "Emotional Needs of the Retired and Elderly." London, England.
Campbell, H. E. (1974). Rocky Mt. Med. J. **71**, 385–386.

Circero. (1967). *In* "Selected Works," pp. 211-247. Penguin, Baltimore.

Downey, G. W. (1974). *Mod. Healthcare* **1**, 56.

Edwardes, A. (1967). "Erotica Judaica." Julian Press, New York.

D'Erasmo, M., and Burger, S. G., eds. (1978). "Training Materials for Citizen Volunteers in a Nursing Home Ombudsman Process," 2nd Ed. National Council of Senior Citizens, Washington, D. C.

Epstein, L. M. (1967). "Sex Laws and Customs in Judaism." Ktav Publishing House, New York.

Ferdinand, T. N. (1969). *Med. Aspects Hum. Sex.* **3**, 34-46.

Finkle, A. L., Moyers, T. G., Tobenkin, M. I., and Karg, S. J. (1959). *J. Am. Med. Assoc.* **170**, 1391-1393.

Ford, A. B., and Orfirer, A. P. (1967). *Med. Aspects Hum. Sex* **1**, 51-61.

Fox, N. L. (1977). *J. Pract. Nurs.* **27**, 22.

Freeman, J. T. (1961). *Geriatrics* **16**, 37.

Glover, B. H. (1977). *Hosp. Pract.* **12**, 101-113.

Goldberg, M. (1972). *Med. Aspects Hum. Sex.* **6**, 142-149.

Gordon, C., Gaitz, C. M., and Scott, J. (1976). *In* "Handbook of Aging and the Social Sciences" (R. H. Binstock and E. Shanas, eds.), pp. 310-341. Van Nostrand-Reinhold, Princeton, New Jersey.

Horn, L., and Griesel, E. (1977). "Nursing Homes: A Citizens' Action Guide." Beacon Press, Boston.

Jacobson, L. (1974). *Nurs. Outlook* **22**, 50.

Kaas, M. J. (1978). *Gerontologist* **18**, 372.

Kassel, V. (1972). "Private Practicing Geriatrician Looks at Nursing Homes," U. S. Congr. Rec. S975 (reprinted p. 2313). U. S. Govt. Printing Office, Washington, D. C.

Kassel, V. (1973). "Geriatrics Today," Radio Ser. KSXX, Salt Lake City, Utah.

Kassel, V. (1974). *53rd Annu. Meet. N. Engl. Hosp. Inc., 1974.*

Kassel, V. (1975). *Med. Aspects Hum. Sex.* **9**, 71.

Kassel, V. (1976). *Med. Aspects Hum. Sex.* **10**, 126.

Kassel, V. (1979). *Geriatrics* **34**, 95.

Kinsey, A. C., Pomeroy, W. B., and Martin, C. E. (1948). "Sexual Behavior in the Human Male," Saunders, Philadelphia.

Kinsey, A. C., Pomeroy, W. B., and Martin, C. E. (1953). "Sexual Behavior in the Human Female." Saunders, Philadelphia.

Miller, D. B. (1978). *In* "Sexuality and Aging" (R. L. Solnick, ed.), rev. ed., pp. 163-175. Univ. of Southern California Press, Los Angeles.

Morris, M. H. (1974). *Religious Humanism* **8**, pp. 31-32.

Moss, F. E., and Halamandaris, V. J. (1977). "Too Old Too Sick Too Bad." Aspen Systems Corp., Germantown.

National Citizens' Coalition for Nursing Home Reform (1978). "Collation." Washington, D. C.

National Enquirer (1972). April 16. *J. Am. Med. Assoc.*

Newsweek (1959). Nov. 23, p. 37.

Newman, G., and Nichols, C. R. (1960). **173**, 33.

Pearlman, C. K. (1972). *Med. Aspects Hum. Sex.* **6**, 92-113.

Pfeiffer, E. (1969). *Med. Aspects Hum. Sex.* **3**, 19-28.

Pfeiffer, E., Verwoerdt, A., and Wang, H. S. (1968). *Pap., 21st Annu. Meet. Gerontol. Soc., 1968.*

Ranulf, S. (1964). "Moral Indignation and Middle Class Psychology." Schocken, New York.

Rubin, I. (1967). "Sexual Life After Sixty." New American Library, New York.

Salt Lake Tribune (1971). Dec. 12, p. 14A.

Shanas, E., and Maddox, G. L. (1976). *In* "Handbook of Aging and the Social Sciences" (R. H. Binstock and E. Shanas, eds.), pp. 592–618. Van Nostrand-Reinhold, Princeton, New Jersey.

Waitzkin, H. B., and Waterman, B. (1974). "The Explotation of Illness in Capitalist Society." Bobbs-Merrill, New York.

Wasow, M., and Loeb, M. B. (1975). *In* "Sexuality and Aging" (I. M. Burnside, ed.), pp. 35–41. Univ. of Southern California Pres, Los Angeles.

Wasow, M., and Loeb, M. B. (1978). *In* "Sexuality and Aging" (R. L. Solnick, ed.), rev. ed., pp. 154–162. Andrus Gerontology Center, University of Southern California Press, Los Angeles.

Weinberg, J. (1971). *Med. Aspects Hum. Sex.* **5**, 216–227.

Weinberg, M. S. (1969). *Med. Aspects Hum. Sex.* **3**, 66–72.

Wolpe, J. (1958). "Psychotherapy by Reciprocal Inhibition." Stanford Univ. Press, Stanford, California.

9

Range of Alternatives

Paula L. Dressel
W. Ray Avant

INTRODUCTION

The focus of this chapter is on the range of sexual orientations in the later years, along with their incidence, their contributions to social adaptation, and the particular constraints surrounding them. Of necessity, an understanding of these issues entails an examination of the concept of sexual orientation both as a theoretical construct and as an operational variable. This examination will be undertaken first. The

SEXUALITY IN THE
LATER YEARS
185

purposes of the sections on incidence, social adaptation, and constraints
are to present the available literature in each area and to critically review
it both theoretically and methodologically. With this basic review accomplished, we shall draw from it substantial directions for further inquiry,
explore the practical implications of the influence of sexualities on
programming and outreach in human services, and posit some future
concerns regarding sexual orientations and aging.

At the outset it is essential to distinguish between sexual *orientation*
and sexual *life-style*. Sexual orientation is but a single component in the
configuration of a sexual life-style. As outlined in this chapter, the
concept of orientation has been used for a number of empirical referents
but is most widely utilized to refer to the sex of one's sex partner. The
notion of a sexual life-style refers to a complex configuration of factors,
including sexual orientation, sex roles, interactional role relationships,
and the situational context in which these are played out. Thus, homosexuality, bisexuality, and heterosexuality represent alternative sexual
orientations, not alternative sexual life-styles. Given this distinction, it
follows that sexual orientations find expression within any number of
life-style forms. At the risk of cliche, then, there are hypothetically just as
many ways of being bisexual or homosexual as there are of being
heterosexual. This understanding will prove crucial as we examine and
critique the available literature.

AN OVERVIEW OF SEXUAL ORIENTATIONS

Before examining the literature on sexual orientations in the later
years, it is instructive to examine the notion of sexual orientation both
operationally and theoretically. There has been considerable ambiguity
with regard to the empirical referents of sexual orientation and ongoing
controversy with regard to its nature as either variable or constant across
the life span.

Dimensions of the Concept

The concept of sexual orientation is not unidimensional. Indeed,
sexual orientation can be determined by a number of factors (Klein, 1978,
pp. 18–19), including:

1. The sex of one's sex partner(s),
2. The sex of the subject(s) of one's erotic fantasies,

3. One's relatedness to a subculture, particularly in the instance of homosexuality,
4. Self-labeling—the orientation that one attributes to oneself,
5. The definition of others, and
6. One's emotional preference

Empirical studies have demonstrated that there are no necessary correlations between some of these dimensions (e.g., Blumstein and Schwartz, 1976a, b).

To complicate the situation even further, the concept of sexual orientation can be viewed as dynamic across the life span. Thus, one's orientation at any single point in time may or may not be one's orientation at another point in time. Sexual orientation, then, can be described as fixed, sequential, transitional, episodic, temporary, experimental, or situational (Klein, 1978, pp. 17–18). The lack of consistency in the definition of the concept of sexual orientation, as well as in the study of individuals cross-sectionally rather than longitudinally, makes the literature on sexual orientation problematic for either seeking generalizations about or comprehending the dynamic aspects of sexual orientations.

The scale that has been utilized most frequently to measure sexual orientation was developed by Kinsey *et al.* (1948). This scale, which ranges from 0 to 6, conceives of sexual orientation as a continuum from exclusive heterosexuality to exclusive homosexuality. The number on the scale assigned to a respondent is a composite score of overt behavior and psychological response. It has been suggested by Gebhard (1972) that the scale could be improved if separate scores were given for each component. The larger the difference between these two scores, it is suggested, the greater the internal conflict that may occur in the individual whose orientation is measured.

Measures on the Kinsey scale have been determined in at least two ways: by the interviewer's assignment of a rating on the scale on the basis of the respondent's answers to various structured questions, and by self-assignment of a scale location by the respondent. Yet, Blumstein and Schwartz (1976a, b), in their studies of bisexuality, have shown that self-assignment is not always consistent with one's sexual history.

The fact that sexual orientation can be defined in a number of ways has caused some writers to utilize more specific terminology for behavioral or psychological referents. Thus, for example, the term *homoerotic* (complemented by *heteroerotic*) signifies psychological response, in contrast to the terms *homosexual, bisexual* and *heterosexual*, which signify behavioral orientation with regard to the sex of one's sex partner(s). In addition, *homosocial* and *heterosocial* refer to the sex of the predominant members of one's interactional field. These latter terms have also been used to distinguish between intimate nonsexual relationships and sexual relationships.

Clearly, the state of the art in studies of sexual orientation is problematic. Yet, the literature reveals increasing interest in sexual orientation as a research topic, utilizing orientation both as an independent and as a dependent variable. This growing interest alone promises to bring improved conceptualization and operationalization. For the purposes of this chapter, sexual orientation, unless otherwise specified, will signify behavioral orientation, for the primary reason that such a conceptualization has direct referents. This choice is in no way meant to diminish the importance of the other dimensions of the concept enumerated earlier, but rather to provide uniformity of meaning in the discussion that follows.

The Nature of Sexual Orientation

One particular difficulty that is reflected in the literature on sexual orientation is the question of whether it is fixed in the early years or variable across the life span. Current research has no solid answers that would allow one or the other perspective to prevail. A variety of empirical studies document the changeability of the gender of sex partners across the life spans of many individuals (e.g., Kinsey *et al.*, 1948, 1953; Blumstein and Schwartz, 1976a, b; Bell and Weinberg, 1978; Kimmel, 1979–1980). Some might argue, however, that this variation is purely situational, temporary, a masking of one's true self, or the emergence of one's true self from previous masking.

It is not the purpose of this section to evaluate the various theories of the etiology of sexual orientation. The reader is referred to sources such as Wolff (1971), Livingood (1972), and Tripp (1975) for extensive discussions of biological, psychological, psychoanalytical, and sociological theories. Thus, both perspectives—that of orientation as being fixed in some individuals, and that of orientation as being changeable in others— can be utilized here. These two perspectives, when related to aging, focus on very different groups of individuals experiencing very different dynamic situations in their later years. The first perspective allows us to concern ourselves with the effect of aging on individuals whose ongoing sexual orientation is homosexual, bisexual, or heterosexual; the second perspective concerns us with those individuals who experience changes in their sexual orientation in their later years.

SEXUALITIES IN THE LATER YEARS

In the later years, as at other times across the life span, sexuality is expressed in various ways, and with various consequences. This section presents data to explore the incidence of homosexuality, bisexuality, and heterosexuality among older persons, examines the various orientations as they relate to social adaptation in the later years, and investigates the particular constraints that may be imposed on sexual expression in its diversity among older people.

Incidence of the Various Orientations

For a variety of reasons it is difficult to assess the relative incidence, and varying degrees of homosexual, bisexual, and heterosexual behavior among the older population. A fundamental problem is the frequent failure of sexuality studies to include older persons as subjects. Often when older subjects are included in such studies, they represent such a small part of the sample that they must be combined with other age groups for statistical analysis, or they must be discarded as a subgroup for analytical purposes. Still another difficulty is the unconscious, yet automatic, assumption by researchers that all older individuals are heterosexual. Coupled with this is the predominant study of older heterosexuals; thus, little data have been available for comparative analysis of sexual orientations in the later years.

Not the least problematic aspect of the question of incidence is the more fundamental question of how to classify respondents on the basis of their behavior. Most arguments surround the interpretation of the Kinsey scale (Kinsey *et al.*, 1948, 1953). One possible means of scale interpretation would designate the ratings from 1 to 5 on the scale to represent bisexual individuals, with the rating of 0 alone identifying heterosexuals, and 6 alone indicating homosexuals. Another possible interpretation would designate the ratings of 2 to 4, which indicate rather equally distributed tendencies, to represent bisexuality. This scheme would leave ratings 0 and 1 to signify heterosexuals, and 5 and 6 to signify homosexuals. Still another means of interpreting the Kinsey scale is to declare that rankings 1 to 6 represent homosexuals (i.e., even a single homosexual act determines that one is homosexual), with 0 alone as representative of heterosexuals.

It is curious to note that these arguments, once exclusively within the realm of methodological debate, have begun to take on ideological overtones with the emergence of social movements related to sexual orientation. Thus, Klein (1978), for example, whose data were collected from individuals at New York City's Bisexual Forum, rejects the latter scale interpretation as a promotion of the myth of the nonexistence of bisexuality.

The major sources of information regarding the relative incidence of sexual orientations are listed in Table 9.1. It should be emphasized that the data described in each source have definite sampling limitations; thus, one cannot readily generalize to the general population. Nevetheless, these data represent the best that are currently available in this area.

It is clear from this table that no reasonable estimates of the incidence of the various sexual orientations in the later years can be derived from current data. Certain persistent patterns of sexual behavior over time do emerge from these data, however. For example, among both males and females who marry, homosexual behavior is most likely to occur prior to marriage, with the highest active incidence of homosexual behavior occurring among older single individuals (Kinsey *et al.*, 1948, 1953; Hunt, 1974). In addition, among both homosexuals and heterosexuals, frequency of sexual outlet tends to decline gradually with age (Kinsey *et al.*, 1948, 1953; Christenson and Gagnon, 1965; Weinberg, 1970; Christenson and Johnson, 1973; Bell and Weinberg, 1978). The singular exception to this latter pattern seems to be black homosexual males (Bell and Weinberg, 1978, p. 281).

TABLE 9.1
Relative Incidence of Sexual Orientations

Source	Findings
Kinsey *et al.*, 1948	50% of overall male sample was exclusively heterosexual throughout adult life; 4% was exclusively homosexual; 46% engaged in both heterosexual and homosexual activities or reacted to persons of both sexes. Data are subdivided into age groups only through the age category of 46–50.
Kinsey *et al.*, 1953	72% of overall female sample was exclusively heterosexual throughout adult life; approximately 2% was exclusively homosexual; approximately 20% was distributed in the 1 to 5 ratings on the Kinsey scale. Data are subdivided into age groups only through the age category of 56–60.
Verwoerdt *et al.*, 1969	Data obtained on heterosexual behavior only.
Hunt, 1974	7% of all males and 3% of all females have had homosexual experiences during more than 3 years of their lives. Data are not grouped by age categories.

Although realistic assessments regarding the extent of homosexual, bisexual, and heterosexual behavior, or changes in orientation, among older persons cannot be made from existing data, current literature does provide a tenative picture of both the potentials for social adaptation and the constraints encountered, according to sexual orientation, in the later years.

Orientations and Social Adaptation to Aging

An issue that has engaged the attention of gerontological researchers and scholars for well over 3 decades is that of social adaptation in one's later years (Maddox and Wiley, 1976). The specific question raised here concerns the degree to which the various sexualities may or may not facilitate such adaptation. The importance to a number of older people of continued sexual interest and outlet has been documented elsewhere (e.g., Rubin, 1965; Christenson and Gagnon, 1965; Verwoerdt *et al.*, 1969; Weinberg, 1969; Pfeiffer *et al.*, 1972; Christenson and Johnson, 1973; Petersen and Payne, 1975; Silverstone and Wynter, 1975; Wilson, 1975; Butler and Lewis, 1976) and will not be discussed here. Central to the present inquiry, however, is whether the various sexual orientations entail relative advantages or disadvantages with regard to social adaptation to old age.

There are few explicit arguments in the literature stating the advantages of heterosexuality in growing old. The dearth of such discussion is probably attributable not so much to the lack of advantages as it is to two mistaken assumptions: first, that older people are generally uninterested in sex (see "Generalized Myth of Sexuality and Aging"); and, second, that, if they *are* interested in sex, they are heterosexual in orientation. Thus, there would be little need for comparative assessments of sexualities as they impact on aging. Currently, however, there is an emerging literature on homosexuality and aging that has made salient the issue of comparison. Indeed, in recent studies of aging homosexuals, a central argument proposed is that being homosexual facilitates adaptation to old age.

Table 9.2 lists the major variables that have been hypothesized or investigated with regard to sexual orientation and adaptation in the later years. Our primary interest in this section is in the relationship between sexual orientation A and adaption to aging R; however, gender B, as it combines with sexual orientation, allows distinctions to be made between homosexual males and females and heterosexual males and females, as well as between homosexual and heterosexual males and homosexual and

TABLE 9.2
Major Variables Hypothesized or Investigated Regarding the Relationship between Sexual Orientation and Adaptation to Aging

Independent variables	Intervening variables	Dependent variables
A Sexual orientation	*C* Life-style	*R* Adaptation to aging
	D Self-interest	
B Gender	*E* Self-image	
	F Opportunity for meeting partners	
	G Pool of eligible partners	
	H Social discrimination	
	I Anticipatory socialization	
	J Role consistency	
	K Development of coping strategies	
	L Sex role flexibility	
	M Extent of social network	
	N Psychological adjustment	
	O Presence of partner	
	P Accelerated aging	
	Q Extent of sex life	

heterosexual females. Additionally, the relationship between orientation and adaptation is usually posited to operate through various intervening variables *C–Q.* In Table 9.3, sources are listed that address variable relationships presented in Table 9.2. An overview of the many variable relationships and of the claims of the studies is presented in this chapter.

Anticipatory Socialization

One theme that recent literature examines is the degree to which sexual orientation, especially homosexuality, prepares one for the later years through anticipatory socialization. Thus, Francher and Henkin (1973, p. 673), in an analysis of the life histories of 10 homosexual men over the age of 50, conclude that adjustment to homosexuality "implies an early coping with the problems of loneliness and alienation" thereby providing anticipatory socialization for aging. The path of variables plotted is that of sexual orientation *A*→development of coping strategies *K* and anticipatory socialization *I*→adaptation to aging *R.* A similar argument is offered by Friend (1980) in a study of 43 self-identified older

TABLE 9.3
Literature Examining the Relationship
between Sexual Orientation and Adaptation to Aging

Relationships among variables in Table 9.2	Sources examining the relationships
A—C—I	Bell and Weinberg, 1978 (males, females)
A—C—I—R	Kimmel, 1979–1980 (males)
A—C—J	Bell and Weinberg, 1978 (males, females)
A—C—M	Bell and Weinberg, 1978 (males, females)
A—C—M—N	Bell and Weinberg, 1978 (males, females)
A—C—M,N—R	Weinberg, 1970 (males)
A—C—M—O—R	Laner, 1979 (females); Raphael and Robinson, 1980 (females)
A—C,E—M	Raphael and Robinson, 1980 (females)
A—H—R	Kelly, 1977 (males)
A—I,K—R	Francher and Henkin, 1973 (males); Friend, 1980 (males)
A—J—R	Francher and Henkin, 1973 (males); Laner, 1978 (males); Kimmel, 1979–1980 (males)
A—L—R	Kimmel, 1979–1980 (males); Friend, 1980 (males)
A—M	Friend, 1980 (males)
A—M—N	Berger, 1980 (males)
A—O—Q—R	Kelly, 1977 (males); Berger, 1980 (males)
A,B—C—M—R	Gagnon and Simon, 1973 (males)
A,B—D—K—R	Francher and Henkin, 1973 (males); Friend, 1980 (males)
A,B—E—R	Gagnon and Simon, 1973 (males); Laner, 1979, (females); Berger, 1980 (males)
A,B—F—O	Nyberg, 1976 (males, females)
A,B—G	Laner, 1979 (females)
A,B—G—O	Treas and Van Hilst, 1976 (males, females)
A,B—O—Q	Pfeiffer and Davis, 1972 (females)
A,B—P—R	Kelly, 1977 (males); Minnigerode, 1976 (males); Friend, 1980 (males); Laner, 1978 (males); Laner, 1979 (females)

gay men. Friend maintains that the coming-out process results in the development of crisis competence for future stressful situations. Kimmel (1979–1980) makes a similar argument, but his relationship of variables is sexual orientation A→life-style C→anticipatory socialization I→adaptation to aging R. The life histories of 14 aging gay men provide the data on which Kimmel bases the conclusion that earlier experiences of living alone provide anticipatory socialization to old age. Data from Bell and Weinberg's (1978) massive study of male and female homosexual life-styles makes the point strongly that in the pattern, sexual orientation A→life-style C→anticipatory socialization I, life-style is a stronger predictor than is sexual orientation. In other words, it is the particular role configuration in which one plays out his or her close relationships (regardless of the sex of one's partner) that is most strongly related to anticipatory socialization. Only insofar as different sexual orientations promote specific life-styles does the relationship between orientation and anticipatory socialization persist.

Role Consistency

A second predominant theme in the literature is the grouping sexual orientation $A \rightarrow$ role consistency $J \rightarrow$ adaptation to aging R. Kimmel (1979–1980), Francher and Henkin (1973), and Laner's study (1978) of advertisements for partners by male homosexuals and heterosexuals concludes that aging homosexual men have greater role consistency from middle age to the later years because of a lack of family responsibilities and a lack of subsequent role loss. Presumably, the same statement could be made about aging lesbians. However, this analysis fails to take into account the fact that some homosexuals marry persons of the other sex and have children. Additionally, other homosexuals live in family-like arrangements that may be accompanied by traumatic role loss. Thus, the path that Bell and Weinberg (1978) posit, sexual orientation $A \rightarrow$ life-style $C \rightarrow$ role consistency J, perhaps specifies the variable relationships more adequately.

Social Networks in Adaptation to Aging

Closely related to the discussion of role consistency is the function of social networks in adaptation to aging. Gagnon and Simon's (1973) contention that heterosexual males have advantages in aging because of children and wives who act as sources of support (sexual orientation A and gender $B \rightarrow$ life-style $C \rightarrow$ extent of social network $M \rightarrow$ adaptation to aging R) has been challenged by recent empirical studies. Although Schroder's (1981) article is not aging-related and includes only hetero-sexual relationships, it does lend support to the opinion that life-style ("social style") impacts the degree of satisfaction experienced in couple relationships. Social styles, he says, reflect the expression of the major needs and need-gratifying methods of the individual. Again, data from Bell and Weinberg (1978) demonstrate the importance of life-style over and above orientation in predicting the extent of social networks $(A \rightarrow C \rightarrow M)$. By identifying the five major life-styles of their homosexual male and female respondents, Bell and Weinberg (1978) are able to show a range of ways of being homosexual and ways in which the various life-styles impact on social activities. Kelly (1977) notes that none of his gay male respondents over the age of 65 had disengaged from activities in the gay subculture. Further, Friend (1980) reports that in his sample, there existed a net gain in support systems of gay males, who supplemented family supports with friendship networks. In addition, Berger (1980), who studied a convenience sample of 112 homosexual males ages 40 and older, reports a positive significant relationship between integration into the gay community and psychological adjustment $(A \rightarrow M \rightarrow N)$. Weinberg (1970) found that the older male homosexuals in his study had less association with other gays than did the younger homosexual respondents; however he also found a strong positive relationship between the age of the respondent and psychological adjustment $(A \rightarrow C \rightarrow M,N \rightarrow R)$.

With regard to lesbians, Raphael and Robinson's (1980) study of 20 women between the ages of 50 and 73 noted that the extent and nature of social networks is mediated by factors such as life-style and openness about one's sexual orientation, which has changed historically $(A \rightarrow C, E \rightarrow M)$.

Bell and Weinberg (1978) discuss the relationships between sexual orientation, life-style, social networks, and psychological adjustment $(A \rightarrow C \rightarrow M \rightarrow N)$. In interviews with 979 homosexuals and 477 heterosexuals of all ages in the San Francisco area, they found that homosexual respondents, both men and women, were more likely to have more close friends than their heterosexual counterparts. On the other hand, heterosexual men and women were more likely to be involved in family commitments. The main difference in these social networks is that contact with family members allows greater opportunity for intergenerational interaction, whereas friendships are more likely to be established with one's peers. Nevertheless, although older homosexuals may utilize social networks for their support systems that differ from those of older heterosexuals, it does not seem reasonable to conclude that aging homosexuals are more likely than aging heterosexuals to be lonely and isolated.

An elaborate variable relationship regarding the role of social networks can be derived from Laner's (1979) study of advertisements for partners by homosexual and heterosexual females. Sexual orientation A appears to operate through life-style C to affect the extent of one's social network M. The extent of the social network, in turn, is positively related to the presence of a partner O, perhaps with a negative relationship between the two variables when the presence of a partner impacts on the extent of the social network. (Such a finding appeared in Raphael and Robinson, 1980). Presence of a partner, O, in turn, is positively related to adaptation to aging R $(A \rightarrow C \rightarrow M \rightarrow O \rightarrow R)$.

According to Nyberg (1976), there are differences between gay males and females in the variables involved in the presence of a partner. Thus, sexual orientation and gender combine to affect the opportunity for meeting a partner and, ultimately, the presence of a partner $(A,B \rightarrow F \rightarrow O)$. Nyberg claims that the subculture of the gay community is much more facilitative and important for lesbians in meeting a partner than it is for gay men.

Pool of Eligible Partners

Another stream of variables that focuses on the presence of a partner is that which examines the pool of eligible partners. Laner's (1979) study posits a relationship between sexual orientation and gender and the pool of eligibles $(A,B \rightarrow G)$. According to her study, the pool of eligibles is less constricted for lesbians than it is for heterosexual women because heterosexual women adhere to societal standards regarding the appropriate age of one's partner—a standard that is not evident among lesbians. The unbalanced ratio between older men and women, along with older heterosexual men's tendency to marry younger women, constricts the pool of eligibles for older heterosexual women, thereby leading to lower rates of marriage and remarriage for this group (Treas and Van Hilst, 1976) $(A,B \rightarrow G \rightarrow O)$. Finally, Kelly (1977) describes an interesting relationship: sexual orientation $A \rightarrow$ presence of a partner $O \rightarrow$ the extent of one's sex life $Q \rightarrow$ adaptation to aging R. Despite the fact that many of Kelly's older gay male respondents were not involved in an ongoing relationship of a year or more, they characteristically reported quite satisfactory sex lives.

This is generally not the case for heterosexual women, however. It is reported that "the extent of an aging [heterosexual] woman's sexual activity and interest depends heavily upon the availability to her of a societally sanctioned, sexually capable partner" (Pfeiffer and Davis, 1972, p. 158) $(A,B \rightarrow O \rightarrow Q)$. Even among those older women who are married, "the husband [is] the determining factor in the cessation of sexual intercourse" (Pfeiffer et al., 1968, p. 758), with women evidencing little indication of any aging in their sexual capabilities until very late in life.

Accelerated Aging and Adaptation

Another major theme in the literature of adapation to aging according to sexual orientation is the question of accelerated aging. The popular myth is that gay men particularly experience an early crisis of aging (Gagnon and Simon, 1973) $(A,B \rightarrow P \rightarrow R)$. Friend's (1980) self-identified "older" gay male sample lends some support to this argument. In his study, 39 of the 43 respondents who labeled themselves "older" were below the age of 64, with a mean sample age of 48 years. Kelly's (1977) gay male respondents, on the average, viewed the onset of old age as being around 50, which is somewhat later chronologically than the claim of Gagnon and Simon (1973). Minnigerode (1976), whose sample included 95 gay men between the ages of 25 and 68, found no substantial difference between his respondents' designations of middle age and old age and the responses obtained by Neugarten et al. (1965) in their middle-aged sample from the general population. Moreover, Laner's companion studies of males and females (1978, 1979) found no evidence of accelerated aging among gay men and women.

Self-Image and Sexual Orientation

A related topic is that of one's self-image with regard to aging and sexual orientation. Gagnon and Simon (1973) maintain that the emphasis on youth by the gay subculture causes a crisis for gay men with regard to adaptation to aging $(A,B \rightarrow E \rightarrow R)$. On the other hand, Laner (1979) states that lesbians are not subject to the double standard of aging and attractiveness (Sontag, 1972) faced by heterosexual women in relation to men. This would allow the older lesbian advantage over her heterosexual counterpart in adapation to aging. In fact, Raphael and Robinson (1980) note that older lesbians prefer and seek out other older women as partners.

The other variable relationships identified in Table 9.3 have been addressed by only one or two studies to date and will be discussed here only because they offer additional hypotheses for future research.

1. Kimmel (1979–1980) and Friend (1980) claim that being homosexual allows sex-role flexibility, thereby facilitating adaptation to aging $(A \rightarrow L \rightarrow R)$.

2. Francher and Henkin (1973) and Friend (1980) describe the gay

male subculture as encouraging self-interest and narcissism, which offer support in coping with many aspects of aging $(A,B \rightarrow D \rightarrow K \rightarrow R)$.

3. Kelly (1977) enumerates various forms of social discrimination experienced specifically by homosexuals in later life, making adjustment to various facets of aging problematic $(A \rightarrow H \rightarrow R)$.

It must be noted that, to date, the limited literature on bisexuality has not explored the impacts of aging on bisexuals or the relative advantages and disadvantages of being bisexual in the later years. This, coupled with the nature of this section as a review of available research, accounts for the exclusion of bisexuality in the present discussion. The authors hope that such exclusion does not fan the flames of controversy surrounding the myth of the nonexistence of bisexuality.

Some qualification of the preceding arguments is necessary before we examine the constraints on sexualities in later life. First, it must be cautioned that not all studies cited actually tested the hypotheses that have been derived from them in this chapter. In some cases we have taken liberty to infer from the findings presented certain causal relationships that were not articulated by the authors, but were suggested by their data. Second, we have employed summary variables as organizers of the material in this chapter with full realization that they are operationalized in various ways across the literature. Third, the bulk of empirical studies reported here employ, virtually of necessity, convenience samples, the findings from which may not be generalizable. Fourth, it is difficult to make comparative statements about groups of elders according to sex and sexual orientation because (a) most data are not categorized in such a fashion, and (b) those that are tend to examine only a single group. Thus, the arguments in this chapter must be viewed as tentative at best.

The foregoing overview of issues in the literature regarding the relative adaptabilities of aging homosexuals and heterosexuals necessitates an examination of the concomitant constraints experienced by those older persons expressing variant sexual orientations. Only from an examination of combined potentials and problems can an adequate view of aging and sexual orientation be derived.

CONSTRAINTS ON SEXUALITIES IN THE LATER YEARS

Despite the growing attention given sexuality in the later years, constraints persist to check, restrain, or inhibit sexual expressiveness on the part of older persons. The constraints that will be explored here are the generalized myth of sexuality in the later years and specific restrictions on various orientations through values, regulations, and demographic imbalance.

Generalized Myth of Sexuality and Aging

One such constraint is the mythological perception of old age as the sexless years. It is incorrectly supposed that the older person, regardless of sexual orientation, is neither interested in sex nor sexually active. A recent unpublished paper (Corby and Brecher, 1981) describes a survey of a nationwide sample of middle- and upper-class Americans over 50 years of age to determine the nature and extent of their sexual and affectional interests and activities and to assess the factors that influence them. Among the 1845 women, 91% indicated present sexual interest, 84% reported that they were currently coitally active, and 14% revealed an increase in sexual interest since age 40. In addition, three major research studies clearly document the importance of sexuality to older persons: Kinsey *et al.* (1948, 1953), Masters and Johnson (1966), and the Duke University Longitudinal Studies (Newman and Nichols, 1960; Pfeiffer *et al.*, 1968, 1972; Verwoerdt *et al.*, 1969; Pfeiffer and Davis, 1972). Of these three major studies, Kinsey's alone addresses the sexual orientation of homosexuality. A comparative analysis of these studies reveals consistent themes regarding the sexuality of older persons (Avant, 1976). In addition, more recent case studies from institutions (Pease, 1974; Silverstone and Wynter, 1975; Miller *et al.*, 1975), along with initial studies of homosexual men and women (Weinberg, 1970; Wolff, 1971; Francher and Henkin, 1973; Lee, 1976; Kelly, 1977; Bell and Weinberg, 1978; Laner, 1979; Kimmel, 1979–1980; Raphael and Robinson, 1980), support these themes:

1. In the presence of reasonably good health and available partners, sexual activity among older people continues into the seventh, eighth, and ninth decades. Among those who are no longer sexually active, it is not uncommon to find a continuation of sexual interest.

2. Within the older age group, the range of sexual drive varies from very great to very little. Sexual capacity varies from individual to individual and from time to time in a particular individual.

3. There is an overall pattern of decline in sexual interest and activity with advancing age. However, sexuality continues to hold a place of importance in the lives of most older persons. Although there is a gradual decrease in sexual activity and interest, there is definitely no sudden cessation at any fixed chronological point.

4. Among older men and women, sexual interest and activity are directly related to individual sexual histories. The sociosexual environment of the sexually formative years, past sexual habits, and former sexual experience all strongly correlate with sexuality in old age. Those who describe their sexual urges as strongest in youth tend to describe them as moderate in old age. Those who describe their sexual feelings in youth as weak to moderate describe themselves as being without sexual feelings in old age.

5. The maintenance of sexual capacity and activity is dependent upon the opportunity for regular sexual expression. A willing and cooperative partner is essential to continued sexual activity.

Particularized Constraints on Various Orientations

Coupled with the myth of sexless old age are certain particularized constraints, including public attitudes and values, social regulations, and demographic imbalance.

Public Attitudes and Values

Behavioral expectations and social sanctions stem from the dominant cultural values held by members of society. In American culture, certain of these values and resulting attitudes act as constraints on perceptions of sexual attractiveness in the later years as well as on nontraditional sexual life-styles and orientations across the life span.

Throughout social gerontological literature, the value placed on youth and physical attractiveness has been recognized as a cause of the denigration and devaluation of older people. An overriding assumption, adopted by society at large, including many older persons, is that loss of youth entails loss of attractiveness and sex appeal (see, e.g., Bell and Weinberg, 1978, p. 103). This belief has been documented by a number of studies related to sexuality in the later years, most of which have focused predominantly on heterosexuality. Studies involving older homosexual men and women now reveal that youth may be a dominant value within those subcultures as well. However, the homosexual male subculture appears to value youthfulness more than the lesbian subculture does (Bell and Weinberg, 1978, p. 105; Raphael and Robinson, 1980).

Older persons generally encounter these prejudices regardless of sexual orientation; however, differences are noticeable among heterosexuals and homosexuals. Sontag (1972) describes a double standard experienced by older women that defines them as less attractive and less sexually appealing than older men. There is no indication that she considered women of different sexual orientations. However, within the homosexual subcultures the reverse appears to hold. Youthfulness may be more valued among homosexual males than it is among females, which results in the constraint of a double standard of age and attractiveness for homosexual males not unlike that which exists for heterosexual females (Francher and Henkin, 1973; Goldberg, 1977; Bell and Weinberg, 1978; Raphael and Robinson, 1980).

In addition to varying constraints related to age and presumed sexual attractiveness, constraints also exist with regard to life-style issues. In American society, heterosexual monogamy is a dominant cultural value. Weis (1976) found little or no change in American attitudes toward extramarital sex during the last few decades. He found that approximately 70% of contemporary Americans disapprove of all extramarital sexual relations, and that nearly one-half of those remaining believe that extramarital relations are almost always wrong. Of specific relevance to the issue of sexuality in the later years is the finding that increasing age is associated with support for the traditional norm (Weis, 1976; Klemmack and Roff, 1980). In light of the demographic imbalance among older men and women, particular concern may arise from the indication that older females are the most likely age–sex group to support the traditional norm against extramarital sex (Weis, 1976; Snyder and Spreitzer, 1976). Moreover, there is an indication that within heterosexual monogamy, coitus is the norm for sexual expression, with a predominant negative attitude toward alternative sexual activity (Wilson, 1975). The limited data available suggest that monogamy, or at least serial monogamy, is a preferred life-style among homosexual males and females.

In heterosexual marriage and mate selection, the acceptable norm is for men to select and/or marry women who are younger than themselves and for women to select and/or marry older men. This is found to carry over into the later years. In an examination of mate selection through mail order magazines, Jedlika (1978) found that older men preferred women who were from 1 to 7 years younger than themselves, and that older women preferred men who were from 4 to 10 years older than themselves. This, of course, results in greater constraint for older heterosexual women than for older heterosexual men, given the differential mortality rates of men and women.

Heterosexual monogamy is established as a dominant cultural value in our society; it is similarly observable that, in terms of sexual orientation, heterosexuality is the dominant value (Reiss, 1981; Ludeman, 1981). Until recently, study and research in human sexuality focused predomi-

nantly on heterosexuality, to the near exclusion of other sexual orientations. This appears especially to have been the case with sexuality in the
later years. As mentioned earlier, it has often been assumed that the
sexual orientation of all older persons is heterosexual. The obvious
consequence of the valuation of heterosexuality is a predominant negative attitude toward other sexual orientations, which results in ignoring
them altogether, identifying them as aberrant behavior, and/or declaring
them to be taboo. On the basis of a 1974 sample of National Opinion
Research Center (NORC) data, Nyberg and Alston (1977) found that the
percentage of respondents (72%) believing homosexual behavior to be
always wrong did not change between 1970 and 1977. Although variables
other than age may be involved, older people tend to be more disapproving of homosexual behavior (Nyberg and Alston, 1977). However, variables and correlates other than age may produce that effect (Wilson, 1975;
Snyder and Spreitzer, 1976; Willits et al., 1977; Nyberg and Alston, 1977).
Although it may be argued that generally conservatism does not increase
with advancing age, there is some evidence that sexual conservatism may
be a mark of the later years (Wilson, 1975; Snyder and Spreitzer, 1976;
Weis, 1976). The important question, however, is whether such conservatism or traditionalism is an aging, period, or cohort effect. It is beyond the
scope of this chapter, or the aforementioned cross-sectional studies, to
deal with that question. Currently it can be argued that sexual traditionalism does exist among the general population, particularly among older
persons. Such conservatism can operate to constrain nontraditional
sexual life-styles or orientations. The result may be suppression of
sexuality among some older people (Jedlika, 1978; Weinberg, 1969),
sexual conflict within families and between generations (Miller et al.,
1975), and inappropriate and seemingly bizarre sexual expression
(Weinberg, 1969).

While looking at present attitudes among the general population and
among older persons, one might consider future changes in values and
attitudes. If today's older generation subscribes to sexual conservatism,
what may be expected of future generations? Realizing that age alone as a
variable may be insufficient to predict sexual attitudes (e.g., Snyder and
Spreitzer, 1976), let us nevertheless examine what various researchers
argue regarding subsequent cohorts of elders. Within that literature there
appears to be considerable disagreement regarding expectations of future
changes in sexual attitudes. Wilson (1975) and Klemmack and Roff
(1980) suggest that we may expect a liberalization in society's orientation
toward sexual life-styles in the future. Bell and Weinberg (1978) list
indicators of what may be seen as promises of change in the direction of a

more liberal attitude toward homosexuality; however, Nyberg and Alston (1977) discourage the anticipation of a more tolerant attitude toward homosexuality. Finally, Treas and Van Hilst (1976) see little reason to expect changes in values and attitudes that might allow for late-life heterosexual marriages to rise above their present low levels.

Social Regulations

There are still other constraints on sexualities in the later years in the forms of laws, policies, and practices. Reports have documented restrictive legislation regarding private behavior among consenting adults and institutional policies that neglect the needs for privacy, intimacy, and sexual expression among patients and residents (Dressel and Avant, 1978). Treas and Van Hilst (1976) have pointed to social pressures against marriage and remarriage in old age, particularly on the part of offspring. Kelly (1977) has outlined numerous unique discriminations in policy, such as inheritance difficulties, experienced by older homosexuals. Such social regulations, formal and informal, serve to constrain individuals who would violate traditional societal expectations regarding sexual expression and orientation.

Despite the operation of such constraints, there are some indications that social policies may be changing, albeit slowly. Recent successful court challenges relate to "palimony" and to child custody for homosexual parents (e.g., Atlanta Journal–Constitution, 1978) suggest that judicial agents may be coming to view with greater latitude those intimate arrangements considered to be acceptable and legitimate within certain segments of society.

Demographic Imbalance

Older heterosexuals find themselves faced with demographic imbalance with regard to sex and marital status (Dressel and Avant, 1978). Women tend to live longer than men do, and they tend to marry older men; as a result, women over age 65 outnumber men over 65, and the sex ratio of men to women decreases with advancing age. Marriage and remarriage rates among older people present a major problem for that population, especially for older women. Treas and Van Hilst (1976) report that although more older people are marrying today, due to the growth of the population, the propensity of older people to marry remains low. There were 60,000 marriages among the elderly in 1970, but that represented only 3 of every 1,000 older, single women and 17 of every 1,000 older, single men. The U. S. Bureau of the Census (1981, Table 1) reported that in 1980, single women outnumbered single men 65 and over three to two; for the 85 and over age group, women outnumbered men three to one. Added to this is the fact that older men are six times more likely to marry than are older women. Such situational character-istics function as constraints on heterosexual life-styles in the later years. For older lesbians, however, no such problem exists.

In summary, both older homosexuals and older heterosexuals experi-ence various constraints on their sexualities through certain predominant social values, the expression of these values in formal and informal regulations, and demographic imbalance in the sex ratio in later life. It is not accurate to maintain that any one sexual category of older persons is more or less constrained than another. First, it is necessary to recognize that both aging heterosexuals and homosexuals experience constraints on their sexual expression. In addition, the great diversity of role relation-ships, means of expressiveness, and self-images within categories of sexualities are differentially affected by the various constraints men-tioned in this section.

IMPLICATIONS OF THE REVIEW

Given this overview of the literature on sexual orientation and aging, as well as other related literature, certain general statements can be made that will facilitate future investigation in this area and aid practitioners in the field of aging.

Much of the aforementioned literature provides data that strongly question popular beliefs and images of heterosexuality as well as homo-sexuality. The general assumptions that heterosexuals, if only because of their more culturally accepted sexual orientation, find adaptation to aging an easier process and are less constrained in the expression of their sexualities can no longer be taken at face value. Claims regarding the relative ability of various groups of individuals to adapt to old age, as well as claims regarding the degree of proscriptions on certain categories of persons, must be based on empirical evidence rather than folk wisdom.

In this regard, available literature tends to indicate that *life-style may be a far more important predictor of adaptation to aging than the variable of sexual orientation. Similarly, life-style may be equal in importance with sexual orientation in the determination of constraints on sexual expressive-ness in the later years.* These findings lend credence to the claim of diversity among older people, whatever their sexual orientation, and destroy the simplistic arguments for the superiority of one orientation over another.

Despite the fact that there is a growing research interest in sexuality and aging, *the studies reported here, for the most part, lack comparability.* However, comparability is essential in order for generalizations to emerge and for more specified research to be conducted with regard to the generalizations. Although the current lack of a representative sample of older homosexuals and, by implication, of older heterosexuals, may persist, comparability can nevertheless be achieved in areas such as the designation of intervening, dependent, and control variables and the operationalization of those variables. The present literature is diffuse in focus; this reflects the relative newness of interest in the area of study. There are gaps to be filled (both theoretical and methodological), replications to be undertaken, group comparisons to be done, and refinements of variable relationships to be made.

It was noted earlier that sexual orientation would be viewed in this chapter as fixed in some individuals and variable across the life span in others. We have no knowledge of literature on the latter topic, despite the fact that such studies would tap very different situational dynamics than those reported earlier in the sections on adaptations and constraints. Moreover, we have no awareness of work on bisexuality in the later years. It is only very recently that bisexuality has emerged as a research topic for social scientists. Also, as is usually the case, studies in many areas of human sexuality focus only belatedly on older people as research subjects. Here, then, are two topical areas that are ripe for investigation.

Imperfect as our knowledge of sexual orientation and aging is, we can nevertheless conclude that since sexual orientation operates through a multiplicity of other variables, *intervention strategies to alleviate constraints on expressiveness and promote adaptation to aging must be multifaceted,* recognizing diversity within sexual categories of older people. Some issues affect all sexual categories of older people by virtue of the fact of their age alone (e.g., the generalized myth of sexuality and aging). Other issues affect some sexual categories, but not others, because of discrimination on the basis of sexual orientation [e.g., Kelly's (1977) enumeration of discriminatory social policies regarding older homosexuals]. Still other issues affect certain persons across sexual categories because of common life situations (e.g., the adequacy of social supports for older single people, both heterosexual and homosexual).

What does the future hold regarding sexual orientations and aging? If available data are accurate, *we should not expect a significant change in the* incidence of sexualities in future aged cohorts (Hunt, 1974), despite the increased visibility of homosexuality in American society. It has already been mentioned that *researchers hold differing opinions on the possibility of liberalization of sexual attitudes and values* (Wilson, 1975; Treas and Van Hilst, 1976; Nyberg and Alston, 1977; Bell and Weinberg, 1978); as a result, a definitive statement is not forthcoming in that area. It does appear to be the case, however, that *the topic of sexual orientation and aging is emerging as a viable and fertile area of investigation.* This should lead to an improvement in our understanding of the complexity of the topic. In that regard, it is hoped that the consolidation and critical review of studies in this chapter will motivate others to make the next effort in addressing the research needs highlighted here.

REFERENCES

Atlanta Journal-Constitution (1978). "Lesbian Mom Given Custody of Two Children," Oct. 22.

Avant, W. R. (1976). "Sexuality and Older Persons" (unpublished).

Bell, A. P., and Weinberg, M. S. (1978). "Homosexualities." Simon & Schuster, New York.

Bell, R. R. (1971). "Social Deviance." Dorsey Press, Homewood, Illinois.

Berger, R. M. (1980). *J. Homosexuality* **5**, 161-175.

Blumstein, P. W., and Schwartz, P. (1976a). *Urban Life* **5**, 339-358.

Blumstein, P. W., and Schwartz, P. (1976b). *Arch. Sex. Behav.* **5**, 171-181.

Butler, R. N., and Lewis, M. I. (1976). "Sex After Sixty." Harper & Row, New York.

Christenson, C. V., and Gagnon, J. H. (1965). *J. Gerontol.* **20**, 351-356.

Christenson, C. V., and Johnson, A. B. (1973). *J. Geriatr. Psychiatry* **6**, 80-98.

Corby, N., and Brecher, E. (1981). *Pap., 34th Annu. Sci. Meet. Gerontol. Soc. Am., 1981.*

Dressel, P. L., and Avant, W. R. (1978). *Alternative Lifestyles* **1**, 13-36.

Francher, J. S., and Henkin, J. (1973). *Am. J. Orthopsychiatry* **43**, 670-674.

Friend, R. A. (1980). *Alternative Lifestyles* **3**, 231-248.

Gagnon, J. H., and Simon, W. (1973). "Sexual Conduct: The Social Source of Human Sexuality." Aldine, Chicago.

Gebhard, P. H. (1972). *In* "National Institute of Mental Health Task Force on Homosexuality: Final Report and Background Papers" (J. M. Livingood, ed.), pp. 22-29. U.S. Govt. Printing Office, Washington, D.C.

Goldberg, R. (1977). *Gay News* July, pp. 18-20.

Hunt, M. (1974). "Sexual Behavior in the 1970's" Dell Publ., New York.

Jedlika, D. (1978). *Fam. Coordin.* **27**, 137-140.

Kelly, J. (1977). *Gerontologist* **17**, 328-332.

Kimmel, D. C. (1979-1980). *Int. J. Aging Hum. Dev.* **10**, 239-248.

Kinsey, A. C., Pomeroy, W. B., and Martin, C. E. (1948). "Sexual Behavior in the Human Male." Saunders, Philadelphia.

Kinsey, A. C., Pomeroy, W. B., Martin, C. E., and Gebhard, P. E. (1953). "Sexual Behavior in the Human Female." Saunders, Philadelphia.

Klein, F. M. (1978). "The Bisexual Option." Arbor House, New York.

Klemmack, D. L., and Roff, L. L. (1980). *Alternative Lifestyles* **3**, 137–148.

Laner, M. R. (1978). *Gerontologist* **18**, 496–501.

Laner, M. R. (1979). *J. Homosexuality* **4**, 267–275.

Lee, J. A. (1976). *J. Homosexuality* **1**, 401–418.

Livingood, J. M., ed. (1972). "National Institute of Mental Health Task Force on Homo-sexuality: Final Report and Background Papers." U.S. Govt. Printing Office, Washington, D.C.

Ludeman, K. (1981). *Gerontologist* **21**, 203–208.

Maddox, G., and Wiley, J. (1976). *In* "Handbook of Aging and the Social Sciences" (R. H. Binstock and E. Shanas, eds.), pp. 3–34. Van Nostrand-Reinhold, Princeton, New Jersey.

Masters, W. H., and Johnson, V. E. (1966). "Human Sexual Response." Little, Brown, Boston.

Miller, M. B., Bernstein, H., and Sharkey, H. (1975). *Gerontologist* **15**, 291–296.

Minnigerode, F. A. (1976). *J. Homosexuality* **1**, 273–276.

Neugarten, B. L., Moore, J. M., and Lowe, J. C. (1965). *Am. J. Sociol.* **70**, 710–717.

Newman, G., and Nichols, C. R. (1960). *J. Am. Med. Assoc.* **173**, 33–35, reprinted in Palmore (1970).

Nyberg, K. (1976). *J. Homosexuality* **2**, 29–38.

Nyberg, K. L., and Alston, J. P. (1976–1977). *J. Homosexuality* **2**, 99–107.

Palmore, E., ed. (1970). "Normal Aging." Duke Univ. Press, Durham, North Carolina.

Palmore, E., ed. (1974). "Normal Aging II." Duke Univ. Press, Durham, North Carolina.

Pease, R. (1974). *Gerontologist* **14**, 153–157.

Petersen, J. A., and Payne, B. (1975). "Love in the Later Years." Association Press, New York.

Pfeiffer, E., and Davis, G. C. (1972). *J. Am. Geriatr. Soc.* **20**, 151–158; reprinted in Palmore (1974).

Pfeiffer, E., Verwoerdt, A., and Wang, H. S. (1968). *Arch. Gen Psychiatry* **19**, 756–758; reprinted in Palmore (1974).

Pfeiffer, E., Verwoerdt, A., and Davis, G. C. (1972). *Am. J. Psychiatry* **128**, 1262–1267; reprinted in Palmore (1974).

Raphael, S. M., and Robinson, M. K. (1980). *Alternative Lifestyles* **3**, 207–229.

Reiss, I. (1981). *J. Marriage Fam.* **43**, 271–283.

Rubin, I. (1965). "Sexual Life After Sixty." Basic Books, New York.

Silverstone, B., and Wynter, L. (1975). *Gerontologist* **15**, 83–87.

Schroder, K. H. (1981). *Am. J. Fam. Therapy* **9**, 65–74.

Snyder, E. E., and Spreitzer, E. (1976). *Arch. Sex. Behav.* **5**, 249–254.

Sontag, S. (1972). *Saturday Rev.* **55**, 29–38.

Treas, J., and Van Hilst, A. (1976). *Gerontologist* **16**, 132–136.

Tripp, C. A. (1975). "The Homosexual Matrix." Signet, New York.

U. S. Bureau of the Census (1981). "Age, Sex, Race and Spanish Origin of the Population by Region, Division and State: 1980." U. S. Govt. Printing Office, Washington, D. C.

Verwoerdt, A., Pfeiffer, E., and Wang, H. S. (1969). *Geriatrics* **24**, 137–154; reprinted in Palmore (1970).

Weinberg, J. (1969). *Am. J. Psychiatry* **126**, 713–716.

Weinberg, M. S. (1970). *Soc. Probl.* **17**, 527–537.

Weis, D. L. (1976). *Annu. Meet. Natl. Counc. Fam. Relations, 1976.*

Willits, F. K., Bealer, R. C., and Crider, D. M. (1977). *J. Gerontol.* **32**, 681–688.

Wilson, W. C. (1975). *J. Sex Res.* **32**, 681–688.

Wolff, C. (1979). "Bisexuality: A Study" (Rev. ed.). Quartet Books, New York.

PART **III**

ISSUES IN RESEARCH AND THERAPY

10

Research: Status, Gaps, and Design

Alex Finkle

INTRODUCTION

Prior to the studies of Kinsey and colleagues (1948, 1953), evaluations of human sexual behavior were sporadic and lacked a systematic approach, despite the pioneering work of H. Ellis (1910) and A. Ellis (1979). Kinsey's group evolved a standardized format for eliciting information from both men and women. Questions including 521 items were posed in appropriate terminology so that the interviewers could better relate to the interviewees (e.g., southern prostitutes, male prisoners). In this manner, rapport was established, forthright replies were anticipated, and salient answers were most likely to be given.

SEXUALITY IN THE
LATER YEARS

211

CURRENT DEVELOPMENTS

One-to-one interviewing has been and remains the most effective technique used in obtaining information about sexual activity, as opposed to written questionnaires and reviews of medical records and gynecologic examinations, which were customary prior to Kinsey's studies (Kinsey *et al.*, 1948, 1953). Since it is to be expected that aging persons who consent to be questioned will be more alert and communicative than many of their peers, it is assumed that their replies will generate data of slanted quality and quantity (Masters and Johnson, 1968; Palmore and Kivett, 1977). Nevertheless, skilled interviewers can revise questions as they go, or subtly interject the same question later in the conversation in a way that will lend validity to the data that will subsequently be aggregated. I do not recommend any format exclusively. Effective questionnaires should include age, race, religion, education and occupation, marital status, and sexual history. In the case of married persons, items should include questions regarding the number and duration of marriages, whether marriages ended in divorce or death, present residence (private, institutional, or retirement center), sexual interests, opportunities and performance of at least the preceding year, age of partner, the location of sexual activity, and so on. Cooper (1972) offers a detailed list of essential questions for such interviews.

Recently, from the 1960s on, studies of older persons in the United States have disclosed that sexual interest and competency are not entirely limited by biological age, although they gradually falter during the eighth decade. In the case of a couple, declining potency often ends attempts at sexual intercourse, although women may indeed retain their sexual drive longer than men do. For either sex, an available, willing partner is the best encouragement to continue sexual activity. Older married persons and couples (married and unmarried) have been the subjects of reports by many researchers, such as Berezin (1976), Comfort (1977), Finkle (1976), Kaplan (1974), Masters and Johnson (1968), Pfeiffer (1974), and Rubin (1968), to mention but a few.

It is unlikely that efforts will be made to identify quantity and quality of sexual performances photographically, since Masters and Johnson (1968) have already used this research method. Despite the current spate of pornography (Henderson, 1979), it is improbable that the lay public will consider such visual methods to be of scientific value. Clearly, the interview is the vital first step in gathering information on human sexuality. Objective scientific studies, such as the measurement of penile erections during sleep (Karacan 1978; Karacan *et al.*, 1978), penile plethysmography (Barry and Hodges, 1978), radiographic and temperature recording of the penis (Michal and Popsichal, 1978), and other neurovascular studies (Zorgniotti, 1979), must follow an interview carried out in a way that is conducive to later acceptance by the subject of a scientific evaluation.

DATA COLLECTION

Attitudinal Ambience

Most interviewers who gather information on the sexuality of the aged are younger than the subjects they interview. Thus, the perspective of the interviewer can be very different from that of the subject (Snyder and Spreitzer, 1976). Whereas discussion of (much less participation in) sexual activity was rarely approached openly and was often considered "dirty" as recently as one generation ago, this is certainly not true at this time. Premarital sexual activity is now much more readily admitted, and overt nonmarital cohabitation is much more acceptable than it was 35 years ago (Wall and Kaltreider, 1977). Indeed, so-called permissive attitudes about sexuality in the United States are of substantial concern to religionists, sociologists, and students of human behavior. Additional research on the influence of modern attitudes on sexual freedom and expression would be desirable.

Definition of Terms: Communication

It is necessary that investigators agree upon an accepted definition of sexual potency in men (Cooper, 1972; Finkle *et al.*, 1959). Since 1959 the author has defined sexual potency as the ability to activate psychic (emotional) desire for sexual intercourse and penile erection adequate for coitus and to achieve gratification (usually ejaculation) during the sexual act within the preceding year.

Close similitude in terminology or in questions employed by various investigators is desirable. A seemingly forthright question in one context could elicit a totally different answer in another context. For instance, if the interviewer were to ask a male prisoner with a relatively low educational level how often he sleeps with a woman, he or she might receive no reply, a contemptuous stare, or a sarcastic, ambiguous remark. Perhaps when that man was sexually active outside prison, he would go to bed with a woman in order to have sexual intercourse, not to sleep.

Another example is masturbation—a form of sexual outlet for a college student who might lack the time, money, or aggressiveness to seek a partner for intercourse. However, such erotic self-play within a prison might be treated harshly by guards who are familiar with homosexuality and other "perversions" of prisoners. Therefore, questions regarding masturbation may remain unanswered, or they may be answered inaccurately.

In evaluating their pilot program devised to improve sexual satisfaction among aging couples, Rowland and Haynes reported in 1978 that preprogram interviews and educational measures served to improve sexual satisfaction more than the program itself. Their research was complicated by methods of evaluation based on probable error in definition of normality and functionality. Their results were distorted in some instances by long-existing marital strife between members of participating couples; however, couples with the greatest sexual problems appeared to benefit most from participation in the study. Their report underscored the difficulty of dealing with uncontrollable human variables. However, future refinements in definition and methodology will likely provide much valuable information and will surely determine which couples stand in urgent need of personal sex therapy.

Interview and Interviewer

Statistical analyses might be reckoned as a sine qua non in the summation of data obtained by means of interviews, but perhaps more important would be the interviewer's appraisal of the subject's attitude. In particular, did the latter appear alert, and was he or she interested in the interview? Did the subject appear to be embarrassed or unduly aggressive, perhaps withholding vital information in the former situation, while exaggerating it in the latter? Finally, were the questions sufficiently simple to avoid misunderstanding on the part of either the interviewer or the interviewee? Objectivity is a prime requisite for the interviewer and for the reviewer of data. Moreover, realistic interpretations of data would undoubtedly be enhanced by annotations as to the circumstances of the interview and the attitude of the subject.

In studies of sexuality in the later years, it is manifestly necessary to ask each individual whether the desire for and participation in sexual activity involves the act of intercourse. Many older men and women are satisfied by the simple warmth of touching and holding, of tender gestures and kisses. These are forms of sexual activity in which intromission is obviously not involved.

It is noteworthy that answers obtained in a recent study were given much more freely *after* the interviewer had put away her pencil and paper than they were when she asked questions while transcribing the subjects' verbal responses (Wasow and Loeb, 1979). It is also important to be aware that some health workers still harbor stereotypical prejudices regarding elderly people (Solomon and Vickers, 1979).

SOURCES OF DATA

In order to obtain up-to-date views of aging persons on many subjects of concern, interviewers could profitably conduct and categorize interviews at community senior citizen centers and retirement residences where patients might be wealthy, middle class, or indigent. These specific determinants would permit extraction and correlation of data to greatest usefulness.

Clearly, it is necessary to differentiate between patients who are in short-term extended care facilities and those who are confined, perhaps for life, in convalescent hospitals (Kassel, 1976; Chapman, 1976). The latter institutions provide domiciliary care; in such settings there is generally no privacy for courtship and sexual relationships. Moreover, the limitations of the physical environment, along with the attitudes of nurses, administrators, and, not least, patients' families, usually stifle interpersonal (and, much more, sexual) opportunities. In contrast, residents of expensive retirement centers usually have their own apartments and the financial means to seek privacy outside the institution, if necessary. Therefore, the latter group offers researchers the opportunity to exclude many inhibiting variables and to better delimit the influences of personal, religious, and other important factors on sexual activity.

New situations that bear on sexual relationships require investigation. For example, loss of self-esteem, coupled with retirement from work and increasing attrition by death within the peer group, adversely affects sexuality.

MEDICAL EDUCATION

As Lief has noted repeatedly (1979), an obvious first step in developing adequate clinical awareness of human sexual function and dysfunction should be the improved, systematic education of medical students in human sexuality (Mace *et al.*, 1974). At this time there is no uniform approach in medical schools to this type of education (Lloyd and Steinberger, 1977). The personal background of each individual student and, subsequently, of each individual physician, is involved in his or her willingness to explore and deal with the sexual foibles of men and women. When physicians are not secure in their own sexuality, they bypass or shun the sexual problems of patients. It is most improbable that such physicians would voluntarily seek out a thorough sexual history. As a result, their patients would remain in the limbo from whence they came, thereby perpetuating the embarrassment and irritability of physicians and patients alike.

Whereas psychiatrists had previously dominated inquiries into the therapy of human sexual problems, others are now entering this field. Each group probably approaches this area with bias, either recognized or unrecognized. Thus, as Masters and Johnson (1976) have noted, psychiatrists believe that sexual dysfunction is caused by an undiscovered psychological problem. If the problem could be found and rooted out, so to speak, the sexual difficulty would promptly disappear. Masters and Johnson (1976) espoused intensive therapy involving two interviewers, which challenged the psychopathologic presumption. In effect, Masters and Johnson utilize an educational program designed to reorient and assist male and female partners in the resumption of sexual intercourse. This program was based on the premise that the couple sought only physiological and emotional improvement in sexual response. More thoroughgoing analyses were neither needed nor appreciated. Reinstatement of sexual function was the goal, pure and simple. Kaplan's approach to sex therapy (1974) endorsed that of Masters and Johnson.

THERAPEUTIC APPROACHES

It is the opinion of the author that, for both men and women, the strictures of an uninformed or proscriptive society at every level—familial, legislative, and financial—are more significant than impaired physical ability in discouraging or suppressing sexual activity in advancing age. It is well known that in later years, sexual activity is reduced in frequency and intensity, although the physical ability to perform is not countermanded by biological senescence in men or women (Finkle, 1976).

Medical treatment of impaired human sexual function on a day-to-day basis in private practice has heretofore been quite casual and hurried, for the most part. For the secondarily impotent male (e.g., a man who was previously potent), the physician will usually prescribe a series of hormone injections rather than carefully hear out the patient. If benefit is to be had at all from male hormone injections, it is the result of a three-way interaction, namely the administration of a purportedly *useful medication* by an *ostensibly knowledgeable physician* to *an expectant patient*, rather than a pharmacologic effect of the hormone per se (Finkle and Finkle 1977). The effects of this latter treatment would be totally ineffective, or would almost invariably wear off, within a matter of days or weeks (Finkle and Thompson, 1972). Repeated intramuscular or oral administration of androgens by the original physician or by other doctors to whom the disgruntled patient turns may regrettably result in a new failure.

Since sexual impotency is generally psychogenic and can be readily identified as such by a sympathetic listener, physician or nonphysician, nothing more than reassurance and encouragement is required to help most impotent men. Even the patient with a history of previous hormonal therapy will benefit from attentive listening and emotional support, thereby reversing impotency within weeks (Finkle and Thompson, 1972; Finkle and Finkle, 1977). Should this sympathetic approach fail, the patient may be referred to specialists for more sophisticated types of therapy, having suffered no harm or loss as a result of the initial encouragement. In the cases of the few men whose emotional problems are obviously complex and whose sexual dysfunction is only the tip of the psychologic iceberg, immediate referral to a psychotherapist should precede counseling for impotence (Finkle and Finkle, 1977). For the male, fear of performance failure is generally a critical factor in sexual impotency. A wife or sexual partner's lack of interest or demeaning attitude may be the reason for sexual conflict (Finkle, 1978a). Similarly, the boredom and lack of interest displayed by a man can cause frustration in a woman (Pfeiffer, 1974). The plight of wives of impotent men and their myriad methods of living with this problem have been reviewed by Renshaw (1979).

Specific situations warrant careful appraisal. In particular, although surgical insertion of prosthetic rods into the penis can simulate erection (as do suprapubic reservoirs from which fluid can be made to flow at will into surgically implanted tubes), these approaches should not be utilized without a prior, unequivocal diagnosis of irreversible impotency (Karacan et al., 1978; Furlow, 1978). Clinical diagnosis of psychogenic or organic impotency, or of both, can now be substantiated by various questioning techniques, as well as by nocturnal penile tumescence (NPT) studies (Karacan et al., 1978) and rapid eye movement (REM) studies (Karacan, 1978). These methods contribute to appropriate clinical selection of patients for operation. Of significance in this regard is a recent report concerning the wives of men who had undergone surgical measures to effect artificial penile erections (Kramarsky-Binkhorst, 1978). Some of these women were far from enthusiastic about the new situation. Moreover, sexual participation after surgical treatment, within either a marital or an extramarital context, could be surprisingly infrequent (Kramarsky-Binkhorst, 1978). Thus, better communication between the urologist and the involved couple might be helpful before the operation is attempted. At times it may not be wise or necessary to invite a man's wife for an interview as part of the appraisal of his candidacy for surgical aid to penile erections. If the man were interested only in extramarital outlets, it could well be his decision *not* to inform his usual partner.

Post (1978) conjectures that neuroendocrinological changes account for the depression of sexual frequency in advancing age. Furthermore, he believes that these changes could be halted as a result of the stimulation provided by a new sexual partner. I consider it more probable that new sexual partners provide mutual psychogenic stimulation and that this single fact is enough to explain increased sexual tempo.

Counseling by a urologist or by an interested therapist can overcome sexual impotency, even in the presence of certain organic illnesses, such as alcoholism and diabetes (Finkle, Finkle, and Finkle, 1975). Renshaw recently noted that the psychologic problems of male and female diabetics can account for decreased libido (Renshaw, 1978). Stated otherwise, diabetes mellitus does not doom a man or a woman to sexual dysfunction. Diabetic women generally experience no diminution of sexual response, whereas 60% or more of male diabetics do (Ellenberg, 1977). Nevertheless, impotency associated with diabetes is not invariably permanent (Finkle, 1979).

Many medications prescribed today have depressive or other side effects than can impair or impede sexual function (van der Kolk *et al.*, 1978). Urologic counseling can help patients to overcome some of these problems. Sometimes nothing but change in medication is needed, particularly with regard to drugs controlling hypertension, some of which are less damaging than others to sexual function (Finkle, 1979; Aagard, 1972). Most drugs have greater impact on older than on younger persons (Vancura, 1979). Clinically significant interactions do occur, but untoward effects are not always clearly manifest (Hansten, 1979). Certain drugs, such as L-dopa, used in the treatment of Parkinsonism, may enhance sexual interest in some patients (Brown, *et al.*, 1978). Special situations, such as long-term dialysis in the treatment of renal failure, are known to diminish sexual potency, although the reasons for this are poorly understood (Thurm, 1975; Milne *et al.*, 1977–1978). Radical prostatectomy performed (usually successfully) to achieve remission of at least 15 years of early cancer of the prostrate gland, does *not* invariably doom a man to sexual impotency, as was commonly believed by urologists and other clinicians during the past 70 years (Finkle and Taylor, 1981).

It is known that topical applications of hormones to the vagina, or local lubrication, or both, can help many elderly women to overcome dyspareunia (Finkle, 1978a; Shearer and Shearer, 1977). An older woman's participation in sexual activity probably reflects her personal experiential history and current opportunity to enjoy privacy and tenderness (Stieger, 1976). Since widows continue to outnumber widowers in later life, the adaptation of older women to a lonely and asexual existence must be understood and ameliorated in any way possible (Friedman, 1978). Relationships between an older woman and a younger man are much more common today. At this time, despite the important contributions of Kaplan (1974), Masters and Johnson (1970), and Pfeiffer (1974), more studies are needed to further elucidate the sexuality of aging women.

SUGGESTIONS

Much remains to be learned physiologically, neurologically, and urologically regarding human sexuality, particularly sexual impotency in the male. The aforementioned objective techniques for evaluation of penile vascular flow (Karacan *et al.*, 1978) and neurodynamic features of penile erection (Zorgniotti, 1979) will doubtlessly increase our understanding of normal and impaired tumescence, as will new instrumentation and investigative techniques. For women, less intensive study is needed, but any expansion of the knowledge of female sexual physiology would be most useful.

Investigators and teachers who seek to study and encourage sexual relationships among the aged should recognize emotional overtones and their numerous ramifications. Amassing clinical knowledge of cultural and sociological concepts is not enough. The sympathetic and interested demeanor of the investigator, counselor, or therapist is invaluable, per se, in establishing the rapport without which favorable outcome is unlikely.

Cultural impediments to sexual opportunities of the aged must be identified in devising, pursuing, and analyzing the course of future studies. Additional information must be acquired regarding the intrinsic and extrinsic influences that affect the self-esteem of elderly men and women. Multifaceted and cooperative research programs should be initiated and pursued intensively, since we will deal in the future with an ever-increasing number of older members of our population. Improved quality of life, rather than mere survival to a ripe old age, must be the goal to which we direct our investigative and therapeutic attentions.

REFERENCES

Aagard, G. N. (1972). *Postgrad. Med.* **52**, 114.

Barry, J. M., and Hodges, C. V. (1978). *J. Urol.* **119**, 575–578.

Berezin, M. A. (1976). *J. Geriatr. Psychiatry* **9**, 189–209.

Brown, E., Brown, G. M., and Kofman, O. (1978). *Am. J. Psychiatry* **135**, 1552–1555.

Chapman, R. H. (1976). *Fam. Plann. Perspect.* **8**, 253.

Christenson, C. V., and Johnson, A. B. (1973). *J. Geriatr. Psychiatry* **1**, 89–98.

Comfort, A. (1977). *Br. J. Sex. Med.* **4**, 22–24.

Cooper, A. J. (1972). *Postgrad. Med. J.* **48**, 548–552.

Ellenberg, M. (1977). *Hum. Sex.* **11**, 30–38.

Ellis, A. (1979). "Brief Psychotherapy for Physicians and Nurses." Springer Publ., New York.

Ellis, H. (1910) "Studies in the Psychology of Sex," Vol. I, pp. 353–391. Random House, New York.

Finkle, A. L. (1976). *In* "Geriatric Psychiatry" (L. Bellak and T. B. Karasu, eds.), pp. 63–74. Grune & Stratton, New York.

Finkle, A. L. (1978a). *J. Am. Geriatr. Soc.* **26**, 443–448.

Finkle, A. L. (1978b). *Hum. Sex.* **12**, 130.

Finkle, A. L. (1979). *Urology* **13**, 39–44.

Finkle, A. L., and Finkle, P. S. (1977). *Geriatrics* **32**, 84–89.

Finkle, A. L., and Taylor, S. P. (1981). *J. Urol.* **125**, 350–352.

Finkle, A. L., and Thompson, R. (1972). *Geriatrics* **27**, 67–72.

Finkle, A. L. Moyers, T. G., Tobenkin, M., and Karg, S. J. (1959). *J. Am. Med. Assoc.* **170**, 1391–1393.

Finkle, J. E., Finkle, P. S., and Finkle, A. L. (1975). *Urology* **6**, 697–702.

Friedman, J. S. (1978). *J. Psychiatr. Nurs.* **16**, 34–47.

Furlow, W. L. (1978). *Urology* **13**, 166–171.

Hansten, P. D. (1979). *Curr. Prescrib.* **5**, 69–71.

Henderson, H. (1979). *Sex. Med. Today* **3**, 32.

Kaplan, H. S. (1974). "The New Sex Therapy." Brunner/Mazel, New York.

Karacan, I. (1978). *Sleep* **1**, 125–132.

Karacan, I., Salis, P. H., Catesby, W., Baris, D., Williams, R. L., Scott, F. B., Attia, S. L., and Beutler, L. E. (1978). *Am. J. Psychiatry* **135**, 191–197.

Kassel, V. (1976). *Hum. Sex.* **10**, 125–131.

Kinsey, A. C., Pomeroy, W. B., and Martin, C. E. (1948). "Sexual Behavior in the Human Male." Saunders, Philadelphia.

Kinsey, A. C., Pomeroy, W. B., Martin, C. E., and Gebhard, P. H. (1953). "Sexual Behavior in the Human Female." Saunders, Philadelphia.

Kramarsky-Binkhorst, S. (1978). *Urology* **12**, 545–548.

Lief, H. E. (1979). *Hum. Sex.* **13**, 44.

Lloyd, J. A., and Steinberger, E. (1977). *J. Med. Educ.* **52**, 74–76.

Mace, D. R., Bannermann, R. H. O., and Burton, J. (1974). *World Health Org.* (Geneva) *Public Health Pap.* **57**.

Masters, W. H., and Johnson, V. E. (1968). *In* "Middle Age and Aging: A Reader in Social Psychology" (B. L. Neugarten, ed.), pp. 355–360. Univ. of Chicago Press, Chicago.

Masters, W. H., and Johnson, V. E. (1970). "Human Sexual Inadequacy." Little, Brown, Boston.

Masters, W. H., and Johnson, V. E. (1976). *Am. J. Psychiatry* **133**, 548–554.

Michal, V., and Popsichal, J. (1978). *World J. Surg.* **2**, 239–248.

Milne, J. F., Golden, J. F., and Fibus, L. (1977–1978). *Int. J. Psychiatry Med.* **8**, 335–344.

Palmore, E., and Kivett, V. (1977). *J. Gerontol.* **32**, 311–316.

Pfeiffer, E. (1974). *J. Geriatr. Psychiatry* **9**, 189–209.

Post, F. (1978). *In* "Textbook of Geriatric Medicine and Gerontology" (J. C. Brocklehurst, ed.), p. 187. Churchill-Livingstone, Edinburgh and London.

Renshaw, D. C. (1978). *In* "Handbook of Sex Therapy" (J. LoPiccolo and L. LoPiccolo, eds.), pp. 433–440. Plenum, New York.

Rowland, K. F., and Haynes, S. N. (1978). *J. Sex. Marital Ther.* **4**, 91–113.

Rubin, I. (1968). *In* "Human Sexuality in Medical Education and Practice" (C. E. Vincent, ed.), pp. 517–531. Thomas, Springfield, Illinois.

Shearer, M. R., and Shearer, M. L. (1977). *Clin. Obstet. Gynecol.* **20**, 197–208.

Snyder, E. E., and Spreitzer, E. (1976). *Arch. Sex. Behav.* **5**, 249–254.

Solomon, K., and Vickers, R. (1979). *J. Am. Geriat. Soc.* **27**, 186–191.

Steger, R. W. (1976). *Perspect. Hum. Reprod.* **27**, 53–57, 62.

Thurm, J. (1975). *Urology* **5**, 5–62.

Vancura, E. J. (1979). *Geriatrics* **34**, 63–73.

van der Kolk, B. A., Shader, R. I., and Greenblatt, D. J. (1978). *In* "Psychopharmacology: A Generation of Progress" (M. A. Lipton, A. DiMascio, and K. F. Killam, eds.), pp. 1012–1013. Raven Press, New York.

Wall, S., and Kaltreider, N. (1977). *J. Am. Med. Assoc.* **237**, 565–568.

Wascow, M., and Loeb, M. D. (1979). *J. Am. Geriat. Soc.* **27**, 73–79.

Zorgniotti, A. W. (1979) *Urology* **13**, 185.

11

Dysfunction: Origins and Therapeutic Approaches

Ivor Felstein

INTRODUCTION

Difficulties in sexual function in middle and later years frequently show multiple factors in terms of their origin, though any one factor may appear to dominate the picture. The close link between psyche and soma seen in the sexuality of earlier years is just as significant in older age groups. When we come to consider the therapy of sexual difficulties in senior age groups, we may conveniently separate the organic from the psychological elements in terms of both short-term and long-term responses. However, the two elements have to be merged in order to achieve a satisfactory result.

THE MALE: LIBIDINAL AND POTENCY DYSFUNCTION

The most widely considered sexual dysfunction in the older male subject is loss of potency. This refers to loss of the ability to experience penile erection and ejaculation. The mature male is potent provided four factors are present. These include a normal intact male sexual apparatus, a normal level of circulating sex hormones (for example, testosterone at a serum level ranging from 4 to 12 ng per ml) and nonsex hormones, an intact nerve supply and blood flow to the male sexual apparatus, and a healthy psychological response or "state of mind." Disturbance, of major or minor degree, to any or all of these factors can result in partial or complete impotence.

The phases of the coital act are influenced in a positive or negative direction by the individual's higher cortical center in the brain, whatever the nature of the sexual relationship with the partner. The majority of individuals in later life, as in the earlier years, who request advice and help on problems of potency, are found to be dysfunctional largely because of psychological or psychiatric problems. Even in this group, however, organic aspects may make a contribution.

Organic Causes

Dr. Bernard Goldstein (1976) has suggested that about 1 in 10 men undergo organic body changes or organic illness that create potency problems. In older people, my own studies suggest a more realistic figure of 15% which rises slowly over the age of 70 years. We can now consider the specific organic factors in later life that interfere with potency.

Congenital problems of the sexual apparatus become apparent long before middle and later life. These problems include the rare infantile organ, or micropenis, and the equally rare "floating" penis, the proximal end of which is unconnected with the urethral outlet (which actually opens into a primitive cloaca). In satisfactory erection for intromission, the penis grows from its flaccid state to an engorged state, rising at an angle as much as 45° to "follow" the path of the vaginal introitus. Ligamentous and muscular changes with the years cause a decline in the erection angle in later life, which may fall to a "straight" penis, or 90° angle.

Another organic problem affecting erection in later life is the condition called Peyronie's disease (after the eighteenth century French physician). Here fibrous scarring develops from a chronic inflammatory process of unknown origin. This starts in the testicular covering, the tunica albuginea, and spreads to surrounding structures. When erection occurs, dorsal bending of the penis takes place, which is painful and reduces potency. Therapy is still a problem today. Some success has been claimed with focal injection of corticosteroid drugs. Zarafonetis and Horrax (1959) have reported on the oral administration of potassium para-aminobenzoate (Potaba®), and improvement has been claimed. Surgery has been used to excise scarfibrotic material, but erection may subsequently fail entirely.

Inflammation and Trauma

Infection in the genital apparatus can interfere with potency, usually on a temporary basis, but sometimes the effect is prolonged. For example, virus infection of the testes may produce pain and interfere with successful erection. Bacterial inflammation of the urethra or of the skin of the penis can similarly inhibit erection until suitable medically prescribed antibiotics heal the infection and clear any ulceration. Inadequate or delayed therapy for gonorrhea infection can result in post-inflammatory scarring, which narrows the urethral outlet. In the presence of this kind of urethral stricture, ejaculation is unsatisfactory, and even maintaining an erection can be difficult. Surgical dilating of the narrowed outlet may then be a beneficial approach. Sometimes, when infection causes sexual dysfunction, adequate doses of pain-relieving analgesics can bring about improvement, especially if specific anti-inflammatory drug therapy is also given.

Inflammation of the prostate is another cause of organic sexual problems in later life. Whether this prostatitis is due to nonspecific infection, or whether it is related to the trauma of constant sitting (as in older taxi drivers and truck drivers), it results in aching and much discomfort in the perigenital area and the groin. Aching and discomfort may then inhibit satisfactory erection with proper ejaculation. Therapy involves adequate prostate massage and tetracycline antibiotic therapy. Unhappily, prostatitis may become a chronic problem, causing ongoing impotence. However, if the infection is cleared and potency does not improve, then psychological factors must be considered as the cause of the problem. The same psychological implications hold true for the individual who has had prostate surgery or surgery in the anogenital area. Such operations include removal of an enlarged prostate gland, removal of hemorrhoids, repair of hernias, and even circumcision. The incidence of postoperative psychological loss of potency is far from certain, but it is made more likely by three factors: a lack of preoperative explanation and reassurance by the surgeon, inadequate postoperative followup, and the age of the man. The older the man, the more likely he is to expect loss of potency. Hence the need for effective counseling. If this has been successful, but potency is not eventually restored, then psychotherapy and sexual counseling procedures may be needed.

Older individuals appear to be at greater risk with regard to trauma from accidents in the home or in the street. These accidents may result in injury to the spinal cord or spinal vertebrae, fractures of the pelvis, or spinal disc disturbance. Any of these may interfere with the central nervous system's input and output control of erection and ejaculation potency. Briefly, the sexual nervous control system is regarded as a reflex arc. The input messages along afferent nerves to the spinal cord are derived from tactile stimulation of erogenous areas. These areas include the skin over the thighs, the genitals, and the breasts. Message stimuli also come from the eyes, ears, and nose, and pass into the spinal cord. The input of all these erotic impulses is augmented by erotic messages coming from the memory and emotional areas of the cerebral cortex.

The output messages are mediated through the autonomic nerves that pass out of the spinal cord in the lumbar and sacral pathways. The parasympathetic section of pelvic splanchnic nerves is a promoter of penile erection, and the sympathetic section of hypogastric and lumbar ganglia filaments (the presacral nerves) is responsible for the ejaculatory phase. A knowledge of this sexual reflex arc allows us to understand the sexual dysfunctions of trauma in older people.

If the spinal cord is damaged and cut across completely above the first lumbar level, the man's coital reflex is maintained. When the man's libido is still functional, a cooperative sexual partner can help him to achieve "woman over man" coitus. Stimulation of the inner thighs and the scrotum, testicles, and penis of the man encourages penile erection. The female partner "captures" this and can rhythmically bring him to orgasm. If the spinal cord is only partly cut by an injury, there is marked increased in muscle tone of the lower limbs, and this spasticity makes the apparent impotence more difficult to overcome.

In spinal disc disturbance of the lumbar vertebral area, temporary impotence may follow as a result of a lifting or pulling injury, mainly because of the pain and its distribution. Bed rest on boards, with or without spinal traction or manipulation, may relieve the pain and disc disturbance. This has usually resulted in the recovery of potency.

In fractures of the pelvic bones, initial pain, shock, and bruising depress libido and limit any demonstration of potency. Associated injury to the urethral outlet may interfere with ejaculation, and, if bones are displaced, the coital reflex arc of nervous supply may be interrupted. Surgical and orthopedic treatment of the fractures should be followed by recovery of full potency. However, when legal claims for accident compensation are being made—whatever the age of the injured person—potency may remain absent until the claims are settled.

Maturity Onset Diabetes

The incidence of diabetes mellitus appears to rise with advancing years. More than 50% of all cases after the age of 50 (Houston *et al.*, 1977) are diagnosed as diabetic.[1] Secondary sexual disturbances may be a feature of this illness. For example, local genital infections in the uncontrolled diabetic may cause painful intercourse and thus inhibit potency in subsequent efforts at coitus. As soon as the diabetes is brought under control, the situation should revert to normal as the infection clears. In all age groups, diabetes can produce disturbances of nervous system function, in particular of the autonomic nerves, which, we have already noted, control erection and ejaculation faculties. The parasympathetic inhibition caused by diabetic changes leads to failure of erection. Such impotence is a risk in later life for diabetics who have had the illness for a period of 5 years or longer. Ellenberg (1974) has emphasized a significant finding in diabetes associated with loss of sexual potency. This refers to the observation that such loss of potency precedes any complaint of loss of libido.

When impotence is closely associated with an abnormally high blood sugar level, even for a diabetic, adjustment of insulin or sulfonylurea tablet dosage (and consequent lowering of the blood sugar) may be followed by improvement in erectile potency. However, when the diabetic state is otherwise well controlled, and impotence is slowly developing therapy has proved disappointing. Riley (1974) has reported moderate success in treating diabetic sexual dysfunction using massive doses of vitamin B and vitamin C complex; 60% of the men treated returned to an acceptable level of potency.

Older diabetics whose progressive loss of potency is noted to be accompanied by lower levels of the hormone testosterone in the blood may respond to injections of this hormone. A few of such patients may

---

[1]Editor's note: There is current controversy surrounding this diagnosis among older persons. A number of researchers are of the opinion that the decreased glucose tolerance with age (frequently labeled "diabetes") is a normal age-related physiological decrement rather than a pathology (Andres, 1971). Moreover, this decline is usually remedied by diet alone.

even respond to male sex hormone given in tablet form, at least in terms of some recovery of libido, which may also have declined. Intelligent diabetic patients who are aware of the potential for loss of potency with their disease may develop   a psychologically based impotence that requires nonorganic therapy. This includes careful explanation and reassurance of the diabetic man that a helpful and effective treatment program is available. Behavioral and relaxation techniques are used, in which the patient and his sexual partner engage in progressive sessions of sexual arousal—first, avoiding genital touching; later, encouraging genital stimulation; and finally evoking and "capturing" erections.

Hormone Deficiency

Hormones play an important role in the normal development of the male sexual apparatus. At puberty, the hypothalamus gives a signal to the anterior pituitary gland in the brain, which stimulates production of adrenal and genital trophic hormones. This is followed by maturation of the testes, which in turn produce a regular level of the male sex hormone, testosterone. However, the exact role of testosterone in the mechanics involved in erection and ejaculation potency is far from clear. Cooper (1974) has noted that antimale sex hormone drug therapy, such as the use of cyproterone acetate, abolishes potency and causes a decline in libido. Potency and libido are restored on withdrawal of the drug and the subsequent return of blood testosterone levels to normal.

In hypopituitary states in later life that are the result of unknown illness, postshock effect, or local hemorrhage into the anterior pituitary gland, the pituitary gland fails to produce its trophic or stimulating hormones, which encourage testosterone output by the testes. There is associated failure of thyroid and adrenal gland hormone production. This means that the individual is impotent, has a low level of libido, and experiences the systemic changes found in hypothyroid and hypoadrenal states. The latter are corrected by substitution therapy using thyroid and steroid hormones; these are administered for the rest of the patient's life. The male sex hormone deficiency can be corrected by thrice weekly injections of testosterone for up to 3 months, followed by testosterone tablets taken on a mainenance basis. With regard to the latter therapy, this writer has reported his observations of improved general health, but without regular and full recovery of potency and libido in many subjects treated. Reiter (1953) has reported similar somewhat disappointing results with testosterone therapy. Crowe (1978, p. 24) confirms these earlier studies, stating that "androgenic hormones have never in my experience restored potency in an impotent man." By contrast, Crowe feels that mixtures of androgens and estrogens can be helpful in women who exhibit a low sexual drive.

The most significant organic change associated with tissue aging is hardening of the arteries, known as arteriosclerosis, which reduces tissue blood supply. Oxygen and nutrition are diminished, and cell decline is accelerated. The rate and progression of arteriosclerosis varies from individual to individual and from one organ to another. The process can and does affect the cellular function of both testes in the older male subject. As a consequence, male sex hormone production may decline in varying degrees. Some degree of compensation may be achieved by the adrenal androgen hormone. However, if the testosterone level of the blood falls sufficiently, then a "male climacteric" picture emerges. General lethargy and fatigue, as well as anxiety and tension, are accompanied by a decline in libido and diminished potency for the older male.

In this situation, the physician can make a 24-hour estimate of urinary excretion of androgen hormone breakdown products (known as 17-oxy steroids) and check whether this has dropped below the acceptable level of 10 mg, the average level from the age of 70 onward. If the figure is lower, then the impotent men can be given a course of testosterone by injection or by implant, or a course of tablets containing fluoxymesterone. Once again, the resuls in terms of regaining libido and improvement in potency are variable and not consistently enouraging.

Better results may be achieved when the individual is also assessed psychiatrically, in order to exclude the presence of an associated depressive illness. Appropriate antidepressant or thymoleptic drugs can be given, along with adequate psychotherapy, when depression is confirmed.

Drugs

Autonomic nervous control of potency utilizes the hormonal nerve–muscle messengers known as the catecholamines, which are functional at parasympathetic and sympathetic nerve endings. These neurotransmitters are involved in individuals who, in later life, suffer from an abnormally raised blood pressure with symptomology that requires drug therapy. The introduction of such drugs to the patient's treatment program assumes that nondrug therapy has not been effective. Such nondrug therapy includes weight reduction and weight control for the obese individual, reduction (or, preferably, cessation) of smoking, low dietary salt intake, and organization of work and social conditions to limit stress and anxiety. The earliest used of these anti-hypertensive-effective drugs, such as mecamylamine and the methonium compounds, interfered with parasympathetic and sympathetic function. Users of these early drugs felt physically better but complained of impotence. The next generation of drugs used to treat hypertension, the sympathetic-blocking agents such as guanethidine, were slightly less troublesome sexually, but they still interfered with ejaculatory potency. Contemporary drugs that effectively lower blood pressure are based on selective beta-blocking agents, or vasodilator mechanisms; as a result, loss of potency in the therapy of hypertension is now at minimal levels.

When antihypertensive drug therapy interferes with potency, the female partner can utilize positional adjustments to help the situation. Adoption of a side-to-side posture, lying first above and then below level position with her partner, produces penile compression as the shaft is moved backward. Again, when the women is in the superior position in coitus, she can initiate and extend the rhythmical movements required. The significance of antihypertensive blocking drugs on female sexual functions should not be overlooked at this point (Beaumont, 1974). The woman with high blood pressure in later life may require alternative therapy, such as diuretics, which do not interfere with sexual phases, including satisfactory orgasm. Male subjects also may be controlled by switching to diuretics. Diuretics lower the blood pressure through the promotion of urine secretion and excretion by the kidneys. These drugs do not usually result in either a total inability to ejaculate or in delayed or retarded ejaculation, as with the sympathetic-blocking drugs described earlier. One of the newest nondiuretic, antihypertensive drugs that is effective but less likely to create sexual side effects is prazosin. Its mode of action affects smooth muscle, not the autonomic channels.

Diuretics are at present the mainstay of therapy in chronic heart failure. As Jackson and Jackson (1981) have pointed out, the thiazide diuretics can produce erectile dysfunction in older men as well as side effects such as lowered potassium levels and gout. This dysfunction is usually reversible, however, on withdrawal or decrease of the thiazide dosage. The mechanism of thiazide impotence is not, at present, fully understood. It may be that the pelvic blood flow is reduced by the drug relative to vasodilator effects in the peripheral blood vessels.

Another important group of drugs—and these may be used in psychological problems regarding potency in some cases—are the mood-changing or mood-elevating drugs, the psychotropics. Unfortunately, these, too, may interfere with ejaculatory function, as Beaumont (1974) has stressed, whether they are the tricyclic antidepressants or the proma-zine and perazine derived drugs. Central depressant drugs—sedatives, or sleep-inducing agents—are known to relax as well as depress libido (Renshaw, 1981). This can be significant in later life, because the individual who suffers from anxiety, insomnia, or epileptic attacks requires therapy with phenobarbitone or other centrally acting anti-epilepsy drugs. A decrease in libido as a result of all these drugs can effectively reduce potency.

An interesting link between the catecholamines and one of the cerebral problems of later life is seen in Parkinsonism. In 1966, Hornykiewicz showed that dopamine, a chemical antecedent of epine-phrine, was much reduced in the relevant brain areas of patients with Parkinsonic tremor and rigidity. This ultimately led to the introduction of levodopa therapy for this medical problem of middle and later life (James, 1978). The body converts levodopa to the required dopamine, and functional improvement occurs.

As part of the clinical picture of Parkinsonism, there is frequently a decline in sexual tension and sexual interest, with a secondary loss of potency. This writer, and many other research physicians (Jewesbury, 1970) who were first able to use levodopa in hospital assessment (before its general release), noted a resurgence of sexual tension in treated Parkinsonic patients. Recovery of libido was followed by improvement of potency in some individuals. This effect of levodopa was hailed by some as confirmation of the aphrodisiac qualities of brain amines noted in animal experimentation (Renshaw, 1981). However, there is no clear evidence that those individuals suffering from Parkinsonism in later life improve sexually beyond the premorbid levels of potency and sexual tension. Neither is there any real evidence that levodopa given to non-Parkinsonic individuals in older age groups leads to recovery from a potency loss among male subjects. To complete the picture, observation of Parkinsonic patients on a long-term basis has shown an overall falling away of the initial improvement and a tendency to "on–off" episodes of clinical symptoms (James, 1978).

Many effective drugs used in the treatment of diseases have been the subject of occasional reports as causal in impotence in older persons. Where there is no clear pharmacological link between the drug effect in metabolic terms and the mechanisms responsible for control of potency, the likelihood of nonorganic and psychological factors creating im-potence is much increased. There is less information on the risks accompanying the use of "psychosocial" drugs in later life, in terms of the effect on potency. Misuse of morphine, heroin, and the related drugs of dependency, as well as chronic self-dosage with alcohol, may eventually affect potency adversely in the older individual. Such abuse leads to personality deterioration, severe intellectual and emotional disturbance, and the falling away of libido. The so-called "soft" drugs used to alter the conscious state—whether they are amines, lysergic acid, hashish, or related chemicals—are sometimes claimed to improve potency and sexual satisfaction. This may be no more than the effect of heightening a sexually inclined mood common to many foods, drinks, and relaxed atmospheres.

Older people, like younger individuals, enjoy social drinking. Moreover, they may use alcohol as a regular "insurance" for a good night's sleep. An experience of incomplete erection or failure of erection after alcohol intake is inevitably upsetting and is sometimes the first instance of sexual dysfunction noted in later life. The aftereffect is invariably disturbing and can sometimes initiate further problems of dysfunction, whether the individual is under the influences of alcohol or not.

In such a situation, the attending physician has to make an assessment of the degree of alcoholism, if any, and whether the effect is predominantly psychological. Acute alcoholic overdose or intoxication can cause retarded ejaculation whether the individual has been a regular "alcoholic" or not. Chronic excess of alcohol intake, especially in association with a diet poor in the B vitamins, can result in alcoholic peripheral nerve dysfunction. Such peripheral neuropathy can in turn produce impotence. This is unlikely to be reversed as a result of the patient becoming free of dependence on alcohol after suitable treatment. A course of intramuscular B vitamins is nevertheless worth trying in an individual case. Psychotherapy using behavioral and relaxation techniques also is worthwhile.

Peripheral neuropathies from sources other than alcohol, such as accidental lead poisoning in industry or vitamin B_{12} deficiency in pernicious anaemia, can contribute to impotence. Corrective medication may or may not reverse the dysfunction.

Small doses of alcohol allegedly lower sexual inhibitions. This has led to the suggestion that female sexual dysfunction in the later years might occasionally respond to the use of small amounts of alcohol in a therapy program. This writer feels unable to recommend such a procedure on a regular basis. As Moss and Davies (1967) have shown, alcohol is not an aphrodisiac, even for alcoholic women.

Surgery

Almost any medical illness of major to minor degree can have a temporary dampening effect on libido and produce some lessening of potency, whatever the age group. The same is true in the preoperative and postoperative phases of a surgically treated illness. Renshaw (1981) has pointed out that damage to the higher centers of the autonomic nervous system in patients who have suffered a stroke may create a variety of sexual disturbances: partial erections, impaired ejaculation, or total dysfunction in the male subject, and decreased lubrication in the female subject. A stroke also can interfere with sensory appreciation and motor activity in sexuality, as well as with the spoken expressions of sexual need and sexual enjoyment. Sexual counselling is therefore regarded as another necessary factor in the program of rehabilitation, regardless of the age of the stroke patient. In the case of men who have undergone operative surgery, the risks of impotence are greater where such surgery has been in or around the genital area. This is not necessarily because ther has been actual trauma to the genital organs themselves. Usually, it is a psychologically based loss of potency relative to fears and anxieties about performance. Because of a lack of full understanding of the elements of sexual control in an organic sense, the older man may exhibit difficulties in erectile capacity and maintenance.

The operation that is classically associated with loss of potency in the minds of those operated upon is the removal of an enlarged prostate gland. The procedure, known as prostatectomy, can genuinely interfere with ejaculatory function when the surgery is of the so-called "open" type and disturbs the function of the internal sphincter. However, the contemporary approach involving the transurethral method seems to reduce the risk of organic change that might lead to postoperative impotence. Proper preoperative counseling and adequate postoperative psychotherapy can decrease the likelihood of nonorganic impotence in all operations of the genital, perigenital, and lower abdominal type. We must not overlook the "opportunist" side of surgical operations. The procedures permit an older individual with low sexual tension and general disinterest to abandon all sexual activity with a "valid" excuse to his partner.

Venereal Diseases

Venereal diseases can interfere with male sexual potency in later life. In its acute stages, gonorrhea may be responsible for infection of the prostate gland, so that later a chronic prostatitis causing secondary interference with potency is produced. Infection of the urethral outlet by the gonorrhea organism, as noted earlier, may cause narrowing by scarring if the sufferer fails to seek early therapy. This urethral stricture can then interfere with proper ejaculation. The incidence of fairly recent infection with gonorrhea in the over 60s age group is not easy to determine, though it is generally assumed to be very small, relative to the incidence among young adults and teenagers. Schofield (1972) has estimated that 3% of the men in the over 60s age group in the developed countries are infected with gonorrhea. It is this group that is at risk to ejaculation problems and erection difficulties.

Syphilis, if untreated in the early states, or insufficiently treated, can affect the brain and spinal cord function in later life. Krishnan and Lomax in the United Kingdom (1970), and Dencker and Nielsen in Denmark (1959) have, in separate studies, discovered a 1.5% incidence of latent syphilis in older communities. This figure is likely to be up to three times greater among senior citizens in seaport areas than it is among those in inland cities. When late syphilis affects spinal cord function, the reflex arc for potency is upset. This late syphilis, known as *tabes dorsalis*, causes disturbance of gait and balance, upset of bladder function, and impotence. Unhappily, neither penicillin nor other antisyphilitic therapy can reverse the loss of potency in this late form of syphilis.

Blood Vessel Changes

Poor arterial circulation to the lower limbs is a medical problem of later life that may be considerably worsened by diabetes mellitus. There are a number of therapies that can be tried in the treatment of this condition. A surgical approach to the problem has been to "interfere" with the automomic control of blood vessel functioning by cutting across the lumbar sympathetic outflow from the nervous system (Singha, 1967). This procedure, when carried out on both sides of the body (bilateral lumbar sympathectomy), may improve blood flow in the limbs at the expense of potency. Ejaculation, in particular, may no longer be effective. In the sexually active older man, therefore, alternative therapies should be considered by the physician.

In 1978, Michal (at the Institute for Clinical Medicine in Prague) reported on the use of blood vessel reconstructive surgery in a series of men under 55 years of age who were suffering from problems of impaired aorta and iliac artery blood flow. This included the problem of impaired potency. The surgical treatment not only improved blood supply to the lower part of the body and the lower limbs, but it also helped restore sexual function. Michal postulates that surgery may, in time, prove useful in treating impotence due to blood vessel changes in men over 55 years of age.

Nervous System Degeneration

Other diseases that induce degeneration of central nervous system and spinal cord function as part of their overall picture can interfere with potency. The demyelinating disease of multiple sclerosis is an example, though this particular illness is uncommon as a new onset illness in later life. Because this condition is characterized by periods of improvement followed by periods of relapse, the loss of potency, at least in the earlier stages of the illness, may prove to be temporary. This writer has observed loss of potency in demyelinating illness that is psychologically induced after the patient learns of the nature of the illness. Psychotherapy and suitable counseling encourage restoration of potency.

Cord compression due to severe osteoarthritic changes in the neck vertebrae can occasionally result in spastic weakness of the lower limbs, sphincter disturbance, and interference with potency in middle and later life. Surgery may be required, but potency may still not be restored when the reflex arc is permanently broken.

A useful test in helping to assess the presence of organic impotence is to check nocturnal penile tumescence (NPT). A penile plethysmograph measures and records erections during sleep. In sleep, erections are not inhibited by conscious psychological conflict.

Psychological Causes

The foregoing organic causes of impotence in the older male subject are seen to be complex; yet, in many instances, they are amenable to appropriate therapy. However, as we noted earlier, organically related dysfunctions represent a minority of cases. The majority of sexual dysfunctions are psychologically based (either entirely or in part), and they contribute to organic causes.

Taylor (1975) has pointed out that psychologically based loss of potency in middle life is most frequently seen in the individual who is "under stress" and who is "socially and financially successful." The stress or anxiety element is a consistent feature that runs as a significant theme in nonorganic dysfunction in later life. This is observed in its most direct fashion when the male partner develops a depressive illness, either of the endogenous variety or as a reactive form. In addition to apathy and low spirits, the ease of distraction and the inability to concentrate lead to erectile failure that is also derived from the associated problem of diminished libido.

Cultural and marital expectations in sexual terms can lead to anxiety and secondary impotence. McKain (1969) has pointed to a steady increase in new marriage and remarriage rates among people over 60 in the past decade. My own study, "Living to be a Hundred" (Felstein, 1973a), considered the tension, shyness, embarrassment, and fear of ridicule that may be engendered in partners who are new to each other: all elements that can result in potency inhibition in the male partner. Moreover, the elderly person who experiences this failure of potency may be reluctant to seek advice from a professional counselor or physician, who may tell him "be your age," or "don't be a dirty old man." Such a response from a professional increases any tension or guilt feelings and augments the anxiety element that has been causal in the first place.

This writer has also reported the ways in which cosmetic change in either partner in middle or later life can contribute to psychological loss of potency. Among those who are already married, the male partner may be discouraged by changes in his own facial and body appearance in the form of wrinkling, sagging, baldness, stooping, loss of teeth, and graying. He may feel that he is less attractive and stimulating than formerly and become tense and anxious about his sexual performance. Slight or temporary failure in potency may be made worse by his partner's critical, hostile, or unsympathetic reaction.

Alternatively, the male partner may be discouraged by age-related changes in the female. He may find that, as a result of wrinkles, graying hair, sagging body, and loss of youthful curves her appearance is no longer an erotic stimulant. This can result in erectile inhibition. To the normal aging body and facial changes may be added the negative cosmetic effects of illness and the effects of surgical therapy, such as mastectomy for breast cancer. This altered body image may be unacceptable to the male partner and create sexual inhibition as part of an overall rejection of physical contact with a changed partner.

For the female, this open rejection by her regular sexual partner is not likely to be readily accepted. If she already has problems of social adjustment to her altered status, the loss of love and affection and sexual acceptance by her partner can only aggravate the tension, anxiety, and emotional upset she is experiencing. Depending on her personality and her needs, she may try to tolerate the situation, or she may seek a separation. Alternatively, she may encourage her partner to join her in seeking professional counseling, a process to which any partnership of long standing would usually be agreeable. In any case, the female herself may already be receiving supportive advice, adjustment counseling, and helpful medication if she is experiencing postoperative, sociosexual difficulties. For example, she may experience reduced libido, diminished orgasm, or a disturbed sense of gender identity and "femininity" following breast surgery or sexual organ surgery.

In the case of cosmetic aging changes alone, judicious use of "de-aging" cosmetic surgery has been considered worthwhile. This surgery cannot guarantee restoration of sexual potency, but it may be considered as a possibly helpful element in a total progam tackling psychologically based dysfunctions.

Premature Ejaculation

A problem that may or may not be classified under the "potency dysfunction" heading is that of premature ejaculation. A familiar feature of early sexual relations in the young, inexperienced male partner, premature ejaculation may recur in remarriage situations during later life. In the otherwise well and healthy older man, this problem is invariably psychologically based and cannot be readily considered under any organic heading, hormonal or otherwise. The corrective approaches used in younger individuals can be safely applied to the otherwise physically sound older man. Behavioral techniques, such as the use of graded responses or successive approximation, as well as thought stopping, can be applied. The technique of penile squeeze described by Masters and Johnson (1970) also is applicable, although, in the older individual, there is an occasional risk that undue pressure might cause a local petechial effect in the penile skin. This could be overcome as a risk by teaching the male subject to practice the technique alone before trying it with his partner.

Taylor (1975, p. 32) has reported the use of reserpine in small doses to correct premature ejaculation: he suggests .1 mg daily, which can effectively "delay ejaculatory response without having any serious effect on the blood pressure." However, this writer has noted a side effect of reserpine, even in small doses, in the form of mild to moderate depression. Such an effect on mood would be unwelcome in the presence of this kind of dysfunction. Any individual who has a history of depression or a tendency to gloomy moods should not be given reserpine therapy in the treatment of premature ejaculation.

Alcohol, Boredom, and Workaholism

The many individual and environmental factors that may be causally associated with psychologically based impotence in younger persons are still wholly valid in later life. Moderate and excessive drinking, and severe and advancing alcoholism can occur in the aged, as Salzburger (1977) and Kay (1965) have separately described. This form of overdrinking can certainly inhibit potency, even if, in the early stages, there is an apparent increase in libido.

The driving, ambitious man of commerce and the relentless, energetic, creative individual who draw on all their physical resources, with little relaxation or leisure time, may suffer physical and mental fatigue that interferes with potency. The older man who exposes himself to the risk of venereal disease through extramarital contacts, and the individual who takes on a regular liaison with a "secret" friend, may both suffer psychological impotence through guilt, tension, and personal fear.

The middle-aged and older career woman is an increasing feature of contemporary society and may be seen to parallel the ambitious man of commerce. Analogously, she may complain of diminished or low sex drive, or of reduced or absent orgasmic experience. Similarly, the creative, energetic older woman may experience libido loss or less effective sexual response and orgasm.

Older women, like older men, may indulge in extramarital or extraregular (in which neither partner is married) relationships. The woman may then discover a problem of situational anorgasmia, in which adequate sexual response is no longer forthcoming from her husband or her regular partner, but only from her secret contact. With the female and the male partners who are involved in such third-party excursions, the progressive stimulation, relaxation, and desensitizing programs along the lines of Masters and Johnson's (1970) therapy are unlikely to be successful. With that exception, such therapy programs, full or modified, can be of much value in the treatment of libido or orgasm difficulties.

There is the individual who suffers a slight failure of potency and is subjected to partner criticism, which sets up the anxiety trait that disturbs subsequent coital efforts. There is the person who loses interest in his or her partner, simply through the familiarity and routine of their interpersonal relationship, so that sexual life becomes dull, flat, humdrum, and boring. As a result, although libido may be present, potency with the all-too-familiar partner becomes inhibited by the sheer weight of years. There is a direct parallel for the woman who finds the partnership dull and uninspiring; indeed, a sexual turnoff. Poor or absent orgasm, loss of libido or reduced sex drive, and vaginismus may be experienced. Other forms of marital disharmony (such as quarrels over family and friends, or disagreements over finances, careers, or social behavior) that perhaps stretch back over a long marriage may inhibit effective potency.

Psychotherapy and Hormones

The range of direct and predisposing causes for psychological impotence implies that an approach to therapy has to combine general psychotherapeutic principles and individually attuned aids and therapies. The 5-point-program approach suggested by Long (1974) can be considered a particularly useful guide with regard to potency problems that are psychologically derived. The program includes the following elements. Both partners are enlisted for therapy by means of separate and conjoint interviews and assessments. Psychotherapy, by whatever means, helps to remove the fear of failure and instill the goal of "hope of success," so that trust, confidence, and new enthusiasm are encouraged. A period during which the partners are encouraged to engage in physical contact of the nongenital variety helps to revitalize and reanimate the sensory elements of the partnership. Direct instructions on coital procedures are given; these are intended to give maximum stimulus to male potency, with full opportunity to achieve and maintain erection.

Partners can and do remain together, even when male or female sexual dysfunction persists after therapy. This writer, in his professional work, is witness to the happy companionship and mutual pleasure achieved by older married partners who are no longer able to experience full or partial sexual congress. Bodily warmth and contact, kissing and caressing, and hugging and stroking may all be pleasurable. The sharing of social pursuits, visits, holidays, hobbies, and interests can maintain the firm bond of a couple's relationship.

The question still arises whether those who suffer from psychologicallly based disturbances or potency might not also benefit from male sex hormone therapy. Reports over the past decade suggest that testosterone may be additionally supportive in this type of dysfunction. Greenblatt and co-workers (1976) have reported nearly a 50% success rate in increasing male sex responsiveness in the over 50s age group when androgens are administered. Both oral and injection therapy were used. Weekly testosterone injections for up to 3 months, followed by a 2-month "rest period," were said to lift the mood, raise the level of libido, and create an improved feeling of well-being.

There is no guarantee that androgen therapy will reverse the normal effects of aging on sexual function, which have been outlined by Norcross (1976), reported by Masters and Johnson (1970). and described in an earlier chapter by Weg. These changes include a slowing down of the speed of erection, a similar delay in ejaculation, and a possible reduction in total ejaculate. The orgasmic force of ejaculation declines, and the postorgasm refractory period increases after more rapid detumescence.

Fear and anxiety following surgical therapy have been noted as possible causes of impotence. However, such major medical illnesses as heart attacks, angina of effort, high blood pressure, and chronic obstructive airway disease may all discourage libido and reduce potency. Initially, this may be the effect of true postillness weakness, but it is then maintained by fears and tension about inducing the return of the illness, encouraging complications of that illness, or even hastening death. Careful medical assessment and appropriate sexual counseling regarding periodicity, positioning, timing, partner aid, and prophylactic measures may permit a return to satisfactory sexual activity.

Arthritis in Both Sexes

The physical disabilities engendered by arthritis have recently received more attention in terms of sexual difficulties in later life. Hamilton (1975) has reported on the problems besetting both sexes where there is limitation in one or both hip movements. Alternative postures or a posterior vaginal entry can be advised. Surgical replacement of the hip may offer a renewed possibility of sexual function for the older person. Here again, partner cooperation is necessary to achieve the most satisfactory results. Problems also can arise with regard to the pain and stiffness of arthritis in the upper limbs.

A range of helpful suggestions offered as counsel for male and female patients with arthritis includes: undertaking sexual activity after a warm shower or bath, or after heat-lamp relaxation; avoiding positions of intercourse that involve bearing the healthy partner's weight; taking medication well before intercourse as a prophylactic to joint discomfort; using a comfortable supporting bed or cushions while enjoying sexual contact; and keeping the partner informed of the most comfortable, loving position.

THE FEMALE

Dysfunction among Female Subjects

Problems of sexual dysfunction among women in later life may be (as they are among men of the same age) either organic or psychological, or a varied combination of both. Dyspareunia, or painful intercourse, can occur at any age. Taylor (1975) has suggested that we should distinguish between those who experience superficial discomfort and those who can be diagnosed as experiencing severe dyspareunia.

Superficial discomfort is experienced as a vulval sensation. Organic causes include: a thick or large hymen in the virgin who comes to marriage in middle or later life; excessive dryness and poor lubrication in the postmenopausal woman whose levels of estrogen hormones have dropped excessively; local infection of the vulvovaginal areas as the result of, for example, nonvenereal infection, poor local hygiene, venereal exposure, or uncontrolled diabetes mellitus; painful postoperative scarring after a local operation; and local skin inflammation. Infection can be treated by means of suitable medication prescribed by a physician— tablets by mouth, and local applications of cream, ointment, or pessaries in the vulval area. A thick or large hymen may be treated through suitable surgery or by the use of special dilators.

Atrophy of the vagina, with thinning of the mucosal surface associated with inadequate lubrication, may or may not cause dyspareunia. The altered nature of the epithelial lining leads to an inability to hold moisture when it is directly applied. This means that standard lubricating jellies, creams, and gels may be unsuccessful in relieving dyspareunia; they certainly do not encourage comfort in the vulvovaginal area, even in the absence of discomfort during sexual activity.

The aim of estrogen cream applied locally to the vulvovaginal linings is to restore healthy epithelium, which is essentially self-lubricating. My regular advice is to use hormone cream. Every evening, the patient inserts cream with an applicator only half full, and smears a little of the cream around her vulva with her finger. This approach gives a lower "dose," with reduced risk of provoking withdrawal bleeding after absorption. This procedure should be followed for 2 weeks; after which, the patient should apply the cream twice a week as improvement occurs. This therapy should be interrupted for 1 month every 2 months. In addition, in cases of dyspareunia, the patient should make sure that the vagina is dilated sufficiently to allow confident penile entry. Glass or plastic graded dilators can be obtained from medical sources.

Local skin inflammation can be treated with a variety of topical creams and ointments, along with with the use of careful hygiene. Venereal exposure requires both medical therapy and social counseling. Painful scars require a surgical opinion and may respond to local pain-relieving measures, if not actual excisive surgery. As a rule, maturity onset diabetes can be treated through diet alone, or through diet and anti-diabetic tablets. Poorly controlled diabetes in older women is often associated with thrush or bacterial infection in the vulvovaginal area. This can cause dyspareunia or reduced libido. Medicated creams and diabetic control clear up this condition. Diabetic neuropathy in women is not the cause of orgasm difficulties, in contrast to diabetic men. This is true even when the diabetes is controlled by insulin and diet therapy.

Some research suggests that, after 10 years of diabetes, women can develop arteriolar changes in the region of the clitoris. Rostlapil and co-workers from Prague were reported to have found such pathology when interviewed for "Diabetes Outlook" in 1978. This writer retains an open mind regarding such evidence. Psychological dysfunction is as much a feature of the older female diabetic as it is of the older male diabetic. Mental upset, anxiety, stress, and depression can contribute to diminished libido, poor orgasmic response, and vaginismus in the diabetic woman. Therapy should include reassurance regarding proper control of diabetes, relaxation and progressive contact programs, an explanation of any "diabetic symptoms" in sexual activity, and discussions with the male partner to focus attention on pleasurable contact.

When the excitement and muscular activity of sexual enjoyment cause fluctuation of the blood sugar levels and a tendency to faintness or feelings or weakness, the patient should seek advice on timing her intake of food and tablets, or her food intake and insulin injections.

Hormone Replacement Therapy

The effects of diminished levels of estrogen can be treated by more than one approach. A local hormone cream, such as dienestrol cream, can be applied to the vulvovaginal area to reverse the effects of loss of cell lining and lubrication. Local cream therapy may be combined with oral female hormone replacement therapy in the form of tablets containing natural conjugated estrogens or synthetic estrogens. Short-term oral replacement therapy for female sex hormones is well accepted, but the long-term or indefinite use of this procedure into later life is still being argued by medical doctors at present.

The champions of continued hormone replacement therapy advise that estrogens not only benefit sexual competence and discourage any decline in libido, but also protect against bone thinning, arterial degeneration, skin bloom loss, and breast and genital tissue atrophy. The antagonists of the long-term estrogen hormone replacement approach emphasize the risks of inducing cancerous changes in the uterus and breasts, with the subsequent hazard of malignant disease.

Gerdes (1981), in research performed at the University of Witwatersrand in South Africa, has suggested that, for consideration of therapy, the climacteric woman might be categorized as either vulnerable or resilient. The vulnerable woman has several severe physical and psychological menstrual symptoms, as well as frequent and/or severe sexual problems. The resilient woman has infrequent or mild psychological symptoms and minimal symptoms in the climacteric; she has a neutral or positive attitude toward the menopause, and she is informed and knowledgeable about the menopause.

Maddison (1973), a pioneer of hormone replacement therapy for postmenopausal females, prefers a sequential therapy using estrogens and progestogens on a 5-week cycle after the age of 55 years; 1 of the 5 weeks is hormone-free. He advises a Pap smear every 3 to 6 months. Side effects such as breast discomfort, cramps, and nausea can occur. Some older women do not like the fact that this therapy causes inevitable periodic hormone-withdrawal bleeding after menopause has passed. In this instance, superficial dyspareunia can be successfully relieved by local estrogen cream therapy as a single approach, or by short-term hormone treatment.

Deep pain in the pelvis at coitus, or soon afterward, usually has an organic cause, which may be determined by a gynecologist. Local organ positional changes can cause dyspareunia. Retroversion of the uterus can entrap the ovaries in the pouch of Douglas, and these glands may then be pushed against the sacral backbone at coitus. In this case, surgical therapy would be corrective. Chronic or more acute pelvic infection also can be causative and require antibiotics and surgery. Lumbosacral problems of an orthopedic nature also may give rise to deep dyspareunia and respond to suitable supportive therapy. This sacroiliac source of dyspareunia can cause from 48 to 72 hours of postcoital pain and result in depression of libido. All such physical corrective measures of organic problems are supported by careful sexual counseling of the older woman and her partner when he is available and his presence is appropriate.

Vaginismus

Vaginismus is a sexual response experienced by a woman when her partner tries to insert his penis into her vagina. Irregular and involuntary movements of the vaginal muscles take place. Each time this occurs, penetration becomes more painful; and eventually it becomes impossible. Delvin (1974) has described the genesis of this condition in relation to cultural and religious background and upbringing, fear and anxiety brought about by early unpleasant sexual experiences, and the influence of parental care or parental aggression. In later life, as in the earlier years, the therapist must first ensure that there is no physical or medical element that needs correction. This involves a doctor's lubricated digital check, followed by encouragement for the woman or her partner to make a digital check with a lubricated small finger. There are subsequent "talking out" sessions that focus on past sexual experiences, sexual needs, sexual attitudes and upbringing, and sexual knowledge and information, as well as ideas received from parents and other sources. An instruction program for self and partner cooperation involves nongenital attention, then genital attention, and finally, gentle insertion exercises using a small finger or well lubricated graded dilators. If such therapy must be excluded, a variety of behavioral desensitization and relaxation techniques may be employed. These may be the more prolonged variety outlined by Masters and Johnson (1970) or more brief therapies, such as those reported by Delvin (1974). Therapists should not overlook the possibility of associative impotence in the male partner.

Orgasmic Problems

Orgasmic dysfunction in women in later life may arise, like failure of potency, from organic factors, psychological factors, or a combination of both. Organic medical factors causing dyspareunia, as already described, can account for secondary orgasmic dysfunction. Moreover, the disturbances of hormonal or nervous system origin described for male potency problems can similarly inhibit the orgasmic phases of the older female's sexual response. Medical examination and assessment for the presence of infection, scarring, hormone depletion, or upset reflex arc, for example, are followed by appropriate medical therapy when available. In order to minimize the postmenopausal possibilities of hormonal decline and imbalance, Maddison (1973) has recommended the combination of estrogen therapy with progesterone therapy in sequential form; the progesterone can effectively contribute to satisfactory orgasm and decrease the potential carcinogenic effect of estrogen alone.

The percentage of decline in libido in later life is just as variable for older women as it is for older men. The studies of Gilmore (1976) confirm a view offered by others—that the presence of a sexually active partner in the marriage setting encourages a continuation of sexual tension and sexual outlet. This means that interpersonal problems or illness of one partner can interfere, in psychological terms, with sexual tension that would otherwise have been present. Libido and arousal to orgasm may subsequently suffer.

Primary orgasmic dysfunction of the female partner in a new marriage and in remarriage in later life has been reported. It may, as in earlier life, reflect cultural, religious, and family factors of sexual conditioning (Crowe, 1978). The Masters and Johnson (1970) sensate focus therapy, as well as the vaginal muscle training techniques of Kegel (1952), may be applied. Older persons of both sexes may have experienced coitus, fathered or produced children, and had a regular sexual partner, yet still be uncertain about the role and sensitivity of the sexual parts of the body. If a woman places a finger in her vaginal entrance, and then tries to contract and relax her vagina around it, she discovers where her vaginal, or pubo-cocygeal, muscles are located. Moreover, Kegel exercises can be used to encourage the return or the attainment of orgasm.

RESEARCH IN THE UNITED KINGDOM

In the United Kingdom, studies of sexual dysfunction in later life and of therapeutic approaches, have been sparse to date. We have already mentioned some of the significant contributors to the British scene. Maddison (1973) was the director of research at the Maddison Clinic for Preventive Medicine in Older People in Teddington, Middlesex. He pioneered the use of sex hormone replacement therapy in the United Kingdom in a program that also sought to improve the general as well as sexual health of older persons. Maddison has retired and has summarized his findings in two articles in the *British Journal of Sexual Medicine* (1973).

Gilmore (1976), a research physician in geriatric medicine at the University of Glasgow, reported on sexual findings and problems in 300 elderly people living at home in northern Glasgow. Her semistructured interviews revealed a full picture of older Scottish individuals' sexual habits and practices, and it confirmed the importance of having an available partner in later life. An important objective finding was that among elderly married partners, reduction in frequency of sexual relations appeared to be determined by the male's sexual capacity rather than by the female's interest and capacity. Gilmore's article gives a fair summary of her research findings.

Research and counseling in sexual dysfunction in later life in the United Kingdom are now being supported by the Committee for the Sexual Problems of the Disabled (SPOD)—an offshoot of the National Fund for Research into Crippling Diseases. SPOD sponsors seminars, workshops, and conferences on sex and disability, and it issues advisory papers.

Fox, a research physiologist at St. Bartholomews Hospital in London, has contributed much new material in the physiology of coitus. His findings are reported, among other places, in the *Journal of Reproduction and Fertility* (1970). His most recent contribution to problems of sexual dysfunction in later life arises from his studies by radiotelemetry of intrauterine pressure during female orgasm. Fox's findings indicate that satisfying orgasm is possible in a woman even when her partner's penis is either not in the fully erect state or is actually flaccid.

Riley (1974), a family physician in England, the former director of the Devon Institute of Human Relations, and a practicing behavioral therapist, has taken a special interest in potency problems of older males. He reports on the use of male and androgenic hormones in several organic conditions.

This writer continues his own personal efforts to promote interest in and study of sexual problems in later life. Through his own practice in sexual and geriatric medicine, through such books as "Sex in Later Life" (Felstein, 1973b) and "Living to be a Hundred," (Felstein, 1973a) and through lectures and articles in the medical and general press, he is adding to the goal of improving the sexual as well as the social and health quality of later life. He hopes that more professionals in health care will join him.

REFERENCES

Andres, R. (1971). *Med. Clin. North Am.* **55**, 835–846.
Beaumont, G. (1974). *Br. J. Sex. Med.* **1**, 10–12.
Cooper, A. J. (1974). *Br. J. Sex. Med.* **1**, 6–10.
Crowe, M. J. (1978). *Br. J. Sex. Med.* **5**, 22–24.
Delvin, D. (1974). *Br. J. Sex. Med.* **1**, 21–27.
Dencker, F., and Nielsen, H. (1959). *Dan. Med. Bull.* **6**, 230.
Ellenberg, M. (1974). *Ann. Intern. Med.* **1**, 21–27.
Felstein, I. (1973a). "Living to be a Hundred." Hippocrene Books Inc., New York.
Felstein, I. (1973b). "Sex in Later Life." Penguin, Baltimore.
Fox, C. A. (1970). *J. Reprod. Fertil.* **24**, 319–336.
Gerdes, L. C. (1981). *Br. J. Sex. Med.* **77**, 35–39.
Gilmore, A. (1976). *Mod. Geriatr.* **6**, 35–38.
Goldstein, B. (1976). "Human Sexuality." McGraw-Hill, New York.
Greenblatt, R. B., Witherington, R., and Sipahioglu, I. B. (1976). *Drug Ther.* **6**, 101–104.
Hamilton, A. (1975). *Br. J. Sex. Med.* **2**, 27–233.
Hornykiewicz, O. (1966). *Pharmacol. Rev.* **18**, 925.
Houston, J. C., Joiner, C. L., and Trounce, J. R. (1977). "Short Textbook of Medicine." Hodder, London.
Jackson, N., and Jackson, G. (1981). *Br. J. Sex. Med.* **73**, 22–26.
James, I. M. (1978). *Mod. Geriatr.* **8**, 65–68.
Jewesbury, E. C. O. (1970). *Br. J. Hosp. Med.* **4**, 230.
Kay, D. (1965). "Oral Report to World Psychiatric Association Symposium." Royal College of Physicians, London.
Kegel, A. H. (1952). *Wes. J. Surg. Obs. Gynec.* **60**, 521.

Krishnan, M., and Lomax, W. (1970). *Gerontol. Clin.* **12**, 2.

Long, R. C. (1974). *J. Ky. Med. Assoc.* **72**, 273–275.

McKain, W. (1969). *Proc. Int. Congr. Gerontol. 8th, 1969*, Vol. 2.

Maddison, J. (1973). *Br. J. Sex. Med.* **1**, 44–47.

Masters, W. H., and Johnson, V. E. (1970). "Human Sexual Inadequacy." Little, Brown, Boston.

Moss, M. C., and Beresford Davies, E. (1967). "A Survey of Alcoholism in an English County." Geigy Monograph, Cambridge, England.

Norcross, K. (1976). *Br. J. Sex. Med.* **3**, 26–28.

Reiter, T. (1953). *Practitioner* **170**, 181.

Renshaw, D. (1981). *Br. J. Sex. Med.* **71**, 34–37.

Riley, A. J. (1974). *Br. J. Sex. med.* **1**, 3.

Rostlapil, J. (1978). "Diabetes Outlook," quoted on p. 1. Scientific and Medical Publishing Co., Alton, Hampshire, United Kingdom.

Salzburger, G. J. (1977). *Mod. Geriatr.* **7**, 44–45.

Schofield, C. B. S. (1972). "Sexually Transmitted Diseases." Livingstone, Edinburgh.

Singha, H. S. K. (1967). "A Pocket Surgery." Churchill, London.

Taylor, R. W. (1975). *Br. Med. J.* **3**, 31–34.

Michal, V. (1978). *Br. J. Sex. Med.* **5**, 13–18.

Zarafonetis, C. J. D., and Horrax, T. M. (1959). *J. Urol.* **81**, 770–772.

PART **IV**

A VIEW FROM OTHER COUNTRIES

12

Continuity of Self-Actualization: Womanhood in the Climacterium and Old Age

Benjamin Maoz
Erika Landau

*To the memory of our great teacher in
humanistic–existential psychotherapy,
Professor Franz Brull.*

INTRODUCTION

This chapter summarizes our general outlook on the continuity of the cycles in female psychodevelopment, with the emphasis on the last third of the life span. It is based on 11 years of experience in clinical work (individual psychotherapy) as well as three empirical studies: (a) a psychosocial investigation of a random sample of 1148 women aged 45–54 from five ethnic groups in Israel (Maoz *et al.*, 1977a, b, 1978; Datan *et al.*, 1981); (b) a treatment inquiry concerning the influence of estrogens on 80 postmenopausal women (Durst and Maoz, 1978); and (c) a study of 25 inhabitants (aged 69–73) of two homes for the elderly to characterize creative attitudes and their correlation with attitudes toward sex and aging (Landau and Maoz, 1978).

In this chapter, *population* refers to studies, and *patients* relates to the psychotherapeutic practice of the authors. The emphasis will be on the insights achieved during this work rather than on the details of the data (facts and figures) (McKinley and McKinley, 1973; Neugarten, 1970; Wilbush, 1981).

PERCEPTION OF MENOPAUSE: TRADITIONAL AND MODERN WOMAN

We believe that the perception of menopause is determined at least as much by the present and the future outlook as it is by the effects of past psychosexual development.

If there is a relationship between psychosexual development and the perception of menopause, then it is partially dependent on the actualization of the three stages in a woman's life: girlhood, womanhood, and motherhood. If, in one of these stages, there was no self-actualization, the experience of climacterium is altered and may be colored by the unfulfilled stage (the phenomenon of mourning in the wake of lost opportunities).

Another important part of our credo is that menopause is perceived as one of the first significant irreversible signs of aging and the beginning of being closer to death. Therefore, we believe that there is a link between the perception of menopause and the approach to old age and death. In addition, the attitude of the society will be, in part, as significant as the individual approach in the acceptance of climacterium and old age.

Although the traditional woman's life cycle appears to be more in keeping with biological realities than that of the modern woman, we found that the first two assumptions of our credo hold for both groups. The first assumption—that the present and future outlook is as decisive as the past in the approach to the climacterium—should be linked with the question of changing identity. In both groups, there are some changes in self-image and identity. A traditional woman is characterized by very conventional concepts of family-hierarchy relations, with a strict and conservative frame of reference. In Israel we found that, for many traditional women, leisure time has to be spent with members of the same sex. Modern women are the opposite: they believe in the equality of partners, with a more liberal frame of reference. In the population studies, we found that traditional women were generally Oriental–Jewish and Arab, whereas the modern women were of European origin.

The more structured the group (such as the traditional large family), the better the middle-aged woman knows her new identity. The less structured the group (such as the modern nuclear family), the less likely the woman will be to find an identity defined by society. As a result, she will have to look within herself to develop role and identity. It is not as it was before: rather than receiving and acquiring experiences, she must create on the basis of her experience and apply her acquired knowledge. Jung (1953) speaks in this connection about the "psyche creating its own future." It is up to the woman to create her new inner and outer identity.

Options for the Postmenopausal Woman

The range of choices the modern woman faces after climacterium appears to be more difficult to handle than the limited goal of the traditional woman—to be a grandmother. The consciousness of a new identity is one of the most important individual differences in the approach to climacterium. Although this period may be a limitation from a biological aspect, it represents an expansion from the spiritual–cultural aspect (Hall and Lindzey, 1970).

Societal Stereotypes, Individual Perceptions

Among the patients, there appeared to be a connection between societal acceptance of climacterium and old age and their own approach. If society identifies womanhood primarily with child bearing, and if it identifies old age with uselessness and mental deterioration, these images become self-fulfilling: the self-image of the woman becomes what society expects of her.

In traditional society, the main role of the woman as a reproducer is replaced after menopause by the role of matron, which has high family and social status. In modern society, the role of the woman is not only a reproductive one; it connotes "femininity" in a broader sense, as well as career success. In a youth-centered society, there is no defined role for the middle-aged woman. Unless the individual is prepared to give the postmenopausal period new meaning, the reaction to change of life could become problematic. Society does not support the modern woman as it does the traditional woman.

As for our second assumption—that perception of menopause is related to the actualization of the stages in a woman's life—patients in psychotherapy indicate that there is less denial of the relationship between growing old, moving toward death, and menopause in the women who actualized themselves in their girlhood, womanhood, and motherhood. This means that they did not leap directly from girlhood to motherhood; instead they lived for a period as women, enjoying a conscious sex life without the connotation of childbearing. There is a chance that those women will go on being "women" during motherhood. The more fulfilled and actualized the womanhood stage, the better will be the acceptance of change of life. This may be a paradox: a woman may not be sorry to lose the womanhood that she enjoys. An actualized potential, with the concomitant minimization of fear of loss, is a necessary condition for the continual creative process of life (Landau, 1973). The "normal" reaction to climacterium is one of mixed feelings. Extreme statements such as "Thank God that I got rid of it" or "I am not worth anything, because I don't have it any more" indicate a neurotic trend in the personality.

What many modern women really mourn in their change of life is not the inability to give birth, but rather what they perceive as the loss of their beauty and sexual attractiveness—the ease with which they received and gave pleasure. The more fulfilled a woman has been, the more she will look for new ways to actualize her existing potentials. She will cling less to the accustomed ways and habits of proving herself to be a woman and become more flexible; she will let old habits go. She will look for new bases for relationships or shift the importance from one aspect of her relationships to another. The "afternoon life" is just as meaningful as the morning; only its meaning and purpose are different (Jung, 1953).

Individual and Survey Data

We had hoped to find the insights from psychotherapy with individual patients verified in the social surveys. However, the surveys provided no correlation that suggested a link between actualized womanhood and adaptation to the menopause and menopausal years. Perhaps the methodology in most social–sexual surveys, including ours, results in questions that are limited to girlhood and motherhood or to perceptions of menopause, to the exclusion of questions about fulfilled womanhood. Another difference may be found in the population sample in the Israeli studies. All the women were married (most of them for the first time), and most of them were mothers of children and could be considered a normal sample, in contrast to our patients.

During interviews, women were asked to respond to the general notions that (a) after menopause, a woman's enjoyment in sexual relations changes, and (b) a husband's interest in his wife is altered during the perimenopausal and the menopausal period. Their answers provided some information on their concepts of womanhood. Modern women, having worried earlier about conception and contraceptive techniques, felt liberated, and they enjoyed sexuality more. However, traditional women, accepting sexuality for reproductive purposes rather than pleasure, stated that enjoyment in sexual expression had diminished.

Concerning husbands' interest in their wives during and after climacterium, modern women answered that they saw no difference. Traditional women perceived some change, either in a positive or in a negative direction. In a particular traditional group, there appeared a typical combination of heightened interest on the part of the husband and less enjoyment in sexual relations on the part of the wife. Here we see a bridge between middle age and old age, when a husband perceives his wife more as a matron of the family and less as a woman. The modern woman reaches this stage much later, because she does not experience the family and social status associated with the role of matron, as does the traditional woman.

PSYCHOLOGICAL CONSEQUENCES
OF MALADAPTATION TO MENOPAUSE

One of the main psychological tasks in the climacterium is the confrontation with the first sign of approaching death. This task is generally denied. It appears to be easier to cope with the end of fertility and menstruation, and the changes brought about by the "empty nest," than it is to cope with the anticipation of death, which is the end of everything.

This denial is stronger in modern, youth-centered cultures than it is in traditional cultures in which old age and death are perceived as natural phenomena. When they were asked to respond to the statement that a woman starts to age with her climacterium, 74% of the traditional women related positively, whereas only 43% of the modern women accepted the statement. Modern women generally denied the statement. However, when they were asked to name the worst aspect of climacterium, modern women often expressed anxiety that the change of life is the beginning of growing old and moving closer to death.

It appears that, for women who cannot adapt to the change of life in their 50s or and cannot visualize themselves as growing old and eventually dying, there is an increased possibility of psychic deterioration, narrowing the range of experiences. On the other hand, those who relinquish former habits and accustomed ways of living during this time will enjoy old age by continuing to actualize their potentials.

This insight stimulated the investigation of a smaller group of both sexes on the question of self-actualization and its relation to sex and death in elderly people (Landau and Maoz, 1978). Self-actualization suggests the existential struggle of the individual to realize potentials (Landau, 1973) as well as the aspiration toward individuation; the harmony between the development of the individual personality and its collective relationships (Jung, 1953). The findings showed that the assumptions related to the approach to climacterium were generally true for old age, too, although there is no long-term outlook. The greater the self-realization of the potentials of old age, the less the denial of death and the greater the readiness to talk, to think, and to enjoy sexual activity, even beyond 80 years of age. Self-realization among the elderly was found in their adjustment to the home for the elderly, their activity within the home and outside it, their ability to create new relationships, and their involvement in social and political issues. As aspects of self-actualization, their creativity, fluency, and flexibility of thinking also were assessed.

The first questions concerning sexuality asked what the subjects thought would become of sexual needs and activity if human beings were created in the laboratory. This question was raised in order to determine the degree to which these older persons were involved in sexual matters. It would have been easy for them to answer this question by the acceptance of laboratory fertilization as a solution to the problem of sex; this would indicate their detachment from sexual issues.

The correlation between self-actualization and a positive approach to sex was very high.

IMAGE AND REALITY OF OLD AGE: TRADITIONAL AND MODERN WOMAN

The social aspect of old age is very similar to that of climacterium. The elderly in the studies mentioned here made the home their society. The more active they were, the higher their status in the home; and the less the denial, the more the activity and thoughts of sex. Here too, two correlations became evident: (a) the link between the perception of the society and the self-image of the personality, and (b) the link between the ability of the individual to be active in a changed environment and the ability to cope with new attitudes toward sexuality. Moreover, there is a positive correlation between activity level in a changed environment and readiness to think and talk about the closeness of death.

In the home for the elderly, there was no possibility for comparison of traditional and modern types, because, in traditional society, old people are usually kept in the family, not placed in institutions. The few traditional persons who were available, such as the traditional climacteric women, approached sex and death in a most natural way. "I thank God every morning that I am alive; that I act and function. Yet, death has become a friend of mine, we are on very intimate terms," said a 79-year-old woman. Another resident, still active in sexual imagination, compared the human life cycle to the course of the sun. Like Jung, she compared the last one-third of life to the afternoon sun, which she liked to observe daily. Death for her was the full, red sun falling into the sea: a symbol of the continuity of the circle of life and death.

CONCLUSION

In summary, it could be said that the manner of acceptance of the climacterium and old age is, to a great extent, determined by actualization of the individual in the stages of girlhood, womanhood, and motherhood. This actualization is also connected with the willingness of the woman to accept change in her identity and understand the perception, in particular, of herself as a middle-aged and older woman. In Israel, there are two clear-cut cultural groups. In the traditional group, the role of matron is offered as a new identity for the woman. In the modern group, similar to that in North America, the woman has to create her own new identity. Fulfilled womanhood will facilitate this process and will help the women to relinquish former habits, accept and enjoy the changed ways, and continue to actualize her still significant potentials even in very old age.

REFERENCES

Datan, N., Antonowsky, A., and Maoz, B. (1981). "A Time to Reap." Johns Hopkins Press, Baltimore.
Durst, N., and Maoz, B. (1978). *Pap., Int. Cong. Menopause, 2nd, 1978.*
Hall, C. S., and Lindzey, G. (1970). "Theories of Personality," 2nd ed. Wiley, New York.

Jung, C. G. (1953). "Collected Works," Vol. 7. Two Essays on Analytical Psychology. Bollingen Ser. II. Pantheon, New York.

Landau, E. (1973). *Am. J. Psychother.* **27**, 566–578.

Landau, E., and Maoz, B. (1978). *Am. J. Psychother.* **32**, 117–128.

McKinley, S. M., and McKinley, J. B. (1973). *Biosoc. Sci.* **5**, 333–554.

Maoz, B., Antonowsky, A., Apter, A., Wysenbeek, H., and Datan, N. (1977a). *Acta Obstet. Gynecol. Scand., Suppl.* **65**, 69–76.

Maoz, B., Antonowsky, A., Apter, A., Wysenbeek, H., and Datan, N. (1977b). *Arch. Gynaekol.* **223**, 9–18.

Maoz, B., Antonowsky, A., Apter, A., Datan, N., Hockberg, S., and Salomon, J. (1978). *Maturitas* **1**, 43–54.

Neugarten, B. L. (1970). *J. Geriatr. Psychiatry* **4**, 71–87.

Wilbush, J. (1981). *Maturitas* **3**, 99–105.

13

Institutional Life: The Canadian Experience

Benjamin Schlesinger

INTRODUCTION

Society has not given genuine recognition to the validity of sexual activity after the childbearing years, creating a dangerous stereotype about the "sexless older years." This stereotype has led to the definition of sexual interest and activity that may continue vigorously into these older years as deviant behavior. Thus, for example, the term *lecher* is coupled only with the old; the young are "lusty" or "virile" (Butler and Lewis, 1976).

Because sexual behavior is not only a function of one's individual attitudes and interactions with a partner, but also a reflection of cultural expectations, the widespread belief about the older person being sexless becomes, for many, a self-fulfilling prophecy (Schlesinger and Mullen, 1977).

There are many other factors that undoubtedly operate to keep alive a strong resistance to the acceptance of sexuality in older people. These include our general tradition of equating sex, love, and romance solely with youth; the psychological difficulty involved in accepting the fact of parental intercourse; the tendency to think of aging as a disease rather than a normal process; the focus of studies on hospitalized or institutionalized older people rather than on a more typical sample of noninstitutionalized persons beset by physical, emotional, or economic problems.

Bowman (1963, p. 375) stated it well.

> Men and women often refrain from continuing their sexual relations or from seeking remarriage after loss of spouse, because even they, themselves, have come to regard sex as a little ridiculous, so much have our social attitudes equated sex with youth. They feel uncertain about their capacities and very self-conscious about their power to please. They shrink from having their pride hurt. They feel lonely, isolated, deprived, unwanted, insecure. Thoughts of euthanasia and suicide bother them. To prevent these feelings, they need to have as active a sex life as possible and to enjoy it without fear. [Copyright © 1963. Published by arrangement with Lyle Stuart.]

Goodstein (1981) states that the elderly are worried about the maintenance of control over their lives and environment and the preservation of adequate physical function. Thus, the loss of sexuality may become part of this fear. He summarizes some of the sexual changes among the aged, including a slowing of the usual sexual abilities and the implication of more global incompetence. Erection and ejaculation may require more time and be of shorter duration. However, sexual ability really is determined by the availability of a partner, the person's past sexual activity, the elderly individual's physical health, and positive support from family and clinician. The elderly are often embarrased by sex and believe the stigma projected by our culture (e.g., for the man, virility at 25 is lechery at 65). Oftentimes, the side effects frm medications with consequences for sexual expression are not recognized as such, and the patient believes that he or she is "over the hill." Actually, these natural physiological changes, if explained and understood, can potentially encourage increased closeness, meaningful touching, and psychological satisfaction, because extra time and communication will be required in the relationship. Further details are provided in this volume in Chapter 3.

STATISTICAL TRENDS IN CANADA

The census of 1976 indicated that there were 2,002,345 Canadians over the age of 65 years (1,126,940 women and 875,405 men). They comprised 8.7% of the population. Among the males, 8.7% of the aged population lived in institutions. By 1980, 9% of all Canadians were senior citizens (Statistics Canada, 1979). Naus (1981) points out that, in 1980, 70% of the men 65 years old and over were still married, as were 39% of the women in that age bracket.

In the 1980s there has been a gradual move to recognize the sexual needs of our senior citizens. Naus (1981) states that, on the positive side, there is evidence that many couples become more compatible the longer they are married, and that they enjoy the greater opportunity for togetherness after retirement. Also, reduced occupational responsibilities, combined with shared decision making and a more flexible definition of marital roles, may relieve pressures either partner or both partners had been experiencing and may facilitate greater intimacy. Thus, their sexuality plays a part in their retirement as well as in their eventual institutionalization, if that becomes necessary.

Looking ahead on the Canadian scene, Rose (in press) feels that most Canadians are now aware of the elemental facts concerning the aging of our population. It is reasonably well known that the number of Canadians who are 65 years of age and over will double, increasing from about 1,710,000 in the early 1970s to more than 3,400,000 in the year 2001. Within the province of Ontario, the identical population group will increase from about 730,000 in 1976 to more than 1,300,000 in the year 2001. Although for many persons, the additional data into the twenty-first century are a matter of no concern by virtue of their current age, the most acceptable population projections suggest that there will be about 6,100,000 Canadians 65 years of age and over by the year 2031. In addition, it is expected that these vast increases in the number and proportion of the very elderly will continue to be dominated by members of the female sex.

SOCIETAL ATTITUDES AND OBSTACLES TO SEXUALLY ACTIVE ELDERS

Labeling

Many of society's attitudes toward the sexually active single senior are subtle. One of the subtle mechanisms used to control undesirable sexual behavior on the part of an unattached elderly individual is placement in an institution.

Another obstacle that pertains to the single older male is the "dirty old man" syndrome, from which married people and single females seem to be spared. Married people are less suspect when they show affection for younger people, because they are seen in the grandparent role. Women of all ages are allowed to express emotion and affection. The single older man is the most frequent victim of this stereotype. It seems that a sexually active older person is condemned twice: once for indulging in nonmarital sex, and again for carrying on like a young person.

Sexual Outlets for Single Seniors

In 1974, Oke and Zage completed an exploratory study of 10 institutions for senior citizens in the metropolitan Toronto area. Selected interviews were held with older inhabitants of these institutions and the professionals who were associated with them. The illustrations used in this chapter have been taken from this study, which was supervised by the author.

Mrs. B., of the Don Vale Community Health Centre, agreed that many single seniors, especially women, had little or no opportunity to engage in nonmarital sex. She added, however, that for those who were willing to pay, it was available. She cited five cases in the area of older, formerly married women who maintained sexual satisfaction with gigolos. We also interviewed a 66-year-old gay widower who told us that young male prostitutes are very accessible.

Whether or not a person pays for nonmarital sex, one should not assume that a single senior has no sex life. We are reminded of an incident that occurred a few months ago. One of my students set out one day on a "mission of mercy" to visit a poor, nearly blind older woman named Ruby. While visiting, the student heard a noise coming from the bedroom, and Ruby's lover, Bill, emerged. Ruby introduced him as her friend, but he quickly explained, "Well, we're a little more than friends." The student soon realized that Bill's affection was doing more for Ruby's well-being than any of the friendly visits of the social workers.

"Polygamy" is another source of sexual satisfaction for many single older adults, whether society wants to think so or not. It is not conflicting that a society that calls this practice the "dating game" when a younger person is involved labels it "polygamy" when it refers to the older single man or woman.

When we talked to May, a 76-year-old rooming house tenant, we found that she sleeps with many men in the house. She had lived in a nursing home for several years but found that her pattern of polygamous behavior was unacceptable in that setting. Even though her health indicated a need for nursing care, she moved out of the house in order to maintain her sexual freedom.

It appeared from our study that society seems to be easing up on the taboo against masturbation, but, for those persons presently in later life, recollections of lectures on the "evils of this sinful, harmful behavior" remain. Nevertheless, the practice is widespread among the elderly, especially among single persons.

Homosexuality is another sexual alternative for single seniors (and some married seniors, probably to a lesser extent). We investigated this by interviewing members of the Canadian Homophile Association of Toronto (CHAT). It is difficult to find accurate figures on what percentage of the older population is homosexual; this population is poorly represented in most studies, even in the major ones. A board member and counselor at CHAT agreed with the literature that the percentage is considerably smaller than it is for the younger population in society.

However, as one older CHAT member whom we interviewed stressed, because older people may not feel that their sexual lives are anyone's business, they may not "come out" and admit their homosexuality. Mr. R., another interviewee, felt that many seniors, like himself, did not discuss and deal with their homosexuality until their middle years, and that many never dealt with it at all.

SEXUALITY AND THE INSTITUTION

Sexual Expression as a Problem

Residents in institutions for the aged limit their sexual expression to flirtation, masturbation, and affectionate touching (hand holding, hugging, and so on). Formal policies and rules in regard to sexual conduct are nonexistent, and the control of disturbances of a sexual nature is left to the discretion of the staff. Sexuality is rarely discussed, except when there are complaints from other residents, or when there is the occasional ensuing wedding. However, most of the rare discussions relate to sex as a problem. None of the counselors ever introduce the topic. When asked about some of the signs of repressed sexuality, the consensus of opinion was that this aspect of behavior was hard to sort out, because institutionalized patients have so many other problems. Dr. M. pointed out that brain damage in some residents, and the accumulation of their problems over a long period of time, make it difficult to decide whether a depressed patient is depressed because of repressed sexual feelings or because of other important reasons.

All of the professional subjects from the institutions verbalize liberal attitudes and a great deal of knowledge about the sexuality of the aged. Mrs. F. is a prime example of this type of person. She said that sexuality can be expressed in many ways other than intercourse, and that the Lord intended to satisfy old age with all good things, including sexual enjoyment.

It is our observation that it is not always such people who have contact with institutionalized residents' daily lives. Dr. M. reminded us that people in the lower socioeconomic class are less conforming than their middle-class counterparts. That is why she felt that, among the workers in public institutions in particular, where this group is most highly represented, the tendency is to be less inhibited.

A slightly more positive word may be said for nursing homes. In our interview with Mrs. B, she said that nursing homes tend to be less rigid than large institutions. For one thing, they are smaller, and, therefore, usually more conducive to intimate or rather very friendly staff–resident relationships. As a result, although there are no written rules, the residents are generally allowed more freedom of sexual expression. Another positive factor relates to the organizational scale of the homes; most of them are semiprivate, moneymaking ventures, and the proprietor is most often a member of the staff. There is, therefore, a personal stake in ensuring the happiness of the residents.

Staff Interviews

Representative responses from our interviews will give the reader some indication of sexuality in institutions.

From a worker in a Jewish home for the aged:

Masturbation is no problem. Residents hold hands openly.

Staff control is really unnecessary. A show of sexuality that is too blatant is usually controlled by peer pressure. Even in the mentally impaired section, unless some sexual practice is extremely offensive to others, little staff control is exerted.

Married people do have their own rooms, but there is an hourly room check by staff, even during the night.

Staff discuss sexual problems when they come up; for example, residents who were going to be sharing a room with someone who masturbates would be asked if they minded. Sexual problems are discussed in the way that any other problem is discussed.

From a worker in a government-run home for the aged:

[There is] no talk about masturbation. Residents complain about homosexuality.

There is privacy. [We have] separate beds, but not separate bathrooms.

Yes, they hold hands. There was a marriage last year, but relatives break up some romances. [They have] no peace. Money concerns them. In one home, a couple ended up living in separate ends of the hall. Senior-citizen apartments are much more private, but the relative problem remains.

As long as people are fit, they should be free to express themselves sexually. [They should have a] personal choice.

From a worker in a private nursing home:

[There are] no specific rules (as opposed to unwritten rules). Old people, especially men, will watch others, for example, on television, then participate. One [man] is in his 80s, loveable and charming, made passes at nurses [and] got himself attached to a special lady. She didn't like it, so [the] center couldn't allow it.

Privacy would be a problem.

Even in private rooms, a confused person may wander [in]. Old women object to me wandering in. [We] can't lock doors because of safety purposes. Senility begins to take over. Some cannot identify [their] spouses.

Older ladies enjoy young orderlies much more than [they enjoy] their peers.

Elder Interviews

A 74-year-old male resident of a nursing home:

I do have sexual intercourse occasionally. Some of the women whose company I have really enjoyed prefer to get married, so the relationships had to end. I would like to marry, but I do not want to lose my daughter and grandchildren. I guess you would say that they are selfish, and I am a coward.

I am in relatively good health, and I keep myself in good shape. There are good women available. They have their standards too. Also, I just want to be intimate with people I really care for.

A 68-year-old widow in a home for the aged:

I do not have a sex life. I know about only one form of having sex [and] that is with another person, a man. I would feel uncomfortable and sinful.

My husband died 16 years ago. Intimacy has been sort of nonexistent since that time. I visit a sister regularly and see a couple of friends, but it is hard to meet people here. A home or apartment does not appeal to me. My health is gradually getting worse, but I do babysitting and other little things to keep me active outside and inside the home. I do not want to be cut off from the young.

Need for Improvements

In relation to the institutionalized life of the aged, Harel (1981), in his investigation of residents, found a reaffirmation of the need for improvements in the psychosocial dimensions of care in most institutions for the aged. The findings suggest that efforts for improvement should focus on those areas that are most preferred by residents in nursing homes and homes for the aged. Emphasis should be placed on the following areas:

1. Providing residents with opportunities for continuing ties with preferred family members and friends

2. Allowing residents to have more privacy and personal life space and more opportunities to exercise choices and personal responsibilities

3. Providing residents with more opportunities for social involvement and social activities

Such findings would support the need to consider the sexuality of the aged.

IMPLICATIONS FOR PROFESSIONALS

Consequences of Professional Attitudes

The practitioner should be aware that sexual expression continues to play an important role in the lives of many older people. Research has shown that the greater a person's sexual activity in younger years, the greater his or her sexual activity will be in older years (Schlesinger and Mullen, 1977).

Many of these who deal with the rapidly growing number of older persons—family and friends, doctors and social workers, and staffs of old-age homes—are either unaware of the data that indicate that sexual interest and capability of the aged continues or they are unable to psychologically accept the data. These helping persons need to be educated to the realities of sexuality in later years.

Counseling on sexuality and sexual adjustments should be made available to older persons. Older people may have difficulty communicating with authoritative figures, such as doctors in institutions. Many older people feel very guilty about sexual feelings and sexual relations. Elderly people need authoritative figures to relieve their guilt about sex and new techniques. A professional person, and his or her attitudes, can directly influence the sexual lives of older patients or clients. If the professional feels that sexuality in unimportant in older persons and that they have no sexual needs, then older people will experience more guilt.

Professionals must realize that a negative attitude on their part can pronounce a death sentence on the sexual lives of older people.

Oke and Zage (1974) found that the age and cultural background of the staff in homes for the aged make a difference in the attitudes and values related to sexuality and age. The doctors interviewed were well into middle age (one doctor was in his 70s). Their views reflected the era in which they were raised. They viewed the aged as being more concerned with such basic physical needs as food, shelter, and bowel function than with sexuality.

Sexually Deprived Elders

From our study, we feel that men and women in nursing homes and old-age homes are probably the most sexually deprived of the elderly. Their environment is almost totally desexualized. Privacy is lost when they walk in the front door. Many homes for the aged are still sexually segregated; even married couples may be separated. (This is changing, but it still goes on.) Such separation is mainly for medical reasons and is a family decision. Most homes have few single rooms or rooms for married couples. Usually there are bed checks at least once a night. For very ill people, this may be necessary, but it seems to be quite an intrusion for people on standard-care floors who can look after themselves.

We tend to treat old people in nursing homes like adolescents. From what are we protecting old people? One director of a hospital felt that older people regress to infancy. Examples of this institutionally stimulated regression can be found in the residents' excessive attention to rather simple needs. Some elderly individuals are interested only in such needs as obtaining food, getting an enema and a back rub, and seeing a visitor. They become passive receptors of attention. Receiving an enema twice a week may be their only level of sexual activity. They regress to anal eroticism.

This seems dehumanizing and pitiful. Such regression represents the major means by which people seek and receive sexual pleasure. Even more regrettable is the fact that society may find only regressive behavior acceptable. Most of the homes for the aged and nursing homes have been structured in such a way that the aged do become dependent and are now allowed privacy. The myths and misconceptions of sexuality in later years are reinforced.

Realities of Sexuality in Older Persons

There appears to be a gradual acclimation to the idea that there is sexuality after age 65, but we are still a long way from allowing older people to express themselves fully and to deal with their feelings about sexuality. Sexual activity can actually be therapeutic for an older person. Researchers focus on quantitative questions regarding outlet, frequency, and response; they seldom seek answers to qualitative questions involving needs, desires, and hopes.

Masturbation should be accepted for those without partners as a normal means of reducing sexual tension. However, there are very uncomfortable responses when doctors are asked whether they ever discuss masturbation with older persons. In their opinion, if the elderly masturbated in their younger years, they probably do so in later life. Judging from the doctors' discomfort in talking about this, one doubts that it is discussed with elderly people at all. Many physicians require additional training in order to function well in this area.

A campaign is needed in sex education for the aged. For example, techniques of intercourse that are especially pertinent to the needs of older people should be clarified. For example, sexual activity in the morning may be preferable for those who tire easily at night. Certain coital poisitions may make intercourse more feasible for those who are disabled by arthritis.

On the palliative level, we feel that brochures, films, books, and magazines dealing with the subject could be inconspicuously integrated into the library resources of institutions for the aged. Films designed to bring different levels of staff, the aged, and even their relatives together on special occasions (e.g., a movie night) could be shown, followed by discussion. The inconspicuous introduction of material over a period of time would most likely lead to conversations among the exposed parties. There would, at least, be an increased potential for those who need counseling to seek the service. Those staffers who had shied away from the topic would be more likely to introduce such conversation.

Clearly, there is more to sexuality after age 65 than the act of intercourse and orgasm. For the older man, there is the satisfaction of still feeling masculine; for the older woman, there is the satisfaction of still feeling feminine. For both, there is the feeling of still being wanted and needed. There is the comforting warmth of physical nearness, the pleasure of companionship, and the rewarding emotional intimacy of shared joys. Professionals can play their part in helping older adults to include positive sexuality in their twilight years.

CONCLUSIONS

There is a dearth of literature related to sexuality in aging in Canada. In searching for sources on sexual behavior in Canada (Schlesinger, 1977), we could not find one resource that discussed this topic in terms that were relevant to Canada. There is the added fact that we have little data about sexuality among the aged in institutions. We need to deal with the following questions:

1. What part does sexuality play in the institutions for the aged?
2. Is the staff trained to deal with this aspect of the lives of the aged in their care?
3. How can we facilitate the satisfaction of the sexual needs of the institutionalized aged? (This may include sex education, masturbation, prostitution, homosexuality, and heterosexual intercourse.)
4. Are we really dealing with a population that has little or no interest in sexuality as described in the widespread stereotype?

We need to answer these questions so that we can deal with the sexual needs of Canada's institutionalized senior citizens in a meaningful, positive way.

REFERENCES

Bowman, K. M. (1963). *In* "Sexual Behavior and Personality Characteristics" (M. F. DeMartino, ed.), pp. 372–375. Citadel, New York.

Butler, R. N., and Lewis, M. I. (1976). "Sex after Sixty." Harper & Row, New York.

Goodstein, R. K. (1981). *Am. J. Orthopsychiatry* **51**, 219–229.

Harel, Z. (1981). *Gerontologist* **21**, 523–531.

Naus, P. J. (1981). "Growing Old." Guidance Center, Faculty of Education, Univ. of Toronto Press, Toronto.

Oke, D., and Zage, D. (1974). "Aging and Sexuality." Faculty of Social Work, University of Toronto (unpublished).

Rose, A. (in press). "Canada's Elderly Population: Macrocosm of Social Policy Issues." McMaster Univ., Office on Aging, Hamilton.

Schlesinger, B., ed. (1977). "Sexual Behavior in Canada." Univ. of Toronto Press, Toronto.

Schlesinger, R., and Mullen, R. (1977). *In* "Sexual Behavior in Canada" (B. Schlesinger, ed.), pp. 66–75. Univ. of Toronto Press, Toronto.

Statistics Canada (1979). "Canada's Elderly," Cat. No. 98-800E. Ottawa.

14

A View from Sweden

Birgitta Gustavii

INTRODUCTION

Every society establishes its own sexual mores; these mores develop in different ways in different cultures. The quality of the emotional tone can be positive or negative, but the "inflection" that we first hear remains with us throughout life; superficially changed perhaps, but nevertheless still basically tuned in the same way.

SEXUAL EMBARRASSMENT FOR THE ELDERLY

In Sweden we have had a dark view of sexuality, filled with taboos. The present generation of older people has witnessed an incredible change in societal attitudes in matters concerning sexuality. In order to understand the difficulties and the possibilities for sexual expression that the older generation experiences, we must explore these changes.

Many people, not only the elderly, regard sexual life as isolated, functioning independently of life-style in order to give satisfaction. This is an unreasonable expectation in such a vulnerable and sensitive sphere.

Confidence, affection, love, and knowledge are the most important prerequisites for a satisfactory sex life. Of these, the older generation has had precious little confidence and knowledge. Sex is still viewed as shameful and illicit for the majority of elderly people; this is a view of sexuality that defeats basic confidence. We first experience confidence in our sex lives when we permit ourselves to feel and to accept our sexual feelings—when we dare to both give and receive. Only then can we perceive that sexuality is a resource, a fountain from which we can tap strength.

People who are elderly now have learned to consider sexuality quite differently. Their fear of unplanned pregnancy was very strong. They learned that the use of contraceptives was nothing other than marital masturbation, and that physical and mental illness would strike anybody who indulged in it. Until 1937 it was a criminal offense in Sweden to spread information about contraceptives. Sexual activity was a wife's duty and a husband's right. Sexual life was particularly shameful for the woman and could lead to exclusion from society (if she were an unmarried mother, for example). Obligatory sex education was introduced as recently as 1955.

Today, we know that there is physical capacity for a sexual relationship throughout life. Nevertheless, we anticipate that such expression will cease sometime between 50 and 60 years of age. This expectation becomes a self-fulfilling prophecy. In my counseling work, middle-aged men suffering from erection difficulties often say "Surely, it can't be over already," implying that it does end, sooner or later. Swedish journalists are amazed by newly published statistical information showing that 80-year-old men retain their sexual desires and capacities and, that they experience sexual fantasies and longings. Such evidence illustrates how far we still have to go before lifelong sexual expression is accepted, especially for older people.

THE LEGACY OF TABOOS

My grandmother asked me one day what my job was really all about. I tried to tell her as gently as I could that I counsel people who experience sexual problems, that nearly all of them could be treated, and so on. "But, does this mean that women can have orgasm? Surely, only a man can experience orgasm," she said. My grandmother's statement does not mean that she has been unhappy or dissatisfied. On the contrary, she and my grandfather had an unusually fine relationship built on mutual respect and devotion. During our continued conversation, I learned that, for my grandmother, it was completely satisfactory to be the giving partner, and that the pleasure of giving her husband satisfaction, and the pleasure of such intimate contact, had been enough.

We can prove that the older generation has many strong taboo-filled conceptions about sexuality that are difficult, and often impossible, to change. These negative, guilt-encumbered ideas make it difficult to adjust the sexual pattern to the different contemporary assumptions that aging now implies for sexual function.

A woman's sex life has been characterized by strong hostility and denial, which, among other consequences, leads to vulnerability of her libido. Many women tolerate sexual intercourse year after year to avoid conflict. Often, the older woman does not know that help is available for dry vaginal mucous membranes. And, even if she did know, she would never dare seek help for that condition. She would be ashamed of showing that she was still sexually active. When the prolapse operation was performed 10 or 15 years ago, it could be done without a thought for her sexual activities and desires.

The sexual life of a man is characterized by a virility demand—a demand for performance. His inclination to isolate his emotional life from his sexual life has been reinforced by sexual attitudes that have been prevalent for many generations. Many older men suffer from high blood pressure, which is often treated with beta-blocking drugs. It has recently been shown that this drug therapy can produce a reduced blood flow in the peripheral vessels, a side effect that results in impotence for some men. Given the shyness of many older men it is doubtful that this difficulty is mentioned to the physician.

Often, an older man needs increased tactile stimulation in order to achieve an erection. Even if he wants his wife to caress his penis, she feels revulsion and cannot bring herself to do anything so "unnatural." More often, he does not know much about the natural changes that come with age, and he regards these changes as a sign of impotence. This is in keeping with his expectations.

A couple in their 60s sought help in the clinic where I practice for the husband's difficulty with erection. For the past 6 months they had not been able to have sexual intercourse. Sexual expression was important to them, and after careful deliberation, they decided to come for help. Both were prepared to find that the husband could be helped by medication;

however, a somatic examination of the man revealed that there was no basis for such therapy. The relationship between the two was unusually harmonious and good. No problems existed with children, grandchildren, or work. The husband's trouble began during a period in which he was exhausted after a bout of influenza. After the very first unsuccessful attempt at intercourse, he was afraid that he had become impotent. They soon made another attempt, acutely conscious of how he functioned. Thus, he continued to make performance requirements, with repeated failure. When we suggested that they should have sexual relations for a period without attempting intercourse, they objected. It appeared that he had never caressed her genital area, and that the thought of touching his penis had never entered her head. We explained the connection between his fear of failure and his present impotence. We tried to explain that the demand for the achievement that he felt so keenly could be eliminated through sensuality–sexuality training. They came back 1 week later and explained that they had done what we had suggested. However, it had seemed very distasteful and unnatural to them. They had both felt that they would never repeat such behavior. The couple rejected the idea of further treatment; they preferred an asexual life if they could not have intercourse in a "natural" way.

NEED AND SATISFACTION CONTINUE BETWEEN PARTNERS

In spite of the difficulties that many older people experience— difficulties that we hope the younger generation will never need to experience to the same degree—many older people enjoy a married life that satisfies them and gives them increased contentment. Even if the physical functioning is not completely satisfactory, the intimacy and closeness shared with a life partner are valuable and fine. This type of sharing creates a confidence that was tender and vulnerable for many years but has had time to develop into a lifelong relationship.

A rural district nurse reports the following experience. She arrived at the home of a 70-year-old man to change his catheter. He asked whether she was married. When she replied that she was not, he did not reveal why he had asked. The explanation came 1 year later, when her vacation substitute was asked the same question. She replied that she was married. On hearing this response, the man dared to ask her to leave the catheter out for a few hours so that he could have sexual intercourse with his wife. Naturally, his request was granted, and now the regular nurse follows this routine. This happened only a year or so ago in Sweden. This example illustrates an unusual degree of patience on the part of a man who still has sexual drive but whose socialization dictates that sexual matters are discussed only with married persons.

INSTITUTIONALIZED ELDERLY

We have been addressing the issues that face people who live with their partners. But what is the situation for older people who spend their final years in an institution, where the aged have not only their own inhibitions to cope with, but also those of the nursing staff? This problem has recently attracted a good deal of attention. Nursing staffs are receiving instruction in human sexuality issues that favor a compassionate and permissive point of view concerning the social rights and needs of institutionalized elderly people.

It is hard to be alone—it is more difficult to be old and alone. I know a man who met a woman of his own age a few years after his wife's death. They found that they had much in common and that their relationship pleased both their fellow patients and the nursing staff. Members of the staff helped them to get a double bedroom. It was then that the difficulties started. The man's children were furious and shocked. They refused to accept their father's newfound happiness. They regarded their father as absurd and as a disgrace to the family, because he demonstrated his feelings and his needs openly in this way.

CHANGING ATTITUDES AND VALUES

It is not only the values of the aged that must change. The younger generation also must develop a more positive view of old people's sexual and emotional lives. But we must not go so far that we frighten old people with our newfound knowledge or impose a way of life that would be a rejection of their lifelong attitudes. We must understand that sexual life and the relationship between two people are formed in accordance with their particular circumstances. We can help when help is needed and asked for, demonstrate our understanding, and refrain from demanding that old people's attitudes undergo radical change. We must learn to respect the shyness and inhibitions of the elderly. We have to realize that, in spite of all the obstacles they have known in the past and still encounter, they are able to enjoy a rich life, even if it is lived on terms other than our own.

PART V

FUTURE PERSPECTIVES

15

Beyond Generativity: Toward A
Sensuality of Later Life

Nancy Datan
Dean Rodeheaver

INTRODUCTION

When Freud was asked to name the tasks of the healthy adult, he replied, "Love and work." The peculiarities of human development exclude the pre-adult from full participation in love or in work: premature engagement in these tasks is defined as a form of social pathology, a violation of laws against child labor, for example, or statutory rape. It is in the best interests of everyone, it seems, to prolong the long childhood of humanity with the "ever longer" childhood of civilization (Erikson, 1963): creative and industrious workers, and patient and responsible

SEXUALITY IN THE
LATER YEARS

279

parents, are the socially desirable outcome of a long, careful socialization process that relies, in part, on the prohibition against adult sexual behavior and adult work, until the time—defined both maturationally and socially—is right.

At the other end of the life cycle, matters are less clear. Both entry into and retirement from the work force are life-cycle transitions in which law lends a hand. However, although it is clear that the prohibition of child labor protects the young, it is not equally clear who is protected by retirement laws. The young benefit from the availability of jobs that would otherwise be held by aging workers. Some workers seem to welcome the leisure that comes at the end of the life cycle. Most studies of retirement, however, show that this is a problematic transition for the aging worker. Thus, although everyone seems to gain from the exclusion of the young from the work force, including the young themselves, not everyone gains from the exclusion of the old—and the old themselves are the most likely to lose.

The laws that govern entry into and retirement from the work force, though they may certainly be challenged, nevertheless represent a social effort to achieve the greatest benefit for the most people. Retirement age, social security legislation, and even preretirement programs all represent responsiveness to the problems associated with retirement. The task of this chapter is to inquire into the problems associated with transitions in the later part of the life cycle of love; transitions that are no less problematic for being less explicit. We shall suggest that people are retired out of sensuality and sexuality just as they are retired out of work and productivity; that this retirement is less explicit but hardly less brutal; that there is no compensating social security for the lost sensuality of earlier years; and finally, that there is no social justification for the exclusion of the old from the world of sensual love. These suggestions need little or no defense, but they require a remedy. Implicit in our discussion will be the new directions we might take toward a sensuality of later life.

LOVE, WORK, AND THE LIFE COURSE

In the late 1960s, it was pointed out in the report of the Committee on Research and Development Goals in Social Gerontology (CORAD) that the life cycle is divided into three parts: apprenticeship, productivity, and leisure (Havighurst, 1969). This sequence, it was suggested, awarded the individual a harvest of leisure years at the end of a life spent deferring the need for leisure—a process, it was suggested, that devalued the prize. It was proposed that these divisions of the life cycle might be made less rigorous, allowing for leisure in young adulthood and reeducation in later life, so that disengagement from the work force might become reengagement to pursuits that had retained their meaning over the entire life cycle.

It is worth mentioning that, in the intervening years, some of these recommendations have come to pass: college graduates have paused for an intermission, perhaps backpacking through Europe, before finding a place in the labor force; older workers do change careers; campuses are finding that the only increase in enrollment is from a group once unknown but now no longer novel in the classroom—the returning middle-aged student. Yet, the motivations of these groups are not articulated in a dynamic, forward-looking force for social change, but rather seem to be the sum of small dissatisfactions; unwillingness to make a commitment to a career; dissatisfaction with a career; and boredom in the home. Although the landscape has changed since the CORAD report was issued in 1969, the underlying tripartite division of the life cycle has not been fundamentally altered.

Sex-Role Stereotypes Persist

We would argue that the three-part succession of stages in the life cycle suggested in the CORAD report is compounded by the traditional division of sex roles. Although women may work outside the home and very often do, men who not do so are stigmatized as failures; corresponding to this stigma is the suspicion that attaches to the woman who is dedicated to her career at the expense of a family. Thus, it is not the expansion of options to which we look, but the penalties that accrue to the man or woman who violates sex-role expectations. One may aspire to the prerogatives of both sexes, perhaps; but, if only one sex role is chosen, it had better be one's own. Moreover, it would appear that the prescription for full human potential—love and work—is divided according to sex roles: men work, and women love.

Women are not, however, exempt from the three-part sequence of apprenticeship, production, and leisure. We would argue that this sequence can also be used to describe the process by which a young girl anticipates and then enters into marriage and childbearing, and then, after years of "producing" children and "making" a home, approaches the years of the empty nest, the increasing possibility of divorce, and widowhood.

We might sum up this three-part sequence as it applies to the domains of love and work by suggesting that the first part of the life cycle is spent in learning, the second in doing, and the third in losing. The poignancy of loss is heightened when we reflect that each sex is denied full access to the domain of the other and, hence, to some of the comforts of compensatory gain in later life. The newly retired man is not reported as rejoicing at a chance to be home, at long last, with his wife: he is described as a nuisance, puttering around, unsuccessfully looking for something to do to keep himself busy. The woman whose children have recently left home, or whose marriage dissolves in later life, or who is newly widowed, may be forced to seek employment as an alternative to boredom or poverty, but she is very unlikely to experience her job as an entry into a new dimension. Thus, many men and women live out a life course that concludes by depriving each of his or her primary role, without the prospect of adequate complementary gain. It is in the context of this irony that we will discuss socialization toward a sensuality of later life.

The Mid-Life Crisis: Anticipatory Socialization?

"The second half of life is compensation for the first," remarked Jung; and those who have studied personality development during middle and later adulthood more systematically might agree, with some qualifications (Gould, 1978; Gutmann, 1977; Levinson, 1978; Neugarten, 1977). Gutmann (1975; p. 170), in particular, has argued that there is an age-grading of sex-role prerogatives initiated by the "chronic emergency" of parenthood, which channels young mothers toward nurturance and young fathers toward aggression in the service of the children's needs. As the children grow into autonomy, the period of the empty nest ushers in the "normal unisex of later life," a time during which husbands may reclaim their surrendered dependency needs and wives may reclaim their surrendered assertive needs.

The literature of crisis, however, is more abundant than the study of transition. Scholarly investigations of developmental transitions over the life cycle are not new; however, the remarkable impact of popularized books such as Gail Sheehey's "Passages" (1977) suggests a developing public sensitivity to—perhaps even eagerness for—change in middle life. The themes of popular crisis resemble the sex-role changes described by Gutmann, but they are highlighted by an undercurrent of urgency and struggle. The men and women in "Passages" leave their spouses or their jobs, move on to new loves or a new passion for work, and aspire to a complete rebirth.

The incidence of rebirth in middle age is considerably less than Sheehey would have us believe; but the hunger for rebirth, to judge from the extraordinary impact of her book, is immense. Let us take the book's sales record, rather than its content, as a social phenomenon that is worth some attention. It suggests a widespread yearning for the prerogatives of both sexes, the satisfactions of love and of work, and, perhaps, a recognition that these are not easily won.

The mid-life crisis, about which so much has been written, suggests that these themes, and the struggles that are less than victorious, are frequently seen in clinicians' offices (Norman and Scaramella, 1980). The deeply committed professional begins to question the "one-life, one-career imperative" in middle life (Sarason, 1977). Although divorce is not yet common in middle life, its salience has grown. Troll et al. (1979) have suggested that we may have reached a "tipping point," a reversal of the belief that marriage should be sustained regardless of the partners' happiness. Instead, there is now a growing belief that unhappy marriages should be terminated, although Troll et al. (1979) note that family researchers suspect that divorces often produce more problems that they solve. Among these problems, though it is yet unexplored, is the effect of the growing number of divorces on those marriages that remain intact; Troll suggests that unhappy couples now feel apologetic if they do not divorce. Moreover, for those couples—probably a majority—whose feelings are mixed, we might surmise that one consequence of the rising divorce rate, and the still more rapidly rising visibility of divorce, is that dissatisfaction, rather than stability, is highlighted.

Developmental theorists have remarked that the sense of time undergoes a change in middle age: Neugarten (1968; p. 97) characterizes this change as a transition from "time-since-birth" to "time-left-to-live." The awareness of personal mortality is a catalyst of this transition (Erikson, 1963; Jaques, 1965; Neugarten, 1968). It is a small speculative leap to the suggestion that the mid-life crisis may be a kind of anticipatory socialization to old age. The forewarning of finitude is also a foreclosure of opportunity, lending urgency to change. Clinicians and researchers alike may be moved to ask whether lessons learned when it seems too late might not be learned earlier at less cost.

THE SENSUALITY OF LATER LIFE: LOCKER ROOM TRUTHS AND THEIR CONSEQUENCES

In 1977, we presented an unpretentious little paper called "Dirty Old Women: The Emergence of the Sensuous Grandmother" to the American

Psychological Association. Our goals were modest: we described to a professional audience what boys have been saying in locker rooms for generations—that there are good girls and bad girls, the former for marriage and the latter for pleasure—and considered the consequences of these distinctions for the sensuality of later life. To judge from the remarkable reception the paper enjoyed, ranging from extensive newspaper coverage to abstracted reprints in several in-house psychiatric journals, we must have said something that struck a public nerve. Yet, we said very little that was new. What, indeed, did we say?

Socialization and Social Roles

We observed that contemporary medicine has made it possible to effectively distinguish between sexuality for procreation and sexuality for pleasure, though, of course, they are not mutually exclusive. This distinction has rendered obsolete the sexual socialization of girls, which, until very recently in human history, was focused exclusively on the procreative potential of sexuality. Small girls were not reared to anticipate the intense pleasures of sexual intimacy, but instead were taught to maintain control, not to go too far, not to acquire a bad name and, when eventually sexuality was licensed by marriage, to plan their families.

The inequities of the double standard of sexuality have their origins in the inequities of biology. Family stability is threatened by casual sex; folk songs have for centuries lamented the dilemma of the woman left to mind the baby who is the byproduct of a brief encounter. It seem to us that the network of protective prohibitions on women's sexuality stems from the simple fact that, in a casual encounter, it is the woman who becomes pregnant. Although contemporary social critics condemn the double standard as being oppressive to women, we believe that the historical oppression has been the simple probability of abandonment. The unilateral nature of this threat is seen when we apply the notion of "seduced and abandoned" to a man: it loses much of its force. Folk mores tell us that women are deceived by men; we would argue that there is no deception at all, but merely sexual inequality, which will not yield to legislation.

If sexual inequality is insoluble, its significance is greatly diminished by conception control. But deeply rooted values die slowly, and the double standard, though it may have a limited future, has some poignant consequences for present cohorts of women. Those women who in their youth earned the status of "good girls," and later earned the status of wife and mother, cease childbearing, on the average, in their late 20s and are without a sexual mandate for the rest of their lives, living in a culture that treats middle age and aging as diseases to be fought off with Geritol and Oil of Olay.

Moreover, these are women who were chosen for their restraint in sexuality. A frequent clinical problem in middle life is the marriage that is broken as a man discards his wife for a younger, newer model (Gould, 1980). It might seem that these middle-aged women are devalued as sexual partners, but we have argued that it is more likely that they were never valued as sex partners in the first place (Datan and Rodeheaver, 1977). It is obvious that the first steps toward a sensuality of later life must be taken very early in life, through the teaching of the reciprocity of sexual intimacy. Kastenbaum speaks intensely about the fate of men: "All the dirty old men jokes in the world do not dilute the poignancy of love and sex in later life" (1973, p. 705). We would go further: All the poignancy of the fate of dirty old men does not dilute the tragedy that the solitary sexless old are mostly women, for whom the world has not even granted sexual identity in jokes (Ludeman, 1981). We coined two phrases: "dirty old women" and "the emergence of the sensuous grandmother." We now suspect that the wide impact of this paper simply testifies to a need for these phrases. Moreover, we believe these tragedies will not be touched by anything less than a revolution in the language of boys' locker rooms and in the lessons taught young girls.

Education for sexuality at any age may become obsolescent in the next developmental stage. The expression of sexuality across the life cycle must be seen as a succession of developmental tasks, reflecting the interaction of maturational and social processes. More important and more difficult, if men and women are to learn to love across the life span, they must learn to value a companionship that reflect changes in the nature of love. This lesson must begin in childhood, as boys and girls are taught to cherish one another's friendship.

Toward a Sensuality of Later Life: The Double Standard Revisited

Efforts to encourage the sexuality of later life are rare, but not unknown: for example, Butler and Lewis's "Sex after Sixty" (1976) is a valuable guide for those who are willing to use it. Our concern is that the women and men who are willing to use such a guide are too rare—that the sexual climate of our times too closely resembles the tripartite division of the life cycle condemned in the CORAD report. When a justice of the Supreme Court is praised for his "productivity" in siring a child at an advanced age, it occurs to no one at all to condemn him for creating an orphan—a novel version of an old theme, seduction and abandonment. In this case, perhaps both husband and wife were seduced by the notion that the only effective proof of virility is pregnancy. But it is precisely this notion that must be unlearned for a rewarding sensuality to be experienced in later life.

The existential tragedy of the desexing of aging women and men is compounded by the biological irony of later life. It has long been noted that menopause is frequently accompanied by a heightened sexuality in women; this has long been interpreted as a "denial" of aging. As Malkah Notman (1980) has pointed out, it has evidently not occurred to anybody to interpret this common occurrence at face value. Clinicians have observed, however, that the heightened sexuality of the aging woman may be threatening to the aging man whose potency is declining. Yet no one seems to have concluded that there might be a biological logic of later life that shifts the burden of initiative and ingenuity to women and releases men from performance demands, allowing sensuous leisure.

If a reciprocity of sexuality is revolutionary, the sexual reversal we suggest here is utopian. Perhaps this radical suggestion might stimulate a rethinking of the biological logic of sexual expectations over the life cycle and eventually lead us to behave in tune with our natural rhythms.

The Seasons of Human Love

The supreme triumph of our humanity over our biology is that we do not only make babies, we also make love. We suggest that human love, like human sexuality, has two manifestations. The first, corresponding to sexuality for procreation, is generative love: a love of family, home, and hearth; a love of young creatures; a love that makes sacrifices today for the sake of tomorrow's generations. Generative love may, perhaps, represent our belief in an eternal future.

The second manifestation of human love, which we shall suggest has some parallels to sexuality for pleasure, is existential love. If generative love reaches out for immortality, existential love seizes the brief moment of mortality. We are not speaking of young, romantic love, which hopes to be eternal but proves to be transient. By existential love, we mean a love that reflects a poignant awareness that all life is transient, that existence is brief, and that our days are numbered—an awareness that comes to us in maturity and old age, when we can no longer deny our own mortality. Existential love is the antithesis of generative love, for generative love is an affirmation of faith in the enduring future, whereas existential love represents a recognition that all things pass away, and that life is more precious because it is fleeting.

We believe that existential love, the capacity to cherish the present moment, is one of the greatest gifts of maturity. Perhaps we first learn this love when we first confront the certainty of our own personal death, most often in middle adulthood. Generative love is characteristic of parenthood, a time during which sacrifices are gladly made for the sake of children. However, it is existential love, we feel, that creates the unique patience and tenderness so often seen in grandparents, who know how brief the period of childhood is, since they have seen their own children leave childhood behind them.

We have not yet awakened to the potential for existential love between old women and old men, just as we are not yet prepared to recognize the pleasures of sexuality as natural to the life span, particularly to the postparental period.

Those old people who have had the misfortune of spending their last days in nursing homes may learn that love can be lethal. We have been told of an old woman and an old man who fell in love. The old man's children thought this late flowering was "cute"; however, the old woman's children thought it was disgraceful, and, over her protests, they removed her from the nursing home. One month later she registered her final protest: she died.

In speaking of love and its seasons to an audience in Paris—where, naturally, French sophistication with regard to mature love was anticipated—we learned instead that the censoring of sex among the old is not peculiar to Americans (Datan, 1977). Indeed, the telling of this tale has never shocked an audience: all have had their own versions of similar stories. This is a measure of how far we have to go toward acceptance of sensuality and love among the old, who, ultimately, if we are not unlucky, our ourselves.

We believe that the social changes that have led to our present widespread dissatisfactions with aging will soon lead us to expect and to create new satisfactions and, finally, to accept the natural rhythms of the life cycle and the expressions of sexuality and love that are uniquely appropriate to each of the seasons of human life.

REFERENCES

Butler, R. N., and Lewis, M. (1976). "Sex after Sixty." Harper & Row, New York.
Datan, N. (1977) "Women of a Certain Age and Beyond: Aging, Family and Society" (invited address: "La femme agée dans la famille et la société"). Session d'étude, Le Vieillisement de la Femme, Paris.
Datan, N., and Rodeheaver, D. (1977). "Dirty Old Women: The Emergence of the Sensuous Grandmother" (invited contribution to symposium "Socialization to Become an Old

Woman" (M. Seltzer, chairman). Am. Psychol. Assoc., San Francisco.

Erikson, E. (1963). "Childhood and Society," 2nd ed. Norton, New York.

Gould, R. (1978). "Transformations: Growth and Change in Adult Life." Simon & Schuster, New York.

Gould, R. (1980) *In* "Mid-Life Crisis: Developmental and Clinical Issues" (W. H. Norman and T. J. Scaramella, eds.), pp. 110–127. Brunner/Mazel, New York.

Gutmann, D. (1975). *In* "Life-Span Developmental Psychology: Normative Life Crises" (N. Datan and L. H. Ginsburg, eds.), pp. 167–184. Academic Press, New York.

Gutmann, D. (1977). *In* "Handbook of the Psychology of Aging" (J. E. Birren and K. W. Schaie, eds.), pp. 302–326. Van Nostrand-Reinhold, Princeton, New Jersey.

Havighurst, R. J., ed. (1969). *Gerontologist* **9**, Part 2, 1–90.

Jaques, E. (1965). *Int. J. Psychoanal.* **46**, 502–514.

Kastenbaum, R. J. (1973). *In* "The Psychology of Adult Development and Aging" (C. Eisdorfer and M. P. Lawton, eds.), pp. 699–708. Am. Psychol. Assoc., Washington, D. C.

Levinson, D. J. (1978). "The Seasons of a Man's Life." Alfred A. Knopf, New York.

Ludeman, K. (1981). *Gerontologist*, **21**, 203–208.

Neugarten, B. L. (1968). *In* "Middle Age and Aging" (B. L. Neugarten, ed.). Univ. of Chicago Press, Chicago.

Neugarten, B. L. (1977). *In* "Handbook of the Psychology of Aging" (J. E. Birren and K. W. Schaie, eds.), pp. 626–649. Van Nostrand-Reinhold, Princeton, New Jersey.

Norman, W. H., and Scaramella, T. J., eds. (1980). "Mid-life Crisis: Developmental and Clinical Issues." Brunner/Mazel, New York.

Notman, M. (1980). *In* "Mid-life Crisis: Developmental and Clinical Issues" (W. H. Norman and T. J. Scaramella, eds.), pp. 85–109. Brunner/Mazel, New York.

Sarason, S. B. (1977). "Work, Aging, and Social Change." Free Press, New York.

Sheehey, G. (1977). "Passages: Predictable Crises of Adult Life." Bantam Books, New York.

Troll, L. E., Miller, S. H., and Atchley, R. C. (1979). "Families in Later Life." Wadsworth, Belmont, California.

Index